Subtypes:
The Key to the Enneagram

Eric Salmon

Translated by
Heather Brown

Leaping Boy Publications

First published under the title *La Clé de l'Ennéagramme: les Sous-types* by Inter Editions, Paris 2007

Subtypes: The Key to the Enneagram

Published by Leaping Boy Publications
0044 (0) 1525 222 600
partners@neallscott.co.uk
www.leapingboy.com

Cover design and typesetting by Deborah Hawkins

Printed and distributed by Lightning Source UK Ltd

British Library Cataloguing in Publication Data. A CIP record for this book can be obtained from the British Library.

ISBN 978-0-9935947-1-7

CONTENTS

INTRODUCTION

The Enneagram is a framework based on nine personality profiles; it's a model which uses a diagram to sum up some powerful truths about human nature. Its main characteristic is that it is accessible to everyone. I have personally facilitated workshops with uneducated jobseekers, directors of multinationals and nuns and monks in Rome, Pondicherry and Tehran. All of them were astonished at the insights they gained: *"Sure, I got loads of information, but above all, I feel that I have changed the way I look at myself and at other people. It is as though I am inhabiting myself differently."*

When we come to the subtypes, the name they have acquired has been unfortunate. This crucial aspect of the Enneagram, the one that best enables us to move forward as people, has been labelled "sub" as though it were "inferior". In fact, I think that one day someone in a hurry shortened the English expression "subdivision of the type" to "subtype." Ever since then people have tended to use this shortened expression in preference to the more exact term. Whatever the truth of the matter, I encourage you to think of "subdivisions" when you study the subtypes, because there are literally three different manifestations of the same type. The main benefit of the subtype is to reveal the behavioural aspect of the Enneagram. Whereas the type tells us about internal structure, subtype describes where and how we take our place in the world, the focus of our activities, the visible part of our lives. Thus, when we look in from outside, the behaviour of people with the same subtype will look very alike, whereas if they have a different type, they can have very different underlying motivators for their behaviour. Detecting someone's subtype will always be more obvious than finding their type.

While I don't think that it is ever possible to link professions to types, I do think that some professional sectors fit more closely with certain subtypes, for example insurance with "self-preservation" and politics with "social". You can see subtype at work even more clearly in relationship dynamics; if you look at the life of couples, what children are good at, how they choose school subjects or a career, how people respond to coaching and or act in management, you won't go very far before you hit the subtypes. When we go round the group at the end of a course on subtypes, most of the participants confirm that: *"discovering my subtype has been at least as important as, if not more important than discovering my type."*

Almost forty books on the Enneagram have been published in France since 1997. Most of them deal with the Enneagram at the basic level, i.e. how to understand yourself and others better and how to communicate better. But the Enneagram has another dimension – the transformation of Being or, more precisely, rediscovering the essence of your Being: what Carl Jung calls the "Self", Winnicott "the real me" and humanistic psychologists "essence". On this journey, the first stage is to discover our "false me", become aware of our automatic behaviour patterns and notice how the "false me" is limiting us. In the second stage we then start to experience what it feels like to be in contact with "essence" and make the decision that we want to get back in touch with it on a regular basis. The situation becomes even clearer once we identify what we want to leave behind. The transformation of the ego then becomes possible; we can leave behind our automatic behaviours in order to gain more freedom and consciousness.

The Enneagram subtypes are the key to this journey of transformation. They describe precisely where and how we stupidly waste our energy trying to hang on to defence mechanisms that no longer serve us well. And that is essential, because that is what will enable us to interrupt our automatic reactive process and do something different. As Dr Viktor Frankl says in 'Man's Search for Meaning': *"In between stimulus and response, there is a choice"* – i.e. the possibility of being free, of no longer being dependent on our automatic patterns. I hope that this book will contribute to the rediscovery of our instinctive response patterns so that we can expand our consciousness for the well-being of everyone. Our world really needs it.

PART 1: DISCOVERING THE IMPORTANCE OF SUBTYPES

THE DEVELOPMENT OF THE ENNEAGRAM
IN THE 20ᵀᴴ CENTURY

In order to understand the origins and principles of the Enneagram subtypes, it is important to take account of some key strands of personality theory and psychology which influenced the development of Enneagram and subtype theory. This chapter therefore starts with an outline of the psychological movements that impacted on the development of the Enneagram in the 20th century. These movements in psychology led to the development of a theory about how the tiny child builds its defence mechanisms in order to survive life – and this forms the basis of the three centres and the nine Enneagram types. This sets the context for the description of the subtypes which then follows, and helps to make clear why and how the subtypes are the manifestation of our type in everyday life. Noticing, understanding and having compassion for our subtype behaviour is the foundation for our personal development.

1960 – San Francisco Bay

"Psycho-analysis is essentially the result of observing mental activity/life; that's the reason why the understanding of its structure remains incomplete and subject to constant modification." Freud didn't know how right he was – psychoanalysis was only a stage on the journey. Even before the 2nd World War many researchers were digging in different directions in their explorations of the human soul. Most European researchers decided that, given the political context, they were better off moving to the USA to continue their research. Once they got there they stayed, and mixed with their opposite numbers on the other side of the Atlantic. Some of them would revolutionise the study of humanity: Abraham Maslow, Gregory Bateson, Fritz Perls, Carl Rogers, Wilhem Reich, Ludwig Binswanger and others... Their discoveries about human functioning influenced not only the world of

psychology but also other sciences such as quantum physics. Later, the Vietnam War played an important role – it caused most of these researchers to move to the American west coast, as did most pacifists. The result was that during the 1960s there was, to the south of San Francisco, the greatest concentration of "psychology researchers" – psychiatrists, psychologists and philosophers – in human history. Several movements developed, of which the three main ones were humanistic psychology, the Palo Alto school and transpersonal psychology. The researchers of these different schools were starting to revolutionise the way the way we understand other people. A revolution was under way, a pressing need to understand human nature better and to rediscover the essence of Being. It started to become clear that a self-awareness tool was needed; the Enneagram emerged and was successful because of this fertile ground. The three key post-war pioneers of the Enneagram, Oscar Ichazo, Claudio Naranjo and Helen Palmer, saw the Enneagram first and foremost as a way of expanding consciousness.

Humanistic psychology

This discipline brings together luminaries such as Carl Rogers, Rollo May and Erich Fromm. Founded in 1963, the Association of Humanistic Psychology has 5 key tenets [1]: that individuals

- are more than the sum of their parts
- are affected by their relationships with others
- are conscious
- have choice
- and are endowed with free will.

The Palo Alto School [2]

This school was founded on the basis of Gregory Bateson's research on systemic thought. The fruit of this research was a new way of thinking, which could be summarised as *"Think globally, act locally"*.

"Think globally" – what does this mean? In the West, we have always taught our children analytical thought processes, i.e. that in order to understand a phenomenon, we need to break it down into its constituent parts. Systemic thinking, on the contrary, holds that each element can only be understood by referring to the global context of which it is part.

"Act locally" – this consists in taking practical action at the point where prompt action can lead to the greatest change.

Over thirty years, systemic thinking has been transposed with great success into sectors as complex as unemployment, the environment or understanding violence. From a psychological point of view, this way of thinking has three key applications: family therapy, brief therapy and Gestalt. The five principles of the Association of Humanistic Psychology apply equally well to this school.

Transpersonal psychology

The transpersonal movement was set up in the USA in 1969 around a statement of C. G. Jung that the intellect is just a small part of the psyche, whereas the psyche itself has a cosmic dimension. For Jung, every soul needs transcendence; the individual needs to connect with the sacred. Jung was the first of the psychologists who didn't stop at intellectual and emotional functioning but went beyond the personal to the transpersonal[3]; that is, believing that as humans we are essentially searching for a higher part of ourselves. This Swiss trail-blazer was followed by several humanists such as Abraham Maslow, Viktor Frankl, Charles Tart[4] and Stanislas Grof. They went beyond "classic psychology"; they plumbed the depths of human consciousness, taking further the work of Karlfried Graf Duerckheim and Rudolf Steiner. Without actually being spiritual, this movement was interested in the higher aspects of Being.

Conscious humanity

It was in this context that the Enneagram would really get going, in San Francisco in 1971. Not only did all the research results on the psyche come together, but they started to result in practical applications. For example, all these researchers, and other therapists too, validated the relevance of Gestalt therapy[5] when they went on courses with Friz Perls at the Esalen Institute, one of the first centres for personal development. In this melting pot of new perspectives, the really revolutionary contribution was the idea of considering humans as "conscious", which implies that in therapy, the relationship between a *therapist who knows and a patient who lets themselves be taken charge of* is not necessarily the only possible one. It suggests the desirability of a new form of relationship where the patient becomes co-responsible, the co-creator of their therapy, conscious of themselves and of their own development.

The appearance of the "wealthy and dissatisfied" generation

The other crucial element that came into play at this time was the emergence of the wealthy and dissatisfied generation. A load of people of about forty with a career and a happy family life started to turn up to therapy with requests such as: *"In my emotional and professional life I've got everything I always dreamed of, but I'm looking for something else. The different religions that I know don't attract me or don't fit me any more."* At that time psychotherapists had no strategies to work with people who were doing ok; they didn't know where to send these people who had everything and yet who were looking for more. The birth of the three movements discussed above came out of a whole generation of people demanding to understand themselves more deeply.

Offering a tool for self-awareness

The two strands were converging. On the one hand, therapeutic professionals wanted to make people more autonomous, more conscious of themselves, through a self-awareness tool that would be accessible to everyone. On the other hand, the "wealthy and dissatisfied" generation was demanding a tool to enable their self-development to move forward. Supply and demand were about to join up. But it was a third reason that convinced Claudio Naranjo to push forward with his research into the Enneagram. Claudio's main idea was to offer therapists a tool which would enable them quickly to detect the individual shape of each patient's fragility. In order to develop this, for two years he brought together on weekday evenings in San Francisco a team of about thirty people: psychologists, philosophers, monks, nuns and teachers. This research team was called the *Seekers After Truth*. During their work, this group teased out the links between the nine passions of the Enneagram and the classic psychological pathologies. Crucially, they did this by applying the principle that humans are responsible beings; this group didn't consist of a teacher giving a lesson to pupils, but of a group of people who were seeking together. It was in this group therefore that the "narrative tradition school" saw the light of day: welcoming everyone's testimony in a climate of deep listening, recognising the whole person: body, heart and head.

Claudio Naranjo

At this time the Chilean Claudio Naranjo, through the various strands of his impressive CV, brought together several powerful lines of work, although he was still under forty. As part of his work as a psychiatrist who taught humanistic psychology, his clinical research aimed at replacing certain chemicals used in psychiatry with natural plants producing the same effects. He also taught a course in comparative religion in California and would later be invited to Harvard University sociology department to continue his research. He learned the basics of the Enneagram with Oscar Ichazo at Arica in Chile.

Claudio has written several books, of which *Ennea-Type Structures*, one of his books about the Enneagram, has been translated into a number of languages. In addition to these professional exploits, Claudio has also challenged himself at several levels; he undertook Gestalt therapy with Friz Perls and has practised various types of meditation: yoga, zen and vipassana. He was also Fritz Perls' successor at Esalen for a while, facilitating Gestalt therapy groups.

Helen Palmer

After studying classical psychology and Zen, Helen explored various physical and mental meditation techniques. In the 1960s she undertook research on the development of intuition and identified various types of intuition. When she then came across the Enneagram, she was surprised to find that the different sorts of intuition she had been working on corresponded closely with the Enneagram types. Since then, Helen has contributed significantly to the Enneagram's development world-wide.

In 1973 she took over from Claudio Naranjo the task of developing and structuring the teaching of the Enneagram in the narrative tradition. Helen was careful to keep the Enneagram within the humanist context which had been her starting point, in particular by bringing in techniques such as meditation.

In the 1980s she was at the head of a legal fight to ensure that the Enneagram would continue to be available to everyone and not subject to copyright. She linked the Enneagram to her research on intuition, adding more subtle information which enabled a better understanding of the nine holy ideas. She was part of the creation of the International Enneagram Association, the world-wide Enneagram association which is the forum for key authors and trends.

Helen has written several books, of which: *"The Enneagram Advantage"*, translated into more than twenty languages, is still considered the world-wide reference text. In 2004, she was chosen to be among the first twelve people invited to the Waldzell Institute to reflect on the theme *"Will individual transformation be the key to changing the world?"*, with other guests such as Shirin Ebadi, the 2003 Nobel Peace Prize winner.

David Daniels

In 1988 David Daniels, professor of medicine, specialist in clinical psychology and professor of behavioural science at the University of Stanford, worked with Helen to create the Enneagram Professional Training Program[6]. David's involvement proved to be a decisive step in the Enneagram's evolution; not only is David recognised as an eminent figure in his field on the west coast of America, but he also arranged for Stanford to host the first international Enneagram conference in 1994.

The narrative tradition

David Daniels introduces the narrative tradition in this way: *"Founded by Claudio Naranjo in 1970, the narrative tradition relies on the living witness of people of each type. Groups of people representing the same profile tell their own story in a "panel". In this way you can directly experience their individual observations, their daily preoccupations and the characteristics of each type. The narrative tradition is certainly the best way to teach the Enneagram. It offers every advantage; it brings the system alive, enabling listeners to identify their own profile more easily, and it helps people appreciate differences."* The Enneagram has two key advantages: its down-to-earth approach, and the fact that the narrative tradition brings to the fore the emotional side and the particular energy of each type.

THE ENNEAGRAM

The origins of the Enneagram go far back into history. Some elements seem to come from Pythagoras, but there is no formal proof of this at present. Since then, the diagram has travelled widely back and forth around the world and you can find it in different cultures and in several different historical periods. In this book, we have chosen to focus on the history of the Enneagram since its renewal in the 1970s.

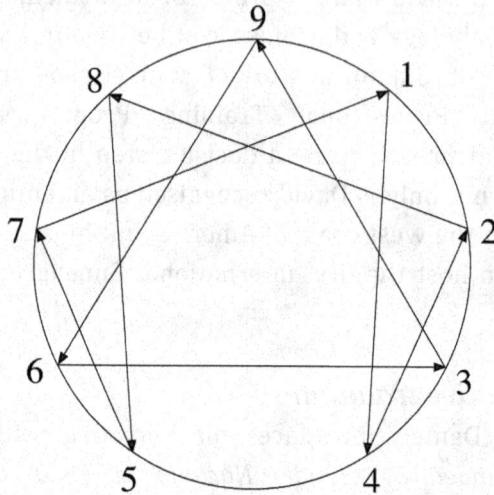

Figure 1 – The Enneagram

The Enneagram is both a diagram and a framework for understanding personality. Its primary purpose is promoting self-knowledge: helping us better to understand the various facets which coexist within us. The system suggests that there are nine points or personality types, each of which corresponds to a pattern of daily habits. Finding our type, our dominant personality facet, is a first and challenging step; to do that we need to explore the shadow side of our personality. We need to start noticing our unconscious motivations, fears and blockages – and the end result is that we start recognising our main fragility and noticing how it keeps repeating itself. But the Enneagram doesn't stop there; it also offers us landmarks for spiritual transformation. It shows us how to move beyond automatic behaviours, fears and blockages in order to rediscover *"the real me"*, or the essence of Being. But beware, there are no miracles or magic solutions; although the Enneagram gives you the landmarks, the map and compass, you still have to take the journey yourself...

Key things to remember

The Enneagram is a model.

It is particularly used as a framework for understanding personality.

It is accessible to everyone.

Its first purpose is to expand consciousness, to make us more aware.

It can also be used to help us know ourselves better and increase our understanding of others.

PERSONALITY – A SHELL TO PROTECT OURSELVES

A metaphor for the human condition

In this section you will find a summary of the different emotional stages of early childhood. If you would like a more academic description, we refer you to the works of Jean Piaget and Margaret Mahler.

Birth

The child comes from a watery world; for nine months it has been immersed in liquid in an undifferentiated world where it is provided with everything it needs with no effort on its part. And then suddenly, all at once, bang, it's born. It goes from a liquid to a solid, real world. If you imagine a new-born baby as incredibly vulnerable and fragile, just imagine its experience of birth: the strangling narrows of the birth canal, compression, blinding lights, a ten-fold increase in noise, cold air...

What pain does the child experience? – Suffering, distress, first experience of bodily tension

Dependence

After birth, the baby is no longer being continuously nourished, and for the first few months is therefore totally dependent on the outside world. In order to survive it either has to put its trust completely in the environment, or it has to learn to show that it is hungry – this is uncomfortable; it can't even provide for its own needs.

What does it experience? – Distress, tension

Coming and going in the world

One day, at the age of between twelve and eighteen months, the child suddenly discovers that things are separate. *"Mummy and I are two people. The chair and the table are two things. In the evening, once she has kissed me goodnight, she might not come back".* These discoveries are major shocks in the child's development. The child comes to realise that its mother and it are two separate beings.

What is the experience? – Distress, doubt, fear, tension

Loneliness

"Because I am a separate being, I am alone, thrown into the human condition, with no defence or protection from my hypersensitivity – alone, forever".

What is the experience? – Distress, tension

Autonomy

A new stage begins. *"Because I am separate, I am independent; therefore I am autonomous. This means that little by little, I can start to explore my surroundings, leave mother for a little and then come back. Then I can go a bit further away from her and come back; I can fall, bump myself, come up against the unknown – and come back. It's risky and dangerous but I have no choice. Since I'm going to have to survive on my own, I need to find my bearings in the world. I will certainly frighten myself as I explore; I will find that the world can hurt me".*

It is probably during this phase that the child discovers that it cannot be itself, do whatever comes into its head, and still be safe. It is no longer in its carefree aquatic period. In this earthly world, nothing can be taken for granted – and the knocks the child takes during its exploration are all the more powerful because it still has no protection. It is still a hypersensitive vulnerable, fragile ball and its suffering gets to an intolerable level.

What is the emotional experience of all this? – *Suffering, distress, fear, tension. "I'm not going to be able to get through this. I cannot be myself, keep all this sensitivity and still survive in the world".*

The wound

One day in the child's development, some event or other proves decisive. It might not be a noticeable moment in time; it might even be something quite small, but it comes on top of years of wounds, frustrations and gaps between ideals and reality. For the child, this particular event is a moment of icy loneliness, a rude awakening, a bitter understanding, a momentary and terrifying vision of the implacable truth; the child discovers that it is not loved for its "true self" and that it probably never will be. In this instant it has to make a decisive choice; in order to survive it has to find a different way of coping with the world. And the first thing it has to do is to insulate itself from the true self's excessive vulnerability and the suffering it causes by setting up a protective shell. In the Enneagram, this episode marks the moment of wounding, whose particular form probably influences the child's choice of type.

Impact on the world

Another major stage is the moment when the child realises that although it can't be freely itself, it can get a sort of compensatory affection as long as it conforms to the expectations of its parents. *"If I pee in the potty, I will be loved; if I pee outside the potty I'll get told off".* This is an interesting discovery – the affection I get depends on my actions. This affection doesn't make up for what the child has lost by not being able to be itself, but it lessens the pain. So from the nine Enneagram types, the child chooses the type pattern that is likely to get it the maximum amount of affection.

What is the emotional result? – Lessening of distress. Lessening of tension. "When I act a part, when I play my role well, part of me is reassured; distress and tension lessen."

Identification

The child identifies with its role. Once it has found this way of surviving, this "not brilliant but better than nothing personality", the child identifies with this role so much that it falls asleep to it – in other words, its awareness of its true self falls asleep.

The result? – Lessening of distress, lessening of tension. "True me" and "false me" are separated.

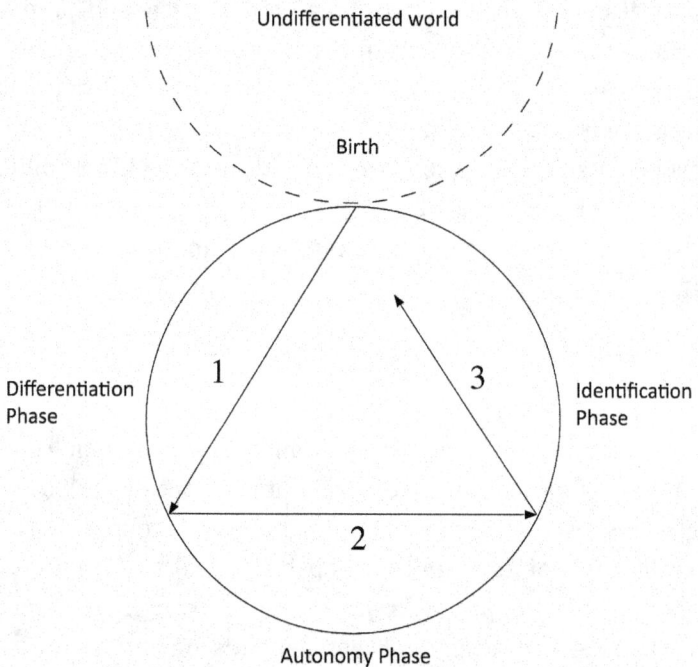

Undifferentiated world

Birth

Differentiation Phase

1

3

Identification Phase

2

Autonomy Phase

Figure 2 – Stages of childhood

NEUROSIS – A GOOD SURVIVAL STRATEGY

After this metaphorical story, here is a rather more academic account of the loss of Being. According to Dr Arthur Janov[7] the tiny child experiences a series of distressful events that result in a raft of needs: to be reassured, fed, cuddled, touched, stimulated… *"These primary needs form the heart of the world of the infant child. The neurotic process is activated when, over a period of time, these needs are not met. The infant doesn't know that someone ought to cuddle it when it cries or that it shouldn't be weaned too young, but if these needs remain unsatisfied, it suffers distress. At first, the child does everything in its power to get its needs met. It holds out its arms for a cuddle, it cries when it's hungry and it wriggles all over the place to make its needs known."*

If these needs remain unsatisfied for some time in spite of its efforts to get the attention of people around it, it will stifle its suffering by stifling its needs. Instinctively, the child will find the only possible solution: to separate its feelings from its awareness. In psychology this splitting off is known as cleavage; the psyche is divided up so that the child can survive. The unsatisfied needs haven't disappeared, but they have been cut off from consciousness. The benefit is that the child no longer has feelings – or rather, it no longer feels pain, because it is separated from it. It has created a protective shield, a suit of armour between it and the pain. It is armoured, it has repressed its true feelings in order to survive, because, as it was, the child was too vulnerable. The child has therefore transformed the satisfaction of its primary need – to be itself – into other needs which are more appropriate to the world in which it lives. In psychological terms, it has become neurotic. Dr Janov[8] says: *"Neurosis is a symbolic defensive compartmentalisation against excessive suffering. It continues because the symbolic satisfactions cannot meet the person's true needs. In order for the true needs to be met, they must be experienced and lived through. Unfortunately, because of the suffering they would cause, they have been deeply buried. When*

13

they are hidden in this way, we are in a permanent state of alert, and this state of alert is tension. It is that which pushes the little child, and later the adult, to use all means possible to get these false needs met."

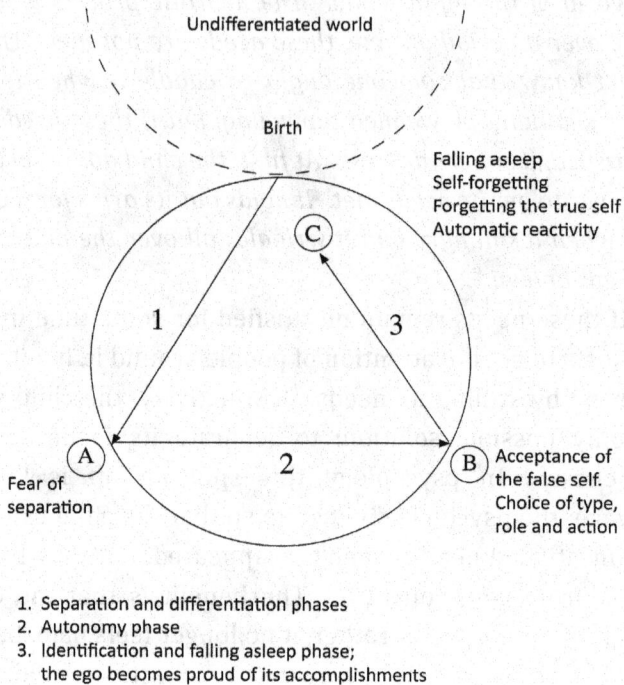

Undifferentiated world

Birth

Falling asleep
Self-forgetting
Forgetting the true self
Automatic reactivity

C

1

3

A

2

B

Acceptance of
the false self.
Choice of type,
role and action

Fear of
separation

1. Separation and differentiation phases
2. Autonomy phase
3. Identification and falling asleep phase;
   the ego becomes proud of its accomplishments

Figure 3 – The construction of the false self

To sum up, it is impossible for the "true me" of the new-born baby to be fulfilled. *As a child, I will try; the "true me" is so important to me that I will go through all kinds of suffering in order to get what I need. But once I get to the limit where I can't stand any more, I make the choice to change my priorities. If I can't have the ideal, I will make do with substitutes; I will choose a personality, the one which will give me at least some satisfaction and make me feel safe – and this personality, this mask I wear, will also enable me to protect my essence, my "true me". The price I pay is that I wear a protective breastplate; I repress my true feelings and I no longer have an objective view of the world. I relocate myself into a "false me" in order to survive psychologically.*

The child therefore enters a vicious circle – becoming something it is not (the personality) in order to get something that doesn't exist – i.e. it tries to find the feeling of completeness by satisfying the needs of the "false self". The decisive event is the tipping point from the true self to the false self. It is the moment when *"the accumulation of all the little wounds, rejections and frustrations sets hard to form a new way of being. Neurosis is the moment where the child begins to understand that in order to survive life it must give up part of itself. This realisation, which is too painful to be borne, never becomes completely conscious, with the result that the child starts to act in a neurotic fashion without having the least idea what has happened inside it."* [9]

THE THEORY OF THE ENNEAGRAM

The Enneagram puts forward the idea that there are therefore nine "disguises", nine ways of playing a role in order to try and survive and get at least a little affection. Depending on the wound of the particular environment, the child chooses the role which is most likely to get it the affection it needs.

Little by little, the role the child is playing comes to dominate its life; the child gets really into the game and plays it to the full. It struggles to make itself loveable, according to the terms of one of the nine patterns. If it can't be itself, it fights to become a different version of itself. Sooner or later, the child ends up believing that this new version is the true one. The game is no longer played consciously; this way of behaving becomes unconscious and automatic. It is neurotic. *"I have identified with my role. I am no longer conscious of the fact that deep inside me there is another me."* The Enneagram sets out nine profiles, with each profile describing the relationship between the wound and the role played out in daily life since that time.

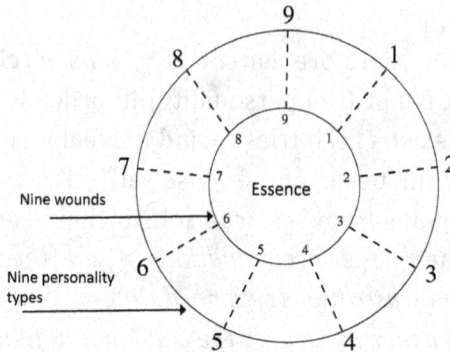

Figure 4 – Relationships between the nine wounds and the nine personality types

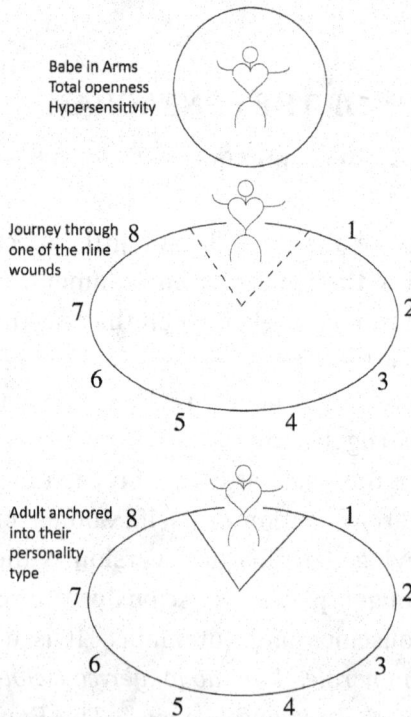

Figure 5 – Choosing a protective survival mechanism Example for Type 9

The role of this survival mechanism is to:

- protect our vulnerability
- turn our attention in a particular direction
- limit our sensitivity

This way of operating enabled us to not disintegrate as children.

Protecting true essence

Essence, that is the "true me" is very well protected. Different layers of resistance act as shock-absorbers against possible attacks from the outside world. Among these forms of protection are:

The Personality Type

As long as the external environment is normal, by staying in their normal type role each person is pretty much able to meet their needs. Because they have their chosen way of adapting to the world, they maintain that they regularly get what they need to feel safe, included or acknowledged. The false needs are met so there is no reason to examine their inner life. The body feels no great tension – they are in their Enneagram "type".

The Defence Mechanism

Each type has a preferred way of protecting itself, even though in certain circumstances others may kick in. These are the "resisting behaviours" that lessen the pain by interpreting objective reality in a particular way, in order to lessen the impact of a suffering which seems too great to be borne. They are called identification, introjection, projection, narcotisation etc. We will say more about these in the second part of this book, where we look at the 27 profiles.

The Passion

In order not to experience our original emotional suffering, we have developed an automatic behaviour which increases tension; everything that might threaten our personality must be fought against, denied, repulsed. The passion is a visceral fear which simultaneously sets up an emotional pressure and a physical tension – it's a physiological mechanism which pushes the human organism to satisfy the needs of the false self. Each time something happens externally, a stimulus pushes us to take on our habitual role, through our automatic behaviour.

When that is not enough, the tension goes up another notch, which lets us know that the first line of defence has been crossed and that the emotion that we are feeling is getting close to essence. That's very dangerous, because getting close to essence also means that we will have to re-experience the feeling of the original wound which was so painful. This brings up a primeval feeling linked to what we feel when our life is in danger; it's beyond fear – it's terror. Because we have abandoned our true self we are in a situation which feels very unsafe; our best protection seems to be to focus on our type needs, identify with our personality and lose contact with everything except the urgency of the present situation. It is as though we lose objective awareness. Over time, the more this repeated pattern of feeling we're in an "emergency situation" becomes automatic, the more we become a robotic slave of our type needs. We are identified with our role and we want to be recognised for our type qualities – and the greater our terror of re-experiencing our wound, the more this desire grows. This is the "Passion" of the type – and it's an enormous emotional energy.

Instinctive responses

Now we are into the territory of instinctive drivers. We are *instinctively* programmed to survive, to protect our living organism. The Petit Larousse dictionary defines a driver as follows: *"Fundamental energy of a being which pushes it to take action in order to reduce tension."*

Figure 6 illustrates how we use shock-absorbers or bumpers to protect essence. In reality there is no difference between the various layers of protection; they all merge into each other. However, naming them enables us to become more aware of our conditioned reflexes and to be less at the mercy of our automatic behaviours.

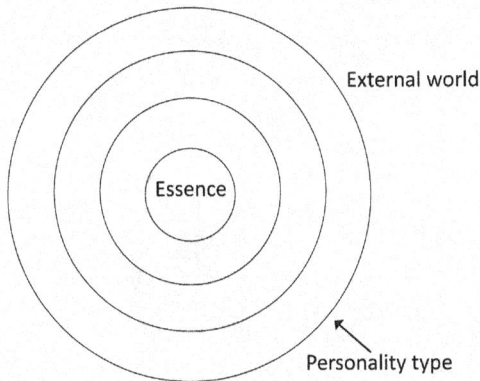

Figure 6 – Essence is protected from the outside world by several layers of resistance

---

Key things to remember

Various protective mechanisms ensured our survival during our childhood. Today, they are so well engrained that we are no longer even conscious of their existence.

Most of the time we operate "on automatic", focused on satisfying our type needs, and we're proud of our behaviour.

THE THREE CENTRES OF PERCEPTION

According to the Enneagram, we have three centres of perception, three ways of communicating with the outside world:

- the mental centre, situated in the head
- the emotional centre, situated in the heart
- the instinctive centre, situated in the belly.

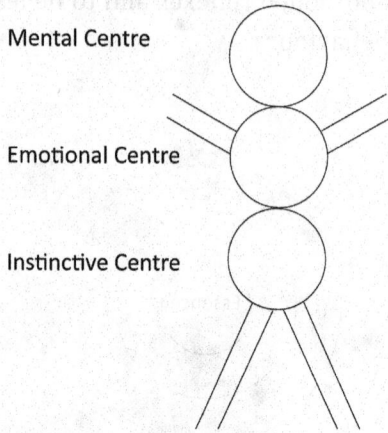

Figure 7 – The three centres of perception

These three centres work differently according to whether we are "on automatic" (in our habitual type function) or whether we are in essence, free of our armour.

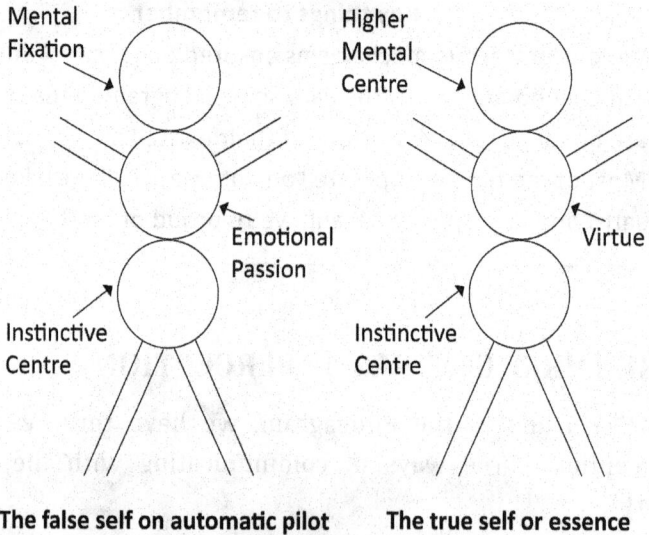

The false self on automatic pilot   The true self or essence

Figure 8 – The extent to which we perceive the three centres varies according to our ability to be present to ourselves

The mental centre[10]

"The mental centre has two extremes, the fixation and the holy idea[11]. The fixation is the name given to the mental preoccupation, to the principal way in which each type pays attention. The state of pure receptivity is the quality of the mental centre when it is freed from its habitual patterns, when the fixation is no longer there. When our mental centre stops its chatter, there is no emptiness or vacuum. On the contrary, peace of mind takes over and what can then emerge is the mental talent of each type: that intuitive knowledge which is beyond our usual mental habits". For each type, names have been given to each of the nine fixations and also to the holy ideas, which is when the mental centre is completely receptive and no longer focused on the type's habitual direction.

The emotional centre

Found in the heart, the emotional centre is the one which enables us to express and receive emotions, to let ourselves be touched emotionally, to create relationships, to charm and convince others. Again, two extremes are in operation: the passion and the virtue. The habitual reaction of each type is called the "passion"; it can be seen as the motor, the force which drives the personality. At the other extreme is the state of well-being, linked to detaching from the passion, which is called the "virtue." When the energy of the passion no longer sinks into its habitual reaction this energy can be remobilised, which enables us to gain access to the virtue of the type. At this point a state of inner peace settles in, because the person has moved beyond the worrying level of tension caused by the passion. This state feels different for each type; the names which have been given to the nine passions and virtues come from very ancient concepts and can be found in several different traditions and cultures.

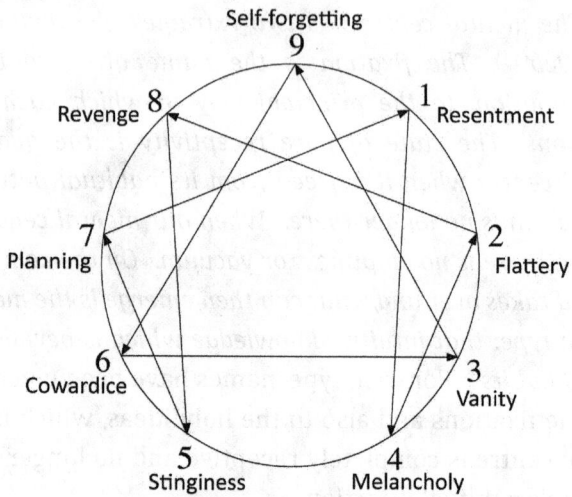

The Fixations – or nine types
of mental distortion

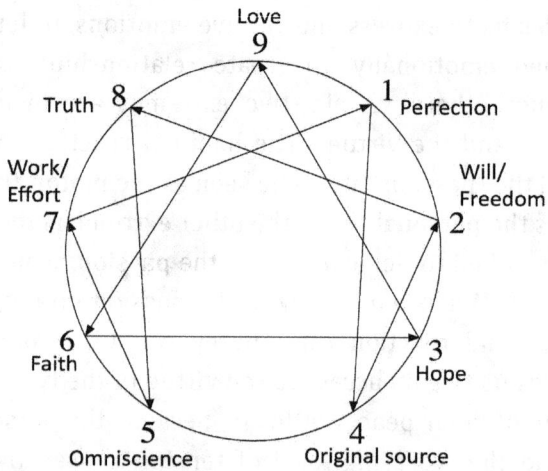

The Higher Mental Centre or nine
receptive mental states

Figure 9 – Fixations and Holy Ideas

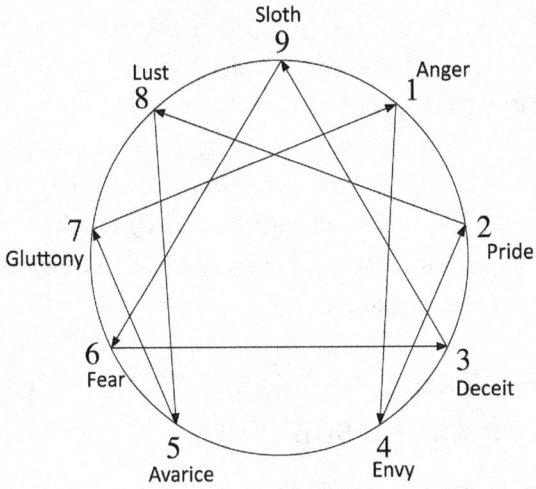

**Passion - nine types of
emotional reactivity**

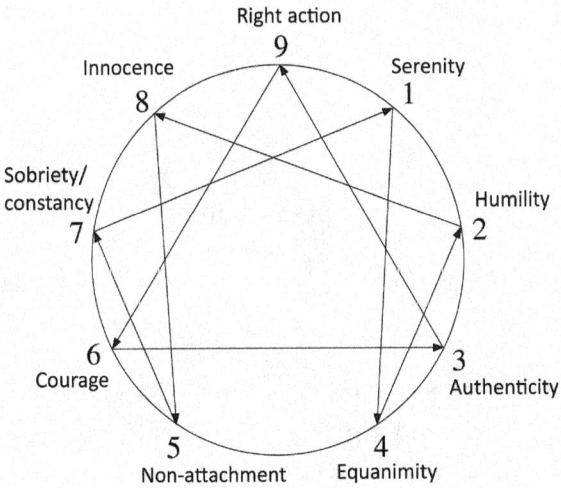

Virtues – nine ways of opening the heart

Figure 10 – Passions and Virtues

The instinctive centre

The instinctive centre is a primeval, ancient, visceral life force, which can't be transformed through conscious effort. Rather it can either be polluted by the passion and programmed to satisfy the type's needs, or be free and capable of acting spontaneously. Those who have practised sport, martial arts, dance or who have run marathons at a high level know the feeling of the special intelligence of the instinctive centre – that feeling of being in the zone.

THE IMPORTANCE OF THE INSTINCTIVE CENTRE FOR DETERMINING SUBTYPES

The instinctive centre is itself sub-divided into three basic instincts:
- self-preservation
- sexual or one-to-one
- social

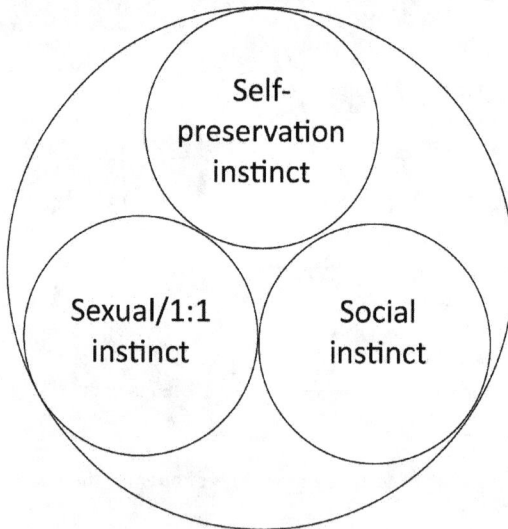

Figure 11 – The instinctive centre is composed of three fundamental drivers

The self-preservation instinct concerns our need for food, shelter and warmth: *"I will survive if I have somewhere to live, something to eat and a way to keep warm"*. The sexual/one-to-one instinct is about our instinct to procreate, to perpetuate the human race. *"I will survive if I can form a relationship with someone and have children."* The social instinct governs our need to belong to a group. *"I will survive if I am welcomed by a community."*

All of us have all three instincts but depending on the experiences of our early childhood, one of them will have been damaged and will therefore have been activated more than the others. This gives us a particular sensitivity in the area concerned; we all have a dominant instinct. It is difficult to detect because it is affected by reflexes which are deeply rooted in the unconscious. For example, on the first day of a subtypes workshop, everyone tends to think that their three instincts are balanced until, as they listen to the stories of people who already know their dominant instinct, they have an "aha!" moment where they realise their preference. It often takes a workshop lasting at least three days to arrive at this powerful acceptance of the self, of the instinctive drivers which have been buried away in us even more deeply than our type.

The self-preservation instinct

For Peter O'Hanrahan[12] self-preservation is our primary driver: finding the food, shelter and warmth that will enable us to survive. This is about our security in the physical world. During the first months of our existence (until the age of about two) we were completely dependent on our mother or her substitute to feed us. The level of material comfort around us was also crucial for our well-being. If the principal wound of our early childhood happened during this period, it is probably the self-preservation instinct which will dominate. Its key characteristic is the need to look after your physical needs and it leads to pre-occupations focused around:

- Food – worrying about having enough to eat, the contents and times of meals, the need to go shopping
- The house: the importance of the home, its comfort and furnishings
- Nature: the need for regular contact with trees, flowers and the elements
- Body rhythms, having a good relationship with your body: health, how much sleep you get, physical exercise
- Clothes: having good shoes, warm clothes, that everything is well made
- Money: worrying about having enough
- The family unit: worrying about the safety and the future of your nearest and dearest.

If this instinct is your dominant one, it is likely that you will have concerns in most of the areas above.

The sexual/one-to-one instinct

The next phase following early childhood is the differentiation phase, between the ages of two and four – realising that mummy and I are two separate people. *"Because I realise that I exist separately from you, I can start going away from you – all on my own – and come back to you."* This period of coming and going intensifies the relationship between the child and its mother. *"It is an intense relationship, leaving you and finding you again, being your preferred person to talk to, having a special relationship with you."* In the same way, in the physical world we were fascinated to discover that every object exists separately. This one-to-one relationship therefore holds true for the relationship between an object and me as well as for a person and me. This object is not me; I can have a particular relationship with it; it and I are separate.

Most recent theory holds that if the principal childhood wound took place during this phase, the sexual/one-to-one instinct will be the dominant one. Its key characteristic is the need to be in relationship and therefore it engenders preoccupations around:

- Being more at ease in one-to-one relationships than with groups
- Being able to generate an intense energy when in one-to-one relationships
- Being able, by a single look, to create a strong bond with someone
- Not liking to be alone for a long time and enjoying having someone to spend time with
- Not liking to live alone and needing someone to share my life with
- Wanting to be the centre of the world for the other person when we are together
- Considering sexuality as important, if not essential
- Having a passionate side
- Having very good powers of concentration
- Being concerned about being charming and able to attract the attention of others to me.

If this instinct is your dominant one, you will probably have concerns in most of these areas. So, to compare this with the self-preservation instinct: when and what you eat is much less important than your need to be with someone – which doesn't stop you enjoying the meal!

The social instinct

The third phase of childhood is the move into the world: realising the existence of other people, the ability to make relationships with other people and make friends. In order to establish our identity it is essential that we get the sense of security of belonging to a group, whether it is a family, cultural, national or religious group. *"I can live much more freely if I have the support of quite a wide group of friends."* If the principal childhood wound happened during this phase, the social instinct will dominate. Its key characteristic is the need to belong to a group and it therefore sets up preoccupations around:

- How easily I can make relationships with others
- The desire to know who is who and who does what within the group
- Needing lots of friends and liking to spend time with them
- Enjoying taking part in meetings and events
- Knowing how to make relationships when I arrive in a new town
- Being aware of titles and social levels and respecting those who have status
- Being concerned about social duties like voting and other civic duties
- Being interested in what politicians and the government are doing
- Being recognised socially by others.

If this instinct is your dominant one, you will probably have concerns about all the themes above. So to compare this with the self-preservation instinct, the exact time of the meal is less important than the presence of the friends you have invited to dinner. In addition, if this is your dominant instinct, you will be concerned by how an organisation or a country works: how and why responsibilities are allocated, where the power lies, who are the sub-groups within the group, the clans and loyalties.

These three instincts are therefore clearly different parts of our life, and in our daily life our most damaged instinct will determine the focus of our preoccupations, needs and desires. Katherine Chernick Fauvre, in her book *Enneagram Instinctual Subtypes*, considers that *"Just like the nine Enneagram passions, the instinctive drivers act like forces which may be unconscious but which are still pervasive and represent our most fundamental way of being. They will colour the way we act, think, feel and finally the way we express ourselves"*. In theory we are influenced by all three, but almost always one of them dominates and determines where we put our attention – it is as though the dominant driver forces us to live in the territory which suits us best.

Key things to remember

We have three centres of intelligence that link us to the outside world: the mental centre, the emotional centre and the instinctive centre.

The instinctive centre is itself made up of three instincts: self-preservation, sexual/one-to-one and social.

One of these three instincts dominates and conditions the way we live and react to life.

HOW THE SUBTYPE WORKS

We only exist in relation to others. "I" can only exist if there is a "You" or an "It". In other words, we live perpetually in direct relationship with our external environment, and depending on how friendly or threatening that environment is, we will react to it with different degrees of tension.

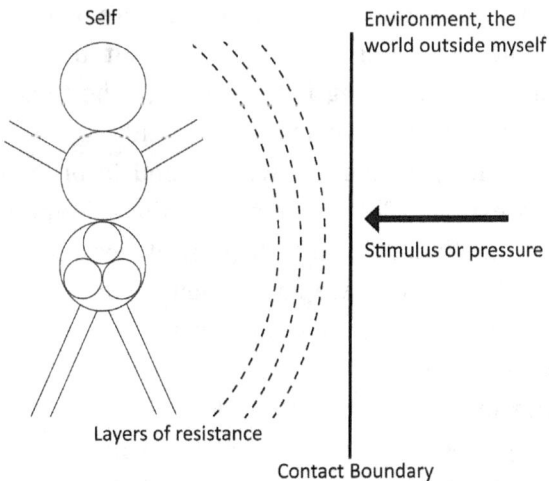

Figure 12 – The relationship between me and the external environment

Tension

For most of us, our different layers of protection are unconscious. They operate according to the level of danger; depending on the degree of threat in the environment, our response will be different.

At the first level, it is mainly about focus of attention. In daily life, we live "on automatic" a bit like robots, focused on meeting our type's needs. Even when everything is normal, there is always an internal tension or vigilance which pushes us to focus our attention in a particular direction.

When the external stimulation goes up a notch, our defence mechanism comes into play – it filters the external event in a particular way in order to make it more psychologically digestible. If the external pressure persists, the tension goes up another notch to force us to react. Our attention fixes itself in the direction concerned – this is the mental fixation. The emotional passion generates a rise in heart rate and muscular tension which pushes us to respond immediately because we must at all costs meet the needs of our type.

If the external threat remains, because the danger is imminent the instinctive centre will also generate tension – so then we must respond from our gut. Different sorts of reaction are possible according to the danger felt by the ego. The principal way of reacting is to discharge the tension in order not to re-experience the pain of the wound.

At each level of tension we respond in order to adapt to external pressure. This movement is the subtype at work; it's the reaction to a certain degree of external threat, the conditioned reflex that we have when the level of our internal tension goes up. The emotional response of the passion is combined with the instinctive response in an act of survival to defend the integrity of the false self.

The subtype is the action which springs into being at the precise moment when the internal tension becomes too great. An external stimulus activates the defence mechanism, the tension rises and the fear of reliving the pain of our wound pushes us to react. The emotional passion and the dominant instinct work together – there is an association between *"If I stay here, suffering will overwhelm me"* and *"physically, if I stay here I will be annihilated."* The passion and the instinct are united in the battle for survival. And while all this is going on the mental centre focuses on analysing the danger through the lens of the type; this is the "fixation".

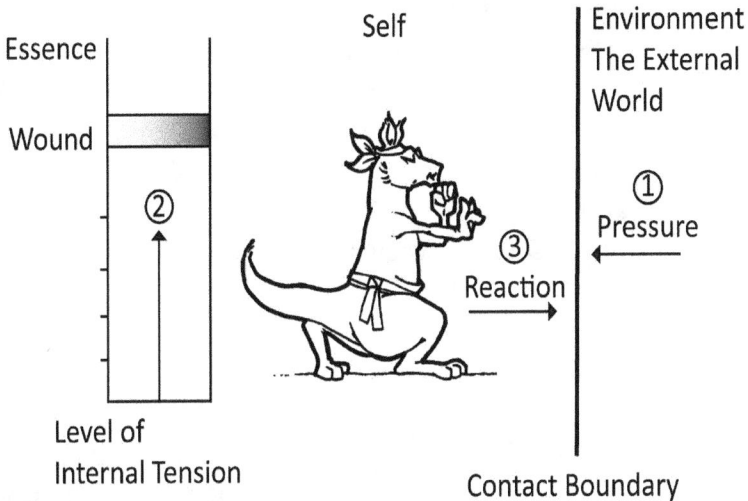

Figure 13 – Subtype is a reaction, an action

Energy and tension

In terms of energy, Dr Janov considers that *"the original forgotten feelings of the true self are like a neuro-chemical energy which turns into a mechanical energy, creating constant internal pressure".* It is clear that any external stimulus leads to raised tension and the generation of energy. Our organism is programmed to get rid of this excess energy. If we don't take action, if we don't react in a compulsive way in line with the beliefs of our personality, this level of tension will put us in contact with our forgotten suffering.

> *When there is a strong threat, our heart accelerates, our body tenses and a visceral energy wells up in the instinctive centre – just as in all stress situations, when we seem to have more energy than normal.*

The three subtypes

There are three subtypes for each type on the Enneagram, and these depend on which instinct was most wounded in the child. So for each type there will be:

- A self-preservation subtype when the passion is allied to the self-preservation instinct – figure 14a
- A one-to-one subtype when the passion is allied to the sexual instinct – figure 14b
- A social subtype when the passion is allied to the social instinct – figure 14c.

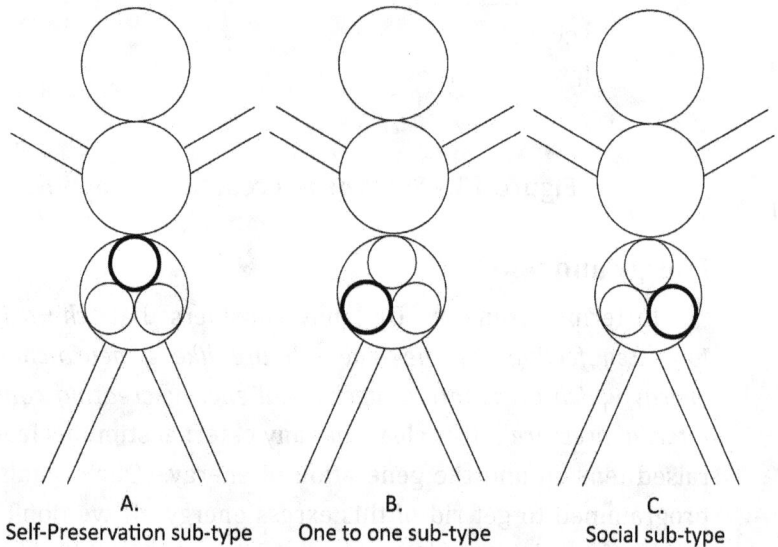

A.	B.	C.
Self-Preservation sub-type	One to one sub-type	Social sub-type

Figure 14 – The three subtypes

Three different ways of operating from the basis of the same type[13]

An example from Type One

Type One anger is internal; with its teeth clenched, it takes a position against reality. It's about not accepting things as they are: a strong internal anger which is not expressed and an irritation against the world. Below are examples of how the Type One passion of Anger can play out through the three different subtypes.

The Self-Preservation Type One

Preoccupations of Type One: trying to do the right thing
Preoccupation of the Self-Preservation Subtype: the home,
security, and material safety
= ANXIETY

Making sure their primary needs are met is so important that it makes these Ones anxious; they can't have fun and feel safe at the same time, they just have to keep working harder and harder. It's a never-ending task, because they feel they are the guardian of the rules and standards. The world keeps changing but they can't see this, so they endlessly take care of the details, want to control everything, try to be disciplined and beat themselves up – which of course just creates more anxiety rather than reducing it.

The One-to-One Type One

Preoccupations of Type One: trying to do the right thing
Preoccupation of the One-to-One Subtype: focus on the
partner
= ZEAL OR JEALOUSY

There's a contradiction here – on the one hand, the Type strives for excellence, on the other hand the one-to-one subtype focuses on relationships. But both are about control: control of material things and control of the relationship with the other person. It's about absolute, complete commitment and self-sacrifice allied to charm, willingness to be controlled and the desire to adapt. The anger of the type is often kept under the surface and comes out in the form of critical comments.

The Social Type One

> *Preoccupations of Type One: trying to do the right thing*
> *Preoccupation of the Social Subtype: focusing on friends,*
> *associations, groups*
> *= SOCIAL INADAPTABILITY*

This is about anger against the world that is not the way it should be – politics, religion or other causes provide opportunities for the reformer instinct. The One sense of duty brings discipline and the repression of spontaneity, the obligation to work hard and to think only in terms of excellence. The social instinct brings a tendency to lecture, to preach, together with dignity and an aristocratic and superior self-concept. Again, the anger is not expressed; it gets transmuted into a critical mind-set, a strong wish to reform anyone who acts against the norms – this is the inadaptability of the social One.

Conclusions

Starting from the same Type (in this example Ones who are driven by a sort of inwardly turned anger linked to "an irritation against the world which should behave better") there are three different ways of operating. Each subtype thinks first about the things that worry them and the core of their preoccupations turns in a particular direction:

- Home, safety and material things for the self-preservation subtype
- The partner or the subject which fascinates them for the one-to-one subtype
- Friends, associations, groups for the social subtype.

Key things to remember

The subtype describes:

✓ The dominant instinct that worries me most.

✓ The shape of my needs, desires and wants.

✓ The flight behaviour that I use when the pressure becomes too much.

✓ The life objective that is most important to me.

APPLICATIONS OF SUBTYPE TO EVERYDAY LIFE

"I use the Enneagram in my helping profession and I would like to know if subtypes will help me to identify my client's type better"

David Daniels considers that *"If you don't know about subtypes, you have about 50% chance of wrongly identifying someone's type."* I am in complete and utter agreement with him. Some examples of how this plays out: when I get into a discussion about the possible Enneagram type of presidential candidates, most people who don't know about subtypes think that most candidates are Threes, because they want to succeed and they are focused on their goals. For people who know the subtypes, it is clear that candidates' behaviour (or what you can see of it) comes in most cases from the social subtype. Once you have taken this into account, you can then try to identify the type which is hidden under the subtype. *"My son is a Three because he is concerned about his image, he likes meeting famous people, being recognised and having a network of influential people who might be useful."* Up to that point, there is nothing here that enables us to decide if the son in question is a Three or whether he sits in another type, but with a social subtype.

Here is another example: *"My wife is a Six because she is continuously anxious about everything to do with safety, the locks, the fire extinguisher, setting the alarm when we go away on holiday."* At this point we don't have enough information to decide whether this woman is in fact a Six or whether she is from another type, but with a self-preservation subtype.

A last example: *"My colleague must be a Four; he is passionate, he even gets carried away sometimes, and he has moods which swing from high to low."* Here again we must be careful; personally I would ask for more information in order to check whether it's likely that he might be a one-to-one subtype, before confirming a type Four.

Essential facts about subtypes

What is type?
This is the structure of the personality, how our inner life is organised, at three levels:

Mental preoccupations: how things work in my head

My emotional wound: the way in which I protect myself emotionally

My direction of instinctive focus: this depends on which of my three instincts has been the most damaged. This area, which preoccupies me the most, is also the area where I have special talents.

What is subtype?
This is the behaviour that is generated automatically when tension rises. This reaction costs me time and energy but the pay-off is that it lowers my tensions and fears. Because the subtype results in movement, you can see it, particularly if it recurs; in any dangerous situation we will tend to use the same response.

When does the subtype kick in?
When tension rises following a stimulus or threat from the outside world, and we feel the need to react, to do something.

Why does the subtype kick in?

To avoid reliving the primary wound of our childhood, with all its great suffering, which we risk if we stay still. Our subtype is the reactivity by which we express and get rid of our excess build-up of emotion.

What is the benefit of the subtype?

It calms us; by reacting we have dispersed energy, the tension has lessened and we feel better.

What are the consequences of the subtype?

On the one hand it makes us get rid of a lot of useless energy. On the other hand it makes us experts in the field of our dominant instinct. Unconsciously, in order to make ourselves safe we tend to prefer the field where we feel most at ease. So self-preservation subtypes tend to be happy focusing on the organisation of material things, such as running the house, but their trap is focusing too much on this area, to the detriment of the quality of their one-to-one relationships or their social life.

Why is it useful to know our subtype?

It helps us to notice the times when tension rises or when we are starting to go on automatic again.

It helps us to recognise that most of our preoccupations or needs are concentrated in these three areas.

It makes us better able to listen to people of other subtypes.

It helps us reduce our tendency to react, so that we are less dominated by our automatic behaviour.

Is one subtype always dominant?

Yes in most cases, but it isn't always easy to flush it out. If you're not sure of your own, ask your partner or children – usually they will know. However, this doesn't stop you hitting all three situations in the same day: for example, having to take care of the house, go to a work meeting and a one-to-one dinner.

Nevertheless you will notice that you are more pre-occupied with and also more gifted and more at ease in one of the three situations.

A good evening at home for each of the three subtypes

Self-preservation subtype: *"My husband and I were at home. We were a bit tired; we had had dinner together. The children had settled down, we lit the fire, we watched a film, the atmosphere was gentle, the cat was on my knee –just the kind of family cocoon that I love. What I feel in those moments is tenderness, a kind of physical tenderness. We are at home, within our four walls, in the warm, and we're safe."*

One-to-one subtype: *"My husband and I were at home. I suggested putting the children to bed early. I gave them their dinner, then I put the youngest to bed and read her a story. Then I put the oldest to bed and had a chat with him about his day. I had a shower and came back into the lounge. We had dinner for two – gazing at each other across the table. His red pullover was beautiful; he looked into my eyes; we talked together, just us two, forget the outside world. Then he wanted to watch a film – it was "The Sound of Music". We shared the high points of the film almost by telepathy, intensely together. What I feel in those moments is the intensity of our relationship as a couple."*

Social subtype: *"My husband and I were at home. As I'm not keen on quiet evenings when nothing happens, I had decided to invite eight or ten friends who I thought would enjoy each other's company. There was a great atmosphere; the guests talked to each other with such animation. As far as what we talked about, everything came in: politics, world religions, the future of our civilisation... I love setting up evenings like this – in fact I'd be happy to be out every evening going to lectures or the theatre or to eat with friends. In fact, that's what often happens; as my husband and I belong to several clubs, our evenings are very busy."*

Comments on the examples above
Instinctively, these people are not looking for the same thing – their needs, wants and desires are not the same.

The self-preservation subtype is really looking for well-being, safety and comfort – it's linked to the self-preservation instinct. So they want to be able to enjoy their possessions and are worried by the prospect of losing them. They are also very conscious of their body, well-being and health. They don't necessarily need to talk a lot when everything is going well. They are happy being quietly at home, and they are sensitive to the atmosphere of the place they are in.

The one-to-one subtype experiences time in sequences, like a series of moments, *"I gave the children their dinner. I put the first one to bed. I put the second one to bed. I had dinner with my husband."* The other characteristic of this subtype is the pursuit of intensity. *"I put the most presence I can into each thing that I do. The day is divided into portions composed of moments which have more or less passion behind them. A good day is a day when there are a lot of highly charged moments one after the other: the smile of one of my children at the breakfast table, the briefing meeting with my boss, the business lunch, the presentation of the project at 5pm, my husband's look when I came home, the quality of his presence that particular evening. A highly charged moment doesn't have to be long, as long as it has a spark of life."* The final aspect is a need to feel they have a special bond with the person they are with, a need to be reassured about their ability to charm.

The social subtype loves to be involved with social events: a first night at the opera, tickets to the hot rock concert at the Albert Hall, cocktails with the mayor, dinner with so-and-so where several well-known people were there, a reunion with old school friends... What matters is going out and meeting people, talking with them about issues in society, communicating, building relationships, being respected, popular and having an honourable status within the group. All this is much better than a boring evening at home.

Consequence 1: The skills of the three subtypes are not the same

Self-preservation subtypes are talented in managing the physical aspects of life; one-to-ones are good at convincing the person they are talking to; socials are the ones with the good address-book. Let's see how this plays out when you're moving house:

The **"self-preses"** will instinctively know how to get organised: the number of cardboard boxes and rolls of sticky tape you will need, the size of the lorry, where to find the right vehicle, the number of journeys that need to be planned for, which room each box will need to go into.

The **"one-to-ones"** will panic; this isn't their field; so either they will charm a self-pres friend into supervising the organisation, or they will find the right removal company who will take charge of everything.

The" **socials"** will call on their gang of friends and will organise an event around the removal and turn it into a memorable celebration.

Consequence 2: We are uncomfortable in our non-preferred fields

Again in the example of the house move, only the self-preses will be comfortable being in direct contact with all the physical stuff that needs to be moved. The other two types will get round it by sub-contracting in some way.

Consequence 3: We often show total incomprehension or even condescension towards the other two subtypes

At the Centre for Enneagram studies (CEE) in Paris, the research we have done over 15 years seems to show that most of our friends are from the same subtype as us; it seems that it is in our preferred field that we find the people with whom we have most affinity. If couples have different subtypes, points where they annoy each other will appear fairly early in the relationship. For example, a self-preservation subtype will fairly soon get annoyed by the demands of a social partner to go out so often. On the other hand, the social partner will ask themselves what on earth can be the pleasure that their self-preservation partner gets from staying at home so often in the evenings. Personally, I think that the misunderstandings that happen in couples probably come more often from a difference of subtype than a difference of type – this is not to say that couples formed of people from the same subtype will never have problems!

Once a year at the CEE we hold a three day workshop[14] where representatives from the same subtype share the things they have in common and describe the qualities and faults of the other subtypes. We then work on our relationships with other people, using the subtypes as our principal model. Some people find out some amazing things about their relationship with their partner. Here is a short summary of the subtype panels from the workshop of June 2006, which had about 50 participants. These are comments in their raw state, which don't take into account the interactive exercises that preceded or followed this exercise.

What the self-preservation and social subtypes said about the one-to-one subtypes

"We like your charming side, your passion, spontaneity, sensuousness, intensity, which are all things which make us feel valued. We don't like your manipulative side, which takes advantage of its charm – that makes us feel as though we don't know where we are with you. We don't like it when you are either too present or too absent from us, and also, you don't seem to realise the effect of the intensity of relationship that you tend to set up."

What the self-preservation and one-to-one subtypes said about the social subtypes

"We really like your ability to express yourselves in a group, to put effort in to help the community, your ambition for the group, your knowledge about how to organise projects, bring people together, and the way you have a broad vision of the world and humanity. We don't like it when you talk too much: words, meetings, requests. We are unhappy with the importance you attach to knowing lots of people, with your pride in being indispensable. We also get fed up when you either disappear completely or you are unavailable (busy on your mobile?) to the point where we can never have a quiet minute with you."

What the one-to-one and social subtypes said about the self-preservation subtypes

"You make us feel safe. We like your practical side, your reliability about physical things, your foresight, your ability to listen to your body. We are touched by the way you simply take charge of all the practical things that need doing while we are away. We do get annoyed when you seem sometimes to have feet of clay, when you think nothing exists in the world outside your house. We are sometimes disappointed by the narrow range of your interests and by your seeming anxiety about the prospect of widening your circle of acquaintances."

Much could be said about the dynamics of relationships between the subtypes; that might be the subject of the next book! In this book however, the main objective is to focus on the transformation of Being.

We will now move on to the description of the 27 subtypes, emphasising the internal tension and the characteristics that can alert us to notice the moment when the reactivity of the subtype kicks in. To make the descriptions easier to understand, we have chosen to illustrate each type with an animal, and each subtype with an easily identifiable sign. So you can spot the self-preservation subtypes by the scarf around their neck, the one-to-one by the little dashes around their head to signal their intensity, and the socials by their bow tie. The diagrams that follow therefore show:

- Figure 15 – The self-preservation subtypes with their scarf
- Figure 16 – The one-to-one subtypes with their intense expression
- Figure 17 – The social subtypes with their bow tie

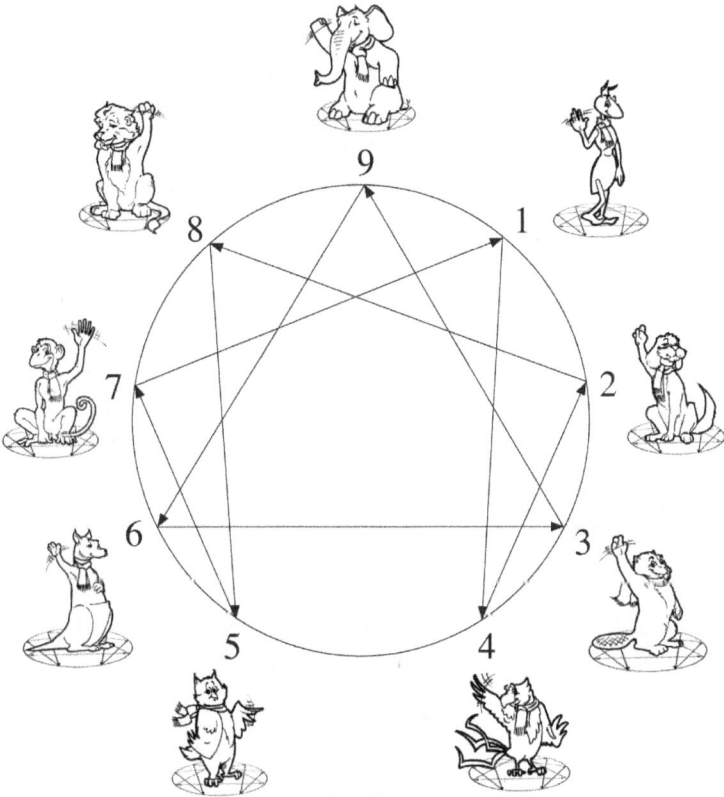

**Figure 15 – The nine self-preservation subtypes
with their scarf**

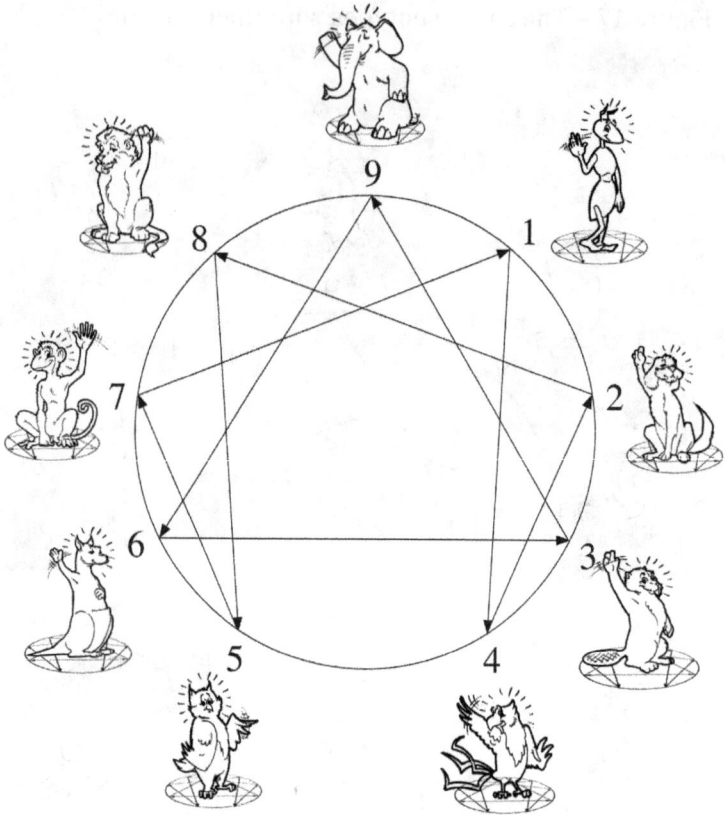

Figure 16 – The nine one-to-one subtypes with their intense expression

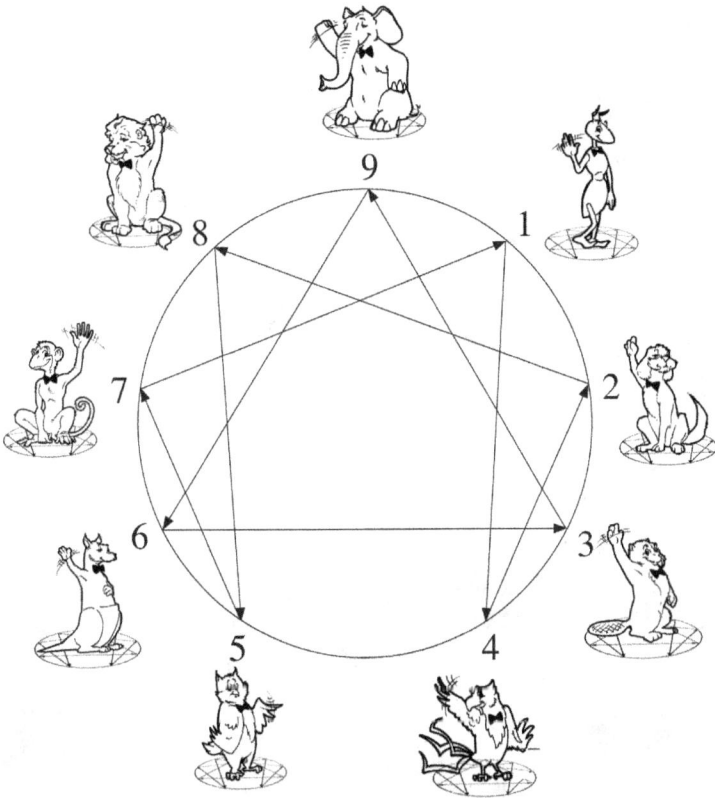

Figure17 – The nine social subtypes with their bow tie

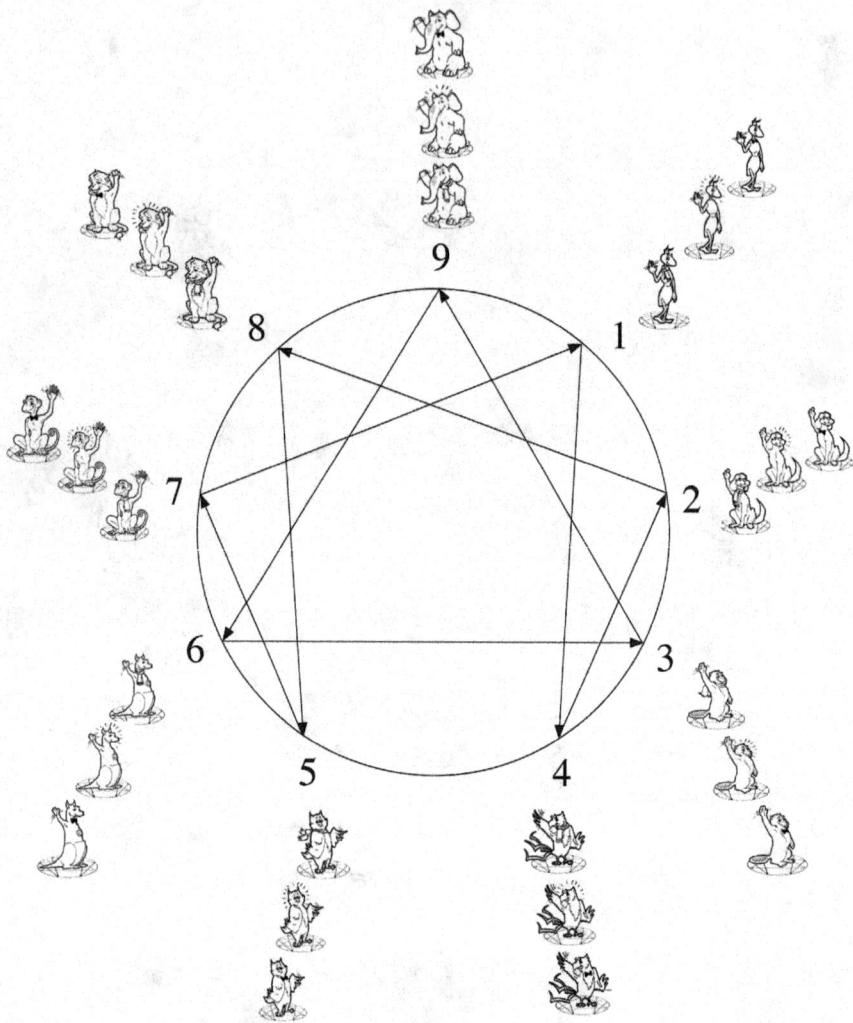

Figure 18 – three subtypes for each type = 27 profiles

References for Part 1

1. Noel Salathé (1995) *Psychotherapie Existentielle*, Institut de Psychotherapie Gestalt Existentielle, Geneva
2. Extract from Edmond Parc and Dominique Picard (2000) *The Palo Alto School*, Editions Retz
3. In German "ueberpersoenlich"
4. Author of (1975) *Transpersonal Psychologies*, Harper and Row
5. Therapy that focuses on the emotions in the present moment and bodily feelings. In order find out more, contact the Paris Gestalt School + 331 43224041
6. This programme exists in France – see www.enneagramme.eu
7. Dr Arthur Janov (1973) *The Primal Scream*, Abacus
8. Ibid
9. Ibid
10. Eric Salmon and Lizbeth Robinson (1998) *L'Enneagramme, Lecture de la Personnalité,* Collection Essentialis, France.
11. The naming of this concept varies according to the author. The original Spanish name has not come down to us. It describes a broadened and objective consciousness, unpolluted by resistance, fear and inhibition and which results in a way of thinking which is both fluid and receptive.
12. See Peter O'Hanrahan's website at www.enneagramwork.com
13. Extracts from the second part of this book
14. See www.cee-enneagramme.eu or +33 1 46430692

PART 2: RECOGNISING YOUR SUBTYPE

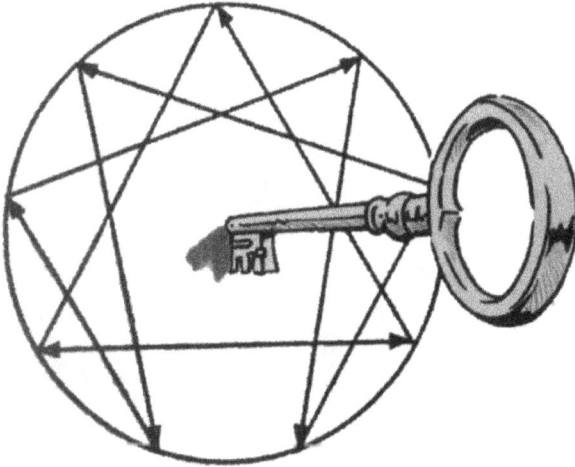

THE THREE SUBTYPES OF TYPE 1

Wound

Somewhere in their past, Type One children were told off the first time they dared to have some spontaneous fun and were deeply hurt because of it. So they gave up their "true self" and adopted instead a correct, polite and disciplined approach to life – in the hope of being loved in return.

Passion: Anger

Ones' anger is internal – it's about *"I clench my teeth, I put my head down and do my best, I set a good example, I focus on achieving excellence."* It's about not accepting things as they are. Oscar Ichazo talks about "taking up arms against reality". The desire to reform the world is so strong that Ones live permanently with a strong internal anger that is not expressed, a resentment that is linked to an irritation against the world *"which should be more virtuous."* This resentment often appears as a sense of injustice about the enormous amount of work that they have put in – they have worked more than others and they have the feeling that they have not been justly rewarded. So they have a sort of self-righteous indignation.

Preferred Defence Mechanism: Reaction Formation

During their childhood, Ones were not allowed their natural impulses and they came to believe that every spontaneous act would be criticised by the outside world. So they learned to criticise themselves first; they look out for and react against every "bad" behaviour, such as desires or anger. When an unacceptable impulse arises, it is blocked – pursuing the idea is forbidden, but the available energy is redirected in another direction. For example everything which is labelled "bad" must be turned into something else; impulses to do with pleasure or relaxation result in a period of tension before they can turn them into efforts to do better in some way. This is called reaction formation. Even sexual desires can be diverted into moral actions, such as paying even more attention to setting the table or cooking a meal. Or the angry energy can be transformed into kindness: *"I want to use a swearword"* becomes *"Put your attention into taking care of others."*

THE SELF-PRESERVATION TYPE ONE

Preoccupations of Type One: trying to do the right thing
Preoccupation of the Self-Preservation Subtype: the home,
security, and material safety
= ANXIETY

For Ones with a Self-Preservation focus, making sure their primary needs are met is so important that it makes them anxious. Ones can't have fun and feel safe at the same time, so they adopt the adage: "Work, work...." There is a vicious circle going on here. They apply the formula "Keep trying for better, keep trying harder..." to an external world in which it seems that every day the same challenges come round; every day there is something new. It's like a bottomless pit when you feel you are the guardian of the rules and standards in a world that keeps changing. Even if you specify the highest standards, it won't prevent unexpected situations arising. Trying to wash things whiter than white won't change the fact that every day the kids will get their clothes dirty again. Ones can't see that they are setting themselves up for a world of endless frustration, so they put their shoulders to the wheel: taking care of the details, wanting to control everything, being disciplined, beating themselves up – and all of that both reduces their anxiety and generates more. *"Playing scales for hours in order to make sure I can do my part perfectly is reassuring, but it still doesn't guarantee that I will be brilliant when I have to play in the concert."*

The Self-Preservation subtype's preoccupation with the realm of survival (maintaining the house, education, preparing food...) takes precedence over other needs. The slightest mistake (using the wrong amount of detergent or the wrong quantity of salt in a recipe) can make them feel insecure and reduce their already shaky self-esteem to nothing. In order to avoid that insecurity they set up more and more control points, checking the details, continually referring to their inner critic and reminding themselves of their duty. Another source of anxiety is the question of time: the feeling that *"I won't have the time to do properly all the things I have to do"* raises their stress and anxiety. The problem is that too much self-sacrifice simply makes tension and resentment even greater. Often they don't think they're good enough to merit getting their needs met, and this belief is the source of their anxiety. The conflict between their personal desire and what would be the correct thing to do generates worry. *"Should I do what I want to do, or should I do the right thing?"* – and this brings uncertainty, anxiety and procrastination.

Their need to control is linked to the need to correct both their environment and their personal appearance – just like a classic French garden where the plants are formally arranged and the trees well clipped.

The Paradox

However much I concentrate and however anxious I become this effort will never actually reassure me.

Metaphor – The Pioneer

This is the pioneer that we see in Western films. They head out to create a new and better world where nature will be tamed, where children will be well brought up: a world of justice. In spite of the continuous wind and dust they sit upright on their horse, a Bible in their hand, correctly dressed with their clothes neat and tidy.

Warning Signs for Type One
- Too much anxiety
- Excess tension in the jaw, back or lips
- Not enough pleasure, having fun, releasing pent-up feelings
- Too much self-sacrifice

Warning Signs for the Self-Preservation Subtype
- Paying too much attention to security
- Spending too much time at work
- Being too concerned with material well-being
- Too many routine evenings at home

A SELF-PRESERVATION ONE'S VIEW – HERVÉ

What I like about my Type

I love the fact that I can sum up situations and people quickly. My present job is as a management and human resources consultant; I facilitate training for companies and coach teams and individuals. The fact that I'm a gut type enables me to identify the needs and intentions of the people I work with. It enables me to tune in to them and adapt easily to their emotions and to the requirements of the immediate situation. These days I find it easier than in the past to be reflective about these feelings and intuitions. I feel that I'm less wrapped up in my instinctive centre than before, and so I can use my mental capacities more clearly in the service of my instinctive intuition.

My type also enables me to achieve things in a well thought through and confident way. I have staying power – I enjoy long-term projects; I feel like a long distance runner. I can give a lot of energy to projects that motivate me, such as, for example, my recent career change, which I achieved at the age of 50.

What I like about my Subtype

I'm very sensitive to the atmosphere of the place I'm in; I make sure that the people around me are comfortable; warmth and light are really important for me. I think that it's thanks to my subtype that I'm able to deal with the automatic behaviour of my type. It's by noticing my physical sensations, being aware of my body and being in regular contact with nature that I can reach more serenity, the virtue of my type, which I'm trying to develop. Five years ago I moved to the country, to be in the middle of the natural world – it nourishes me and I need it; it's essential to me.

Anxiety has always been important and omnipresent, both in my private and professional life; I'm anxious that the material comforts of life will not appear automatically. I went through a time when I lost all objectivity; I was in a permanent state of anxiety about the future, in spite of my beautiful house, my current account in credit and savings that would enable me to survive well if something bad happened. My anger and resentment came out all the time through my preoccupation with practical things, for example my fuel consumption or monitoring petrol prices at the pump.

What I like about the Combination of my Type and Subtype

*As I said above, understanding my subtype was essential in order for me to work on myself; it's the key element which helped me to experience the letting go that I really needed but which I wasn't managing to achieve in real life. People often say that the inner observer helps us to detach from our reactivity – but you have to know where to look, and the discovery of this **anxiety** focused in certain very precise areas around self-preservation was a real eye-opener for me.*

Film Reference[1] – Ben Hur

Jerusalem, AD 26. Prince Judah Ben Hur meets up with his childhood friend Messala, who has been appointed head of the Roman garrison. One day as he is watching a Roman patrol going past below, a slate comes off his garden wall and falls on the head of a Roman officer. This accident leads to a difficult interview between Ben Hur (Charlton Heston) and Messala. Ben Hur wants nothing to do with his ex-friend's political ideas and wants to hold on to his version of the truth. Messala finally decides to interpret the incident as an assassination attempt, which leads to Ben Hur's property being confiscated and him being sent to the galleys.

Ben Hur then starts to show behaviour that exemplifies his preoccupations; he is anxious throughout the film, convinced that this is the only stance that will enable him to vindicate his position; he grits his teeth because he knows that the slightest relaxation would lose him everything he has been working for. This is a film about self-preservation in the sense that it's about survival of the tribe, finding his mother and sister and doing everything he can to enable them to have a home again and to be safe. It's also a question of blood sweat and tears; in the galley he rows, he puts in unimaginable effort with gritted teeth. This film is not about vengeance; Ben Hur could have killed many times, but he never did – even going to the point of saving a Roman commander.

This is a One profile because the hero is upright, irreproachable and exemplary; his will comes from his moral principles. This film is interesting because it gives us a broader understanding of the stereotype of a self-preservation One, who is often described as an obsessive that spends all their time tidying up. This film also shows us a vast array of different expressions of repressed anger.

THE ONE-TO-ONE TYPE ONE

Preoccupations of Type One: trying to do the right thing
Preoccupation of the One-to-One Subtype: focus on the
partner
= ZEAL OR JEALOUSY

Two slightly contradictory drivers can be found here. On the one hand you have the Type One striving for excellence; on the other hand the one-to-one subtype which is focused on the relationship with the significant other. Whereas the self-preservation subtype tries to control material things, the one-to-one subtype tries to control the relationship with the other person. The One energy is about absolute, complete commitment and self-sacrifice; the one-to-one subtype energy adds in charm, willingness to be controlled and the desire to adapt. I have met many one-to-one Ones who thought they were Threes because they were aware that they were trying to charm people. In fact, their concern with their image was simply due to their one-to-one subtype. With Ones, anger is often kept under the surface and comes out in the form of a critical mind-set: *"You're a **tiny** bit late, dear!"* Claudio Naranjo explains this[2]: *"Criticism doesn't only show up as looking for faults, but also shows up as a sort of elitism which leads the other person to feel guilty. There is often a sort of unacknowledged authoritarianism; "I want..." gets transformed into "you ought to..."".* The veiled accusation contains the hope that the other person will change their behaviour in the direction that I desire.

In his book 'Enneagram Structures', Claudio Naranjo gives another example: *"They keep an eye on the other person with a kind of anxious over-enthusiasm. Often they want to tell them off angrily and occasionally they allow themselves to put their desire into practice and adopt a "holier than thou" approach."*

The good side of this subtype is their ability to concentrate. Here you get two drivers coming together: the meticulous concentration of Ones and the great ability to focus of the one-to-one subtype. In one-to-one relationships, because they are trying as hard as they can to be the best possible partner, they will be "jealous" of the fact that the other person doesn't seem to be trying as hard. They will also be jealous of the "time off" that their partner seems to allow themselves. *"He allows himself time with his friends, with his work colleagues, with his tennis partner ... It's always me that sacrifices myself too much for our relationship and I don't think enough about myself. This can get to the point where I'm jealous of the enjoyment he gets out of watching his football match on the telly while I'm there, available to do his bidding, focused on him alone. I experience the football as a rival, and this jealousy simply increases my determination to be an even better partner."*

Somewhere there is a feeling of deficiency; they are jealous and frightened of anyone who is more intelligent, more sexy or more joyful than them, because they represent the risk that one day perhaps, in spite of all their efforts, their partner will leave them for a better offer. Oscar Ichazo explains[3]: *"A relationship is always under threat from someone else who might be even more perfect".* For dating couples, it's the belief that there will always be someone better than them in the eyes of their beloved.

At work, they can be obsessively focused on the tasks they have to get through, on doing the best they possibly can to deliver the tasks they are responsible for. They experience enormous jealousy if their less assiduous but more political rival gets a promotion; they are bitter that they haven't been recognised in due proportion to the number of hours they have worked. At some level they think that if they didn't get the promotion it was because they didn't work hard enough – and this pushes them back into their determination to be even better.

The Paradox

Making all the effort in the world to be the perfect partner risks putting my partner under stress and making them want to leave.

Metaphor[4] – The Preacher

This is the picture of the evangelist or preacher who promulgates high moral principles and whose application of these principles is exemplary. They are jealous and angry towards people who dare to behave more freely.

Warning Signs for Type Ones

- Excess anxiety
- Too much tension: clenched jaws, stiff back, pursed lips
- Lack of pleasure, having fun, letting off steam
- Too much self-sacrifice

Warning Signs for the One-to-One Subtype

- Focus on wanting to prove that you are an intense, passionate person
- Too much focus on the partner: what they are doing, where they are, who they are meeting
- Too much focus on your own actions – not enough wider perspective
- Rivalry between your own goals and your partner's interest in other things.

A ONE-TO-ONE ONE'S VIEW – AURORE

What I like about my Type

Firstly, I love my energy; it's good to go to bed knowing that however tired I am as my head hits the pillow, I will wake up with all the fuel I need to do whatever I have to do tomorrow. I brought up four children, supported my husband when he was working fourteen hours a day, studied psychology and I practise today as a psychotherapist even though my youngest child is still at home. I thank heaven for this drive that I was born with, without which I certainly wouldn't have been able to accomplish all of that to a high standard.

I also like my stickability – I finish what I start; it doesn't matter long it takes. I often think of Penelope, the wife of Ulysses who, during her husband's twenty year absence, wove her cloth by day and unravelled it by night so that she could stick to the choice she had made. It's the same for me; I can find it difficult to make a choice, but once I have made it and it seems like the right one to me, I'll stick to it until the end. My husband uses a different word; he says that I'm stubborn.

The third quality I like is my honesty. I am incapable of lying; I blush to the tips of my ears. And anyway, it suits me always to speak the truth, even if it isn't always easy to be honest; there is sometimes a price to pay. Daring to say to someone "I don't like you when you act like that" will always have consequences.

What I like about my Subtype

I love the intensity of my one-to-one encounters; my day maintains its rhythm through these energy-raising moments. It's as if my internal barometer, which was on "Fair", goes beyond "Good" to "Super-Good". It can be a fleeting instant – this morning, it was me and a sparrow. It lasted, let's say, a tenth of a second in which our eyes met. I can't be sure what it felt, but I felt a brief but strong connection, and in my body it was as though I was filled with a ray of sunlight that recharged my batteries. It's just as true with music; when I like a piece, I let myself be taken by the melody and here we go; for a few seconds nothing else exists in the world except this relationship between the music and me – it's as though I were dancing with someone. Most often though, it happens in person-to-person relationships, but I chose these examples to show that it isn't limited to people.

What I like about the Combination of my Type and Subtype

*Well, I think I experience the up and down sides of the same qualities. If you take stickability on one side and honesty and the desire to experience strong one-to-one bonds on the other, of course it will be with those that I love most that I will want to experience this. An exceptional moment with my husband will raise the level of intensity even more, so I want him to be with me often so that these moments are more likely. And OK, I do tend to be **jealous** of his work or the professional commitments that take him away from me. Coming back to the question; I think that the good side of my type is the faithfulness and the ability to be able to take pleasure in small things.*

Film Reference – No Reservations

Kate is a head chef who does nothing but work. Her sister's death means that she has to take on the task of bringing up her niece Zoe, aged 10. This child coming into her life together with the arrival of a new sous-chef overturns her organised lifestyle and shatters her organised One certainties.

We can see Kate's One profile on several levels: her stiff, rigorous, meticulous side that won't let go, her harsh and sometimes hurtful way of speaking, her enormous reluctance to delegate, because other people won't do it as well as she would – and her principles: "I don't go out with people from my block of flats – it's a rule – and what's wrong with having rules? It's not as though I'm trying to control everything, it's just that I like things to go without a hitch – that's why I end up doing everything myself." We can also see her hypersensitivity when anyone questions the quality of her work: "The customer wants his steak recooked? – I'm saying it's cooked correctly!" She feels incompetent at this new role of adopted mother that she hasn't had time to learn: "I know that I'm not doing well, but I promise you that I'm doing my very best."

Her one-to-one subtype can be seen more clearly in the second part of the film, as we see her passion, her intense looks and also her seductive side (in spite of herself). One example of the union/fusion of the one-to-one subtype with what they are experiencing comes up when Kate is telling her therapist a recipe for quail with truffles and she is so wrapped up in what she is saying that she and the recipe almost become one.

You could look at the film as the story of a One's growth as they access the energy of Types Seven and Four. Because of the shock of her sister's death and the arrival of her niece in her life, Kate experiences Four emotions which she has to accept and which override her One need for control at all costs. Her Seven side also starts to come out slowly; she starts to enjoy playing games like Monopoly; she gradually relearns how to have fun, to laugh and to take life lightly. Here we see the paradox of the one-to-one One; on the one hand we have the One who wants to repeat what's right "if we could write a recipe book for life, all we would then have to do would be to apply it", on the other the one-to-one who is more spontaneous, unpredictable and passionate.

The film shows us these sides of a one-to-one One sequentially, but in fact in this type they're both happening at the same time; this type senses the paradox of the one-to-one who wants to go towards people and the One that wants to restrain impulses and spontaneity.

THE SOCIAL TYPE ONE

Preoccupations of Type One: trying to do the right thing
Preoccupation of the Social Subtype: focusing on friends,
associations, groups
= SOCIAL INADAPTABILITY

This subtype is about anger against the world which is not the way it should be – it's not good enough, we'd better put it right! Politics, religion or other causes will provide opportunities for reform. Jean-Jacques Rousseau is a good example of this; the encyclopaedia tells us he critiques the bases of a corrupting society and proposes principles for ethical public life. Here again, duty brings discipline and the repression of spontaneity, the obligation to work hard and to focus on excellence in everything. There is a tendency to lecture, to preach, and there is also consciousness of their dignity and an aristocratic and superior self-concept. Social Ones are civilised and self-policing; they are not spontaneous beings. Often, their anger presents itself as irritation, as criticism, but they rarely express true anger because it's not the done thing. So this anger gets transmuted into a critical mind-set, and there is sometimes an almost inquisitorial wish to reform anyone who acts differently – this is what inadaptability is about.

Sandra Maitri describes it thus:[5] *"Social Ones express their social awkwardness and insecurity in stiffness. They have rigid ideas about how both they and others should behave socially and their passion of anger arises when other people don't conform to these ideals. They become critical and put others in the wrong for not conforming to their social standards; it's a reaction formation to their underlying sense of not being good enough to belong."* As they have sweated blood to push their cause forward because they deeply believe that it is right, they can only see the world through that cause. This makes them blinkered; being fans of the French team may make them blind to the possible qualities of their opponents! In order to work successfully they have to know the rules, think logically and methodically, and this leads to a lack of spontaneity and difficulty working in non-structured organisations. Because they want to defend the right way to do things, they force themselves to do better at the expense of having a bit of fun. One of the consequences of this is that they can become alienated from their emotional experience.

Ones are disciplined people; they love order, obedience to the law or custom. They are often even more obedient to the principles, customs or rules of the game than they are to the real-life authority of people. Not only do they keep laws and social customs, but they respect them rigorously, because they care about principles, moral rules and ideals. Unconsciously, they impose these norms on others with enthusiasm and determination. They are just like Crusaders; they have the right to break skulls because their cause is excellent and their aspirations are noble. Social rigidity has no place for weaknesses, shades of grey or emotions, which are places where error might creep in.

The Paradox

Putting in too much fervour for a cause may in the end damage the cause itself.

Metaphor – The Reformer

This is the person who has read the rules of the game, knows them backwards, would like to improve them and who feels resentment towards anyone who takes them lightly.

Warning Signs for Type Ones

- Excess anxiety
- Too much tension: clenched jaws, stiff back, pursed lips
- Lack of pleasure, having fun, letting off steam
- Too much self-sacrifice

Warning Signs for Social Ones

- Caring too much about being acknowledged
- Spending too much time maintaining social relationships
- Belonging to too many groups, associations or clubs
- Too much devotion to the cause you espouse

A SOCIAL ONE'S VIEW – CHARLES

What I like about my Type

The power in me – thanks to this incredible energy, people around me can rely on me; I am available whenever someone needs me. Thanks to this energy I can live my values and get enthusiastically involved in what I do. I love my determination too. In my professional life as a managing director, I've got endless patience and obstinacy when it comes to keeping up quality or being consistent in what I require. I know that I'm demanding, but I can't imagine being satisfied with a job done badly. So my critical eye scans what has been done and how it has been done, and I will pick out any ways of doing it better, in a realistic way. My criticism rarely targets the person who did the job; I'm targeting the result rather than the person. I also think I'm good at organising chaos, in fact, the more catastrophic the situation, the more my strengths come naturally into play. I find that I've got a calm strength inside me, which enables me to structure what's going on and re-establish an order that people find reassuring.

What I like about my Subtype

I have a good sense of what's going on in a group – not in a commanding way, but I'm very conscious of the different elements that make up a group; I see how the different people in the group work together to form a whole. Also, I have a great respect for hierarchy; I'm one of those people who think that if someone has got to a certain level in an organisation, it's because they are competent. So my default position is to respect senior managers in an organisation and also those who have been there a long time even if they are not in a senior post; they are part of the history of the organisation. I also admire people who have gone to a lot of trouble to help a business to develop. I like introducing people to each other and I like to do it according to the proper formal protocol, to the point where people sometimes make fun of my conservative style.

What I like about the Combination of my Type and Subtype

What I like is the combination of the responsible, upright, honest strengths of the One and the social idea of the importance of working together. I run my company by imbuing it with my sense of what is right; I try to be exemplary and beyond criticism, in my speech, in the way I dress, the way I respect working hours and holiday rotas. Because I never cheat, I believe that I encourage others not to cheat either. In that way I believe I imbue the organisation with consistency. I hope that my sense of what is and is not correct will rub off on to other people. Before I learned about the Enneagram I didn't realise how demanding I am, both of myself and of others. The downside is that this rigour takes a lot of time, and I find it very hard to balance work and leisure.

Film Reference – The Remains of The Day

The scene is 1936 in Darlington, England. Stevens (Anthony Hopkins) is the butler at Darlington Hall, a luxurious English stately home, where he rigorously rules an army of domestic servants. Dignity, precision, obedience and discretion are his watchwords. He is completely devoted to Lord Darlington, who is a prestigious figure in the British aristocracy of the 1930s. As his second in command he takes on Miss Kenton (Emma Thompson), who is impulsive, playful and lively; she both irritates and fascinates him. Their mutual undeclared attraction is one of the key themes of the film. (I won't comment on the historical aspect of the film, which deals with the negotiations between the great European powers during the 1930s.)

Stevens' social Type One is very clear; in his behaviour, as in his tone of voice, you can detect a stiff, conventional, starchy aspect to him. His speech is politically and grammatically correct, hard and a little cold. His life revolves round his work; he is devoted to the hierarchy of the house and fastidious in applying it. When guests come for dinner, the watchword is "Each one to his job; we will show our foreign visitors that they are in England, where order and tradition still rule." The word "order" could be the key word for the social One, and it can sometimes be pushed to extremes. His father works in the team, and when they speak to each other, they call each other "Mr Stevens". When Miss Kenton tries to call the father by his

THE THREE SUBTYPES OF TYPE 1

first name, because she feels that they are on the same level of the hierarchy, she gets her knuckles rapped: "It is inappropriate to address an older person by their first name."

In a nutshell, Ones know the rules of the game and apply them. In this context the rules are about decorum and social rules. The "right thing" is written into the way things are done as though it were carved in marble – forever – in the same way that the knife goes on the right hand side of the plate and the fork on the left – that's the way it is. There is even one surreal scene where Stevens gets a tape measure out of his pocket to check that the glass is exactly the right distance from the edge of the table!

This character brings out several typical aspects of this type. He is a conservative in the sense that he is the guardian of what is, rather than an innovator. Moreover, he finds it doubly difficult to express his emotions; as a One they would jeopardise the precision of the work that has to be done. As a social subtype, it is not the done thing to express your emotions – until Miss Kenton arrives and arouses his repressed feelings. She is feminine and has a delicate awareness of the attractions between people. One day when she brings flowers into his office he panics: "No flowers; I prefer not to have any distractions and keep things tidy." A crucial scene happens when two employees are about to be sacked because they are Jews. Stevens is concerned to follow his master's instructions and Miss Kenton can't accept orders which take no account of the human factors. Even without the type contrast here, we see a contrast between subtypes; he is clearly social; she is more one-to-one. This film shows how difficult relationships can be when one person is stuck in their subtype; it's a sensitive, charming delicate film that got 8 Oscar nominations in 1994.

THE THREE SUBTYPES OF TYPE 2

Wound

At some point when they were desperately in need of affection, Type Two children came to the conclusion that they had nothing remarkable about them which would entitle them naturally to receive it from others. In other words, they experienced no support from others for the sense that they had of their own value. So they gave up their "true self", but realised that they could get a substitute kind of affection if they identified the needs of others and met them.

Passion: Pride

Pride happens when Twos are so pleased with the service they are giving that they deny their own needs. They want others to have a picture of them as a giver rather than a receiver; in other words, claiming that they are so busy that it's terribly generous of them to offer help. It's the strategy of giving in order to charm others and add to your own perceived value, an unusual alliance between tenderness and readiness to fight. Twos have an enormous need for love which is sometimes hidden by their independence. Their need to keep up some kind of self-esteem leads them to need to make relationships, and in order to achieve that, sexual attractiveness and charm are two of their key strategies.

Twos are impulsive, considerate, charming, warm and self-centred – all at the same time. They are sensitive, don't like being limited and tend to invade your space. They can be possessive and put too much of themselves into relationships.

Claudio Naranjo says[1] *"The repression of needs, associated with pride results in someone who is joyful, who seems to seek pleasure and adventure, but who doesn't realise the distress which drives their compulsive desire to please, and who is in any case too proud to reveal this desire."* They have a natural tendency to feel frustrated, rebellious against routine, discipline and anyone who prevents them from treating life as a game. They have a tendency to flattery, which in this case means focusing on others to the point where they give up their will to act for and on behalf of themselves – and risk losing sight of their own needs.

Preferred Defence Mechanism: Repressing Needs

Repression means wiping your own needs, wants and feelings from your consciousness – they disappear. This helps you to make relationships with others. Your need will be met through the tactic of guessing the need of the other person and doing everything you can to satisfy it. The consequence of this is that your true needs are forgotten or sent into the background because you know that you won't have the time to get round to them anyway.

Peter O'Hanrahan says[2] *"Twos have developed a particular image of themselves; they see themselves as thoughtful and obliging people whose value depends on the approval that they get from others. They focus on the positive to the point where it is difficult for them to recognise faults, particularly their own. They need to do a lot of personal work in order to admit that they also have failings such as envy, anger or fear. They fear being abandoned if their faults are seen, so as a consequence, if something is going badly, Twos will tend to put the blame on to others because it is so difficult for them to take responsibility for their own mistakes. In addition, when they do end up admitting that they bear some of the responsibility for a relationship which is not going well, Twos emit a kind of repressed anger which raises a feeling of guilt in the other person, so that they feel responsible for the Two's unhappiness."*

THE SELF-PRESERVATION TYPE TWO

Preoccupations of Type Two: finding out the needs of other people and repressing their own
Preoccupation of the Self-Preservation Subtype: home, security and material safety
= PRIVILEGE

This energy is about "me first". Managing their material well-being, to which they give all their energy, leads them to demand privileges. *"Given all the time that I spending looking after my family, their well-being and their health, I have the right to have the best seat at the table, to be served first, to get recognition for being the indispensable person in the household. Other people should give due importance and value to the devotion I put in."* It's the idea of preferential treatment, of having rights: *"I give, give, give; I do so many things for other people that I deserve special treatment; I should get interest back on the good works I have carried out."*

At work, they often exercise indirect power like an "éminence grise" rather than overtly, as Francoise X describes: *"I get great pleasure from putting in a lot of time and energy so that my boss has no practical problems. I think I have a natural gift for putting myself in his place, being empathetic to his needs. Given the constraints he works under, I know inside what he would like in terms of flight reservations, car hire and hotel rooms. I know how to manage his diary and rest periods just as he would if he were there. If necessary I can even set things up so that his meal arrives hot, at the ideal time, with his special dietary requirements. In the same way it seems completely natural to me to gatekeep his phone calls, pick out the priority calls, decide myself what is important and know his private phone numbers to help him save time in his relationships with his wife and children. But because I spend a lot of time and energy on that, I really value his appreciation. A smile or a glance, giving me recognition in the weekly team meeting, a friendly word at the annual team dinner, all these little signs of gratitude are absolutely necessary to me. I have too much pride to ask for them overtly, but if I didn't have them, I know that I would soon become very frustrated and aggressive."*

The Paradox

Looking after other people's needs and getting recognition for that, means that I never question what my own needs might be.

Metaphor – The Nursemaid

The nursemaid is naturally gifted for being motherly, comforting and being encouraging. She radiates warmth and nurturing. Another image for this is the Italian mother who is the real boss of the household without appearing to be. Whether they are male or female, they behave like a "nursing mother or father".

Warning Signs for Type Two
- Being too concerned for others
- Too much physical agitation
- Too much need for recognition
- Too much self-sacrifice

Warning Signs for the Self-Preservation Subtype
- Paying too much attention to safety
- Spending too much time at work
- Being too pre-occupied with material well-being
- Too many routine evenings at home

A SELF-PRESERVATION TWO'S VIEW – PASCALE

What I like about my Type

The word that comes to mind is "intuition". Unlike traditional beliefs about Twos, it's not just about "intuition about what is good for other people." It's wider than that; it

71

can also be about material things. For example, at 10 o'clock in the evening I might intuitively think that I won't lock the front door because I sense that for a reason that I don't yet know, I will need to open the door – and most of the time my intuition is right. Since I recognised my subtype I'm better able to manage its key features; I've come to accept that my intuitions always have a meaning, and that my development work is about restraining my compulsion to say or do something about them immediately. For example, when I have an intuitive sense of what would be good for the person I'm talking to, nowadays I manage to restrain my compulsion to tell them straight away. I'm content to stay present and store that information away in a corner of my mind. Over time I've come to realise that the information I get will probably be much more useful a few hours, days or even weeks later. It is as though restraining my first impulse not only improves my emotional balance but also the balance of my relationship with the other person and the use that they will make of my advice.

What I like about my Subtype

I found it hard to accept that I was a self-preservation subtype. At first I found this profile too "small" and lacking in breadth, particularly when it came to relationships. Later I came to terms with it as a sort of base camp: reassuring home territory from which I can go out to explore situations in the other subtypes. Nowadays I'm happy with who I am and I'm in tune with my self-preservation subtype. The result is that I think I go over-the-top less when I do get off-balance, whether it's going into my self-preservation side or when my Two goes off into Eight.

What I like about the Combination of my Type and Subtype

Finding out my combination of Type Two and self-preservation subtype has enabled me to have a better understanding of my spiritual view of the world; it's helped me better to understand the way I see the idea of a universe that's bigger than me, and my relationship to it. In practical terms, whereas I feel that I'm still just as compassionate towards others' suffering, I feel less of an obligation to do something about it straight away, to fling myself into meeting the needs of the first person who comes past, who hasn't even asked for my help. It is as if a sense of balance has come into being between the horizontal axis of the physicality of my Type Two and the vertical axis of the enlightenment that getting to know the subtypes has given me. Nowadays I feel as though the psychological work that I've been doing on my personality is in harmony with my spiritual development.

Film Reference – Fried Green Tomatoes at the Whistle Stop Café

The scene is 1980 in Alabama, USA. Deserted by her husband, 40 something Evelyn is fretting in the monotonous routine of a housewife. Her life revolves round the weekly visits she makes to a relative in an old people's home. There she meets Ninny, an old woman full of joie de vivre who tells her the stirring story of Ruth and Idgie, two inseparable women friends who in the 1920s opened a café whose speciality was fried green tomatoes. As the story unfolds, Ninny's serenity and the moving story she tells give Evelyn back her energy and enthusiasm for life.

Evelyn's Type Two doesn't immediately jump out at you, but we see a succession of delicate caring acts: chocolates, flowers, the way she looks at Ninny. Evelyn's empathy becomes more and more visible. It's easy to see that she operates out of the Heart centre, and when one day Evelyn finds her friend's room empty, we get two scenes of hysteria, one of sadness and the other of joy. We can see how very strong emotions can overwhelm this type. Towards the end, Evelyn's altruism even makes her ask the old woman to come and live with her, although her house is tiny.

In the film the two stories of the 1920s and the present day are superimposed on each other. We see survival in both stories – life and death, a little band of friends who stick together, concerns about basic hygiene and food. The smells of this country café seem to assail your nostrils, starting with fried green tomatoes. Human relationships are at the heart of the Two profile, and here we are surely in Two territory. This film is moving because of the bonds which form between the central characters: not only family bonds but also the friendship between friends and between generations, the bonds between blacks and whites and the bonds of authority between police commissioner and suspect, between suspect under interrogation and the judge. Even leaving the central character out of it, tenderness is the core world of this film. A sort of simple empathy takes you over and you find yourself living the emotions that affect the characters one after the other. Welcome to the world of the Two.

THE ONE-TO-ONE TYPE TWO

> *Preoccupation of Type Two: identifying the needs of other people and repressing their own*
> *Preoccupation of the One-to-One Subtype: focus on the partner*
> *= SEDUCTION/AGGRESSION*

Two lines of energy converge here. The need to create a connection and to be recognised is true of all Type Twos. Added to this there comes a sort of intense presence, which is the special realm of the one-to-one subtype. So for this type, both their type and their subtype need to seduce and to be noticed in order to be valued. It's a case of needing *not only* to establish a connection *but also* to gain approval by using charm and seduction. Pride then comes into the mix through a focus on empathising with the other person: *"getting involved in your interests and tastes in order to please you better."* There is a certain pride in being the favourite, the confidante, the shoulder to cry on when something goes wrong.

Unconsciously, the way one-to-one Twos use their body language and their concerned tone of voice reinforces the attempt to seduce: *"I can't help it; I like to be looked at, to be admired, I like it when people talk to me. I do therefore admit that sometimes making use of my sex appeal and the need to be loved get mixed up. From where I stand, there isn't necessarily a sexual aspect to my one-to-one relationships, but the way I look at people and my thoughtfulness have led to a certain number of misunderstandings. It was a great relief to me when I found out that this confusion is classic for one-to-one Twos. If my external appearance isn't enough to create a contact, it's true that I can then go into "aggressive seduction" mode. It's as though I'm hunting them down; I pursue the other person, demolishing all the barriers that could get in the way of a relationship. I act in a way that ensures that the other person is in the limelight, that they look good. I feel as though I change my stripes for each person I talk to, that I can adjust my approach to embody what they are expecting of me. I've got a whole range of different tactics to make the other person look good. I see myself as living in a world of sensitivity and sensuality rather than in intellect. What interests me is the emotion that's going on right now, the heart-to-heart contact, the intensity of the way we look at each other, the fact that we are sharing the same things at the same time. This comes relatively easily to me; I feel laughter rising in the other person and so of course we start laughing at the same time. This shared moment is not only about recognition of the other person, it's also a great joy."*

The Paradox

No success of my power to seduce is enough to make me feel complete. This intuitive ability, this empathy for the other person, ends up actually being a barrier to finding out what my own true needs are.

Metaphor – The Lover

They will do anything in order to be loved. They can be patient, but they will also move mountains in order to intensify the relationship.

Warning Signs for Type Twos
- Spending too much time caring for others
- Too much physical agitation
- Too much need for recognition from the other person
- Too much self-sacrifice

Warning Signs for the One-to-One Subtype
- Focus on wanting to prove that you are an intense, passionate person
- Too much focus on the partner: what they are doing, where they are, who they are meeting
- Too much focus on your own actions – not enough wider perspective
- Rivalry between your own goals and your partner's interest in other things.

A ONE-TO-ONE TWO'S VIEW – PAMELA

What I like about my Type

I love meeting new people, making a connection with them, feeling good in their company and feeling that with them I can have a wonderful encounter. Each new meeting offers me a new experience, a new opportunity to learn about life. I also love the positive attitude to life that I have most of the time, my ability to adapt to the needs of others, the range of solutions I can come up with to solve problems, the way I can adapt to almost any situation. Equally, I love the fact that I know how to build other people up and put them at ease when they are tense, unsure of themselves or have run out of energy to complete what they want to do. I see the good in a person or a situation long before noticing their faults, and I'm happy to see the world like this because of what I get back from other people.

What I like about my Subtype

The one-to-one focus builds on most of the things I've already mentioned: making contact with someone, knowing how to keep the lines of communication open with most people in most situations. Two characteristics of the one-to-one subtype are particularly true for me. The first is the speed with which I make contact; if you add together my type two and my one-to-one subtype, I seem to be super-gifted in the speed with which I can make a strong connection with someone. It's in the look between us; at the same moment something clicks between us on an emotional level. The other advantage is my ability to get to an unusually intense relationship with people. In my professional life as a human resources coach and trainer it's a real advantage if you can strongly influence a relationship and create a climate of trust.

What I like about the Combination of my Type and Subtype

It's difficult to imagine how things could be different. I'm a person who is both independent and oriented towards others. I spend my time scanning the environment to find out other people's reactions to me. I really believe that most of the time I put on a smile and do everything I can to make their reaction towards me positive and enthusiastic. I simply like people and all that they've got to offer to the world, whether it's individual conversations, outings, meals together or business relationships. I like the person themselves; I like seeing how they tick when they're operating well but also when they're stuck; I can see what's missing in them, what are the cracks which need repairing in order to help the person get themselves back together.

In short, I see what can be improved in someone. And what is more, I'm good at finding the right way to tell them, in such a way that they easily buy into the idea of self-

*improvement. This must be the good side of **seduction/aggression** or aggressive seduction. I manage to make others want to be better, to do better. I can well see how the combination of my Type Two and my one-to-one subtype reinforces the energy of my encouragement. Sometimes after a session a bit of pride comes in and I ask myself: "But how will they manage on their own; where will they get their energy from when I'm not there?"*

Film Reference – Baby Doll

We're in the south of the USA during the 1930s. A bankrupt industrialist is living with his very young wife in the remains of their enormous house. Although the marriage is legal, it is only supposed to be consummated on the young wife's 20th birthday in two days' time.

There's a bit of self-preservation energy in the poverty of the 1930s and a bit of social in the description of the segregation which is still present in the southern states. But the major themes of the film are the one-to-one relationships. The triangle between the three lead characters gives rise to memorable scenes of "jealousy", "competition/hate" and "possession/surrender". In Enneagram books we hear a lot about the altruistic side of Twos; we hear less about their seductive side. The thing is, before you can be useful to another person, you first have to get their attention!

Baby Doll, this 20-year-old child-woman, has both the ability of the Two to seduce in order to make a close contact, and the one-to-one ability to get the other person to turn their attention on to them. These two abilities together multiply into "seduction/aggression". This process seems to have several stages; if your first level of seduction is enough, you stop there. If not, you go to the next level: getting closer, the velvet gaze, the eroticism of words, until you get the intensity of contact you want – and sometimes you get more than you bargained for!

Forced to blow cold after having engendered too much heat, Baby Doll goes from one extreme to the other: "Don't touch me; I don't like to be touched…" while her voice and body are signalling the opposite. The dilemma of the one-to-one Two is that you are sure of your power of seduction and yet at the same time you continuously need to reassure yourself that it's still working; it's about power, lack of confidence, ramping up the seduction, hot glances that drive her husband mad. "It's like a dance: one step forward, two steps back ... But I'm the one who's leading the dance, according to my mood!"

Often the literature describes the failing of the Two as "manipulation". In some senses it's true; the dictionary defines manipulation as: leading a person where you want them to go; getting them to do what you want them to do.   Is she manipulative? Probably.   In reality, like all Twos she has enormous emotional needs, and to fill this bottomless pit she uses her favourite weapon – seduction. And during the course of the film she grows up from a spoilt Lolita to a decisive and desirable young woman.

THE SOCIAL TYPE TWO

Preoccupation of Type Two: identifying the needs of other people and repressing their own
Preoccupations of the Social Subtype: focusing on friends, social links/associations, groups
– SOCIAL AMBITION

Two sorts of energy come together here: the Two's genius for knowing how to create links is multiplied by the social subtype's ability to get to the centre of influential networks. Social Twos achieve self-esteem by getting other people's approval.   Pride consists in achievement of status: being recognised because of the prestige of the people they know, the success of the groups they belong to. They are ambitious by proxy: being close to a business leader or celebrity: *"Oh yes, I know them, I had a drink with them at a friend's house the other evening."*   In addition, they like to identify a protégé with potential; they are ambitious for them and want to be their

79

godparent and be proud because of their success: *"I am the coach of (someone famous); it was I that gave them their first step on the ladder of success."*

Another form of this is someone who becomes the right hand person for someone powerful or influential – it's about making sure that they belong to think-tanks and committees that make decisions. Their ability to invest themselves in the needs of others is used to create an indispensable role for themselves at the heart of the organisation. The most important thing here is not their own success; it's about the success of the organisation or the success of the person they are serving. Being aligned to powerful people is more important to them than being the leader. In an organisation, they will be a mine of information: who does what, who has been having an affair with whom, birthdays, cliques, important relationships. Often they even know everything about what's going on in their competitors' organisations.

The downside is that this leads to an even greater need for appreciation: they need recognition for being a Two *and* for their social subtype, so being ignored is their worst possible fate. In order to avoid this most awful nightmare, the Social Two can expend an enormous amount of energy making and maintaining a vast network of relationships.

The Paradox

The more my social recognition grows, the less I make the effort to focus on my own needs.

Metaphor – The Ambassador

It's about knowing everything that's going on: having good relationships; creating "debts" against a possible opportunity to swing things in their direction. What's important is easy-going directness, looking out for people who've just arrived, smoothing people's ruffled feathers, making each person they meet look good. And above all, it's about always putting the success of their country or their cause before their own interests.

Warning Signs for Type Twos
- Spending too much time caring for others
- Too much physical agitation
- Too much need for recognition by other people
- Too much self-sacrifice

Warning Signs for the Social Subtype
- Caring too much about being acknowledged
- Spending too much time maintaining social relationships
- Belonging to too many groups, associations or clubs
- Too much devotion to the cause you espouse

A SOCIAL TWO'S VIEW – BERNARD

What I like about my Type

I love my ability to help others out. I think that I've always been like that, even though I have realised that this sort of behaviour must be linked to a childhood wound that I'm trying to compensate for. Whatever the case, I like to be helpful; it's more important to me than anything else. I need to help others; it makes me happy. It's innate and obvious, pleasing and compulsive. It's absolutely impossible for me to walk away from someone in need or trouble. When I come to their aid, it somehow reassures me; I feel good because they feel better. I suppose this must also reassure my self-esteem or perhaps my pride.

Another side of this is that it's important for me to get something back from them. I don't set out to get this pay-off, but if I don't get it, I feel insulted and disappointed. What's more, if I don't get any sign of gratitude for what I've done, I don't have a point of reference to tell me whether I'm on the right track. I feel as though they're taking what I've done for them for granted – and it gets to a point where I get stuck, the

81

relationship stalls and I can feel my anger rising. I need other people in order to get through life, and I like the way my personal development comes through relationships with others. I'm not saying that I need to be with other people all the time – I do seek out moments of tranquillity to recharge my batteries, to read or reflect, but my vision of the world is that I am only who I am because of my relationships with others. I build my sense of self through them and vice-versa.

What I like about my Subtype

*Being in the social world allows me to spread my wings. My aim in life is to help to better humanity's well-being on this earth. I see the bigger picture; I am **ambitious** for the future of humankind. I always have more ambition for other people than for myself; my children often tell me off for that. I pushed them to get good marks, to take on exciting projects, to choose good places to go to university – perhaps too much. Thinking back on it, they would probably have preferred me to be more laid-back, to let things take their course, to let them choose their own destiny freely. Being in the social world also means I enjoy groups; I love the big get-togethers that happen at birthdays, Christmas or on New Year's Eve. I love watching others interacting, laughing together, arguing, telling stories. I also love the mixing of generations; for me, relationships between grandparents and grandchildren are natural and very important.*

What I like about the Combination of my Type and Subtype

The combination of my type and subtype makes me effective and dynamic. Professionally, I started my career by setting up my own legal practice, and of course I went into defending the weak against the strong. Fairly quickly I became the preferred lawyer for a number of different professional associations: civil servants looking for work, environmental protection, people suffering from serious burns. These days I'm very independent, and even though I'm a social subtype, the way some of these associations operate or the ups and downs of a large group can become wearing. It has always been important to me to be free to do what I want to do, not to have to work to other people's methods or be accountable to them. On the other hand, it's always been close to my heart to defend and win, whenever a good cause has been defendable. I'm fairly evenly balanced; I love independence and challenge and on the other hand I find it hard to say no. Later in my career I was a mediator; this was good for other people because I usually managed to get the two parties to make steps towards each other, to get them to move from anger to listening to each other. And that was good for me too, because it meant that sometimes I had to speak forcefully, to get on my high horse for a good cause!

Film Reference – The Year of Living Dangerously

The film takes place in 1967 in Jakarta, Indonesia, and illustrates the good and not-so-good aspects of the Social Two subtype. It tells the story of the end of the reign of President Sukarno and the rise to power of the opposition. There are three main characters: an Australian reporter, a young British diplomat and a photographer, Billy Kwan. Billy is a local and knows everyone in both Indonesian and foreign circles. He goes to all the events and diplomatic cocktail parties and keeps cards on all the people he thinks might have potential. He takes on professional projects for others, plots in corridors, handles a lot of information and brings it out at strategic moments that serve his purposes.

The story tells how Billy organises an exclusive interview for the reporter with the leader of the opposition, in particular because he wants to be recognised for being the person who let the outside world know about the awful living conditions of the Indonesian population. For him it's a way of making a contribution to improving the life of his people. Born a dwarf, he has drawn a line under any possibility of emotional happiness for himself and so he lives vicariously. In this story he does everything he can to throw the reporter into the arms of the diplomat. Towards the end of the film, while he's going through a difficult bereavement, he is disappointed by the reporter's behaviour and he cracks: "You are mine – I made you – you belong to me. And because that's true, this woman that I gave you – I take her back!" This film helps us to experience the internal dilemma of a Two: the music, the light and shade, the climate and the atmosphere seep into us from within. The plot turns around feelings and emotions; decisions are subjective, more dictated by the heart than by reason. Be careful; by the end of the film you risk finding yourself in a real altruist's world

THE THREE SUBTYPES OF TYPE 3

Wound

One day when Type Three children expressed an emotion, they came to the conclusion that they were not heard and that they would never be up to what they felt was being asked of them: that they would not be loved for themselves. So they gave up their "True Self" and instead, hope to be loved for the results they achieve and for their accomplishments.

Passion: Trickery, Deception and Vanity

Trickery is about only judging your worth in the world by whether you're successful, to the point where you massage the truth in order to give the best image possible: *"I've got a geography exam the day after tomorrow – already I'm in the future and I got 9 out of 10 – can you understand? – I have done my revision so well that it is as though I had already got this result."* It's auto-suggestion to the nth degree. Because you are pragmatic and effective and because you have to be recognised as such, you *will* get this result – and in order to avoid any doubt, you will claim that you have already got it. Vanity is about being fascinated by your self-image – it's exhilarating to live your life knowing that others are looking at you. So you have to keep up an image that looks good, in order to give substance to the persona you present. Threes need to provide objective proof of their value through all sorts of achievements. But it is not the achievement itself that is important; what matters above all is what others think of it. *"I can imagine nothing worse than winning the 100 metres at the Olympic Games on the day when the television workers were on strike."*

"In fact, it is as though I'm always on stage. I play the role of this dynamic, effective person and I sell it to others. But in order to be really in role, I need to forget myself inside. So my real emotions are hidden to the point where most of the time I even forget that I have emotions of my own. It's not that I set out to deceive others; it's that I wouldn't even know how to describe my own feelings if someone asked me. When I hear people say 'I don't really know who I am,' for me it would be rather 'the only thing that I know is the role that I'm playing – is there anything else?"[1]
In the same way as Twos, Threes have a general desire to please and to seduce, but Threes' reason for doing it is that they want success, for example they want to make their fortune and stand out from their friends. In order to achieve that, they have developed all sorts of talents:

- An ability to complete things efficiently and practically
- The closing off of their true feelings, which enables them to "not do feelings" and drive through for the result; most of the time Threes therefore find it difficult to access their own emotions
- Organising things around them
- Knowing how to build relationships
- Rapidly adapting to the person they're talking to
- Presenting a project clearly
- Keeping up with fashion and the latest trends
- Dynamism (Oscar Ichazo talked about "ego-go" – an ego that dashes out of the starting blocks)
- Happily bouncing back from misfortune

Preferred Defence Mechanism: Identification

One meaning of "identification" is taking on the attributes of whatever image is necessary for success, and playing this role. The second way to understand it is: *"I am like you. I will measure my value by comparing myself with you. To the best of my ability, I will play the role of the hero you would like me to be."*

The third way to understand it is as fitting in with the social norms: *"I play the role written on my business card, for example Director of Marketing. If you ask me how I am, I will tell you how the Director of Marketing is today. But I would be incapable of telling you how I am, underneath this label."* Peter O'Hanrahan says[2] *"Threes have adopted a go-getting approach to life; they want to win, and in order to achieve that they are prepared to work hard in order to succeed. However, in conforming to other people's expectations they sacrifice their true self in order to keep their good image with other people. In general, Threes go through life as though they are playing a role; the crucial aspect is that they are so identified with so many roles that they don't know how to get out of them. Another aspect of this is that identification is a very flexible defence mechanism. It isn't necessarily attached to a particular role, job or kind of relationship; it can change several times during the same day. For example, a male Three might go from the role of good father to that of good husband, then to that of high-flying businessman. The essential factor they are using is a very strong empathy in the emotional centre, which is used to find out what is expected of them. Here you see the chameleon which lives inside each Three: this capacity to melt into the environment they find themselves in, in order to adapt to a new social or relationship situation, allied to the ability to build an image of success wherever they go."*

THE SELF-PRESERVATION TYPE THREE

> *Preoccupation of Type Three: action, success, image*
> *Preoccupation of the Self-Preservation Subtype: focusing on home, safety and material comfort*
> *= SECURITY*

What we find here is two lines of energy which are quite opposed to each other. On one hand you have the dynamism of the Three and on the other the anxiety of the subtype which is about securing their territory and possessions. The more insecure self-preservation Threes feel about whether their possessions will always be there, the more effective they are at making money. Acquiring material possessions reassures them; they feel that money guarantees the future. They are ready to make great sacrifices to get the security that a good job provides. Professional or financial failure is to be avoided at all costs. They believe that money can buy security; their ultimate nightmare would be to be unemployed. Their value as a person is linked to their financial prosperity, to their material possessions.

Self-preservation Threes have a tendency to confuse being financially well-off with emotional pleasure. *"I'll take time to relax once I have finalised my next deal, my next promotion, my next pay-rise..."* Somewhere deep down in their unconscious is the question: *"Could I be loved for myself, independently of my professional success, my money, my drive?"* The film The *Full Monty* shows us a self-preservation Three who has been out of work for several months and who hasn't dared to confess it to his wife; every morning he gets dressed in his suit and tie, takes his briefcase and pretends to go to work. He acts as though his job still exists, because otherwise he would have the feeling that *he* doesn't exist.

The Paradox

Success is never going to be enough to assuage my insecurity. Even if I make millions, the fear of going bankrupt or losing everything still exists – it feels as though no level of fortune will ever be enough to enable me to relax and feel happy.

Metaphor – The Entrepreneur

Their ability to work hard, be efficient and maintain a good image is pressed into the service of gaining material success.

Blessed with great energy, type Threes excel at meeting the targets they set themselves.

Warning Signs for Type Threes
- Too much preoccupation with work
- Too much stress and pressure
- Too much need for recognition
- Too much running around like a mad thing

Warning Signs for the Self-Preservation Subtype
- Paying too much attention to safety
- Spending too much time at work
- Being too pre-occupied with material well-being
- Too many routine evenings at home.

A SELF-PRESERVATION THREE'S VIEW – MARTIN

What I like about my Type
My sense of efficiency – I feel that I know how to organise any given situation in order to achieve the desired objective in the best possible way. This applies to complicated as well as simple situations such as doing the shopping. Organising an impromptu dinner for friends who turn up unexpectedly is almost exciting. If I can't get hold of everything at the same shop, I can make a couple of phone calls, state the time I want to pick up what I've ordered and organise my trip to go from one shop to the next in the most efficient way – and of course I go by scooter to save time. I also like to persuade people: when I want to spend a family weekend at the beach, I know how to convince my wife that two hours in the car isn't as tiring as all that, and that we'll get back fine on the evening of the next day.

What I like about my Subtype
My ability to work hard; I love working; I love making my company move forward. I'm a sales director in an IT company.

Every morning I go to work with pleasure and all day long I get satisfaction from moving things forward – and they do! If a certain course of action turns out to be a dead end, I'll find another way. If a particular lead comes to nothing, I'll spend even more time on the others. I also like the way I work with my body; I need to feel good in my body and I look after it. At home I have an exercise bike that I use every day, but I also go to the gym, pool, and sauna and every Saturday I run round the lake. When it comes to my image, I'm careful to dress well: not particularly outlandish or fashionable, but with well-cut clothes made from good cloth.

What I like about the Combination of my Type and Subtype

The fact that I have the competence to earn enough money so that my family can live comfortably, to feel that they are secure financially, particularly when it comes to the children's schooling. Money is a means to an end; it helps me both to choose a specialism that I like and a job that brings in enough money that I can help my nearest and dearest to live well. I find it hard to imagine how anyone can live happily if they have money worries. So, if my type and subtype talents can help me to free my loved ones from these concerns, so much the better. In the same way, I'm quite hard with my children and push them to get good marks at school, to the point where I spend time helping them revise particular subjects if necessary – although now we have a student that comes in in the evening for them, because I am finding that I have to go away more and more for work. In terms of physical health, I've always encouraged the children to take up one or even several sports and I make sure they have the means to do that. When I see that often my type gets labelled as "Winner" or "Competitor" I find it hard to see what's wrong with those terms; I recognise myself in them. Nevertheless I do try to spend as much time as possible at home so that I can spend time with my family and enjoy the comfort I've worked for.

Film Reference – Sommersby

We are in the southern states of the USA at the end of the American War of Independence. Starring Kevin Costner and Jodie Foster, this film is a remake of the French film The Return of Martin Guerre. The director chose to reposition the film and give it an ending which fits more with the American Three culture.

At the end of the war, Kevin Costner is disgusted by what he was before, and he's sickened by his Three habits of deceit and trickery. So he decides to change identity and take the place of a friend who died in the war. He arrives back at his friend's farm, pretending to be him. Of course, people find him changed, but they put that down to five years' absence, his wounds and traumatic experiences. His wife, played by Jodie Foster, is not taken in for long, but she decides to keep silent because she likes his new sensitivity, thoughtfulness and enthusiasm. He is just happy to be able to be himself again and to live by authentic human values. He gets stuck into this new life at the farm, the organisation of work, ploughing, hard labour, harvesting, living a happy life. And then one day his past catches up with him; the friend whose identity he took is accused of having committed a murder several years previously. Kevin Costner is faced with an agonising choice. Either he confesses that he has committed yet another deception by taking on and taking advantage of an identity which is not his, which will mean that he will be dishonourably discharged. Or he plays out to the end the fact that he has taken on a new self in which he has been able to live out good values, which means that he will find himself condemned for a murder which he didn't commit. This is the choice that he has to make in the end: whether to be true to his new self and not go back to his old demons, even if this means playing his new authenticity through to the end, to the point of losing his life.

This film gives us a rather extreme version of this type, but the fundamental dilemma is a true one for Threes: whether to dare to be who you really are, at the cost of giving up a more superficial image with more apparent pay-off.

THE ONE-TO-ONE TYPE THREE

Preoccupations of Type Three: action, success, image
Preoccupations of the One-to-One Subtype: focusing on
the partner
= MASCULINE/FEMININE

Two lines of energy converge here. The type energy of Threes is about being in relationship in order to succeed; the one-to-one subtype is about being in relationship in order to create a connection with the other person. So here we are dealing with someone who is doubly in the world of relationships: who finds their identity above all through their ability to connect with others. The external impression is of out and out charm: the attentive lover, the on-form competitor, the switched-on producer ... One hundred per cent of their attention goes to having the look which is most likely to be effective.

This subtype is very focused on conquest; physical appearance and sex-appeal are the keys to being desirable, so they will tend to play up the characteristics of their gender. Generally, the men will exaggerate their masculinity and the women their femininity, with the aim of being the ideal companion their partner would wish for. Their empathy is a bit like that of the one-to-one Two; it's an ability to know the needs of their partner. However, their ability to create an image of success focuses on sexual identity and its implications, and often this ideal image hides considerable emotional insecurity. At work, the image they project is the one which will enable them gain the most attraction in any given situation: adapting to the person they are speaking to, giving them the image that they're looking for, persuading and pleasing. It's about adopting the most appropriate image: *"One evening I realised that I did this a lot. That morning I had gone to work with four different suits; I put them in the back of my car and I changed four times according to the circumstances: a normal working day, a cocktail party with friends, a drink with a colleague and an evening at the theatre with my wife. I wouldn't necessarily say that I'm trying to impress other people; I think I'm trying to minimise the risk of not being liked and maximise the quality of the relationship with each person I'm with."*

There is a special quality in this type: the spirit of competition. All one-to-one types have it, but it is particularly true for the one-to-one Three. Jimmy Connors and Andre Agassi are good examples; they are not primarily athletes in search of a record, they are above all in the arena, in face-to-face combat, and they will give their last breath to win – and if they lose they will train twice as hard in order to win the next time.

The Paradox
Embodying the image desired by my partner is not the best guarantee of a good longer term relationship.

Metaphor – The Film Star
Their personal charisma relies on the fact of being an attractive man or woman – and of knowing how to play the right role, whether in personal or professional relationships.

Warning Signs for Threes
- Too much preoccupation with work
- Too much stress and pressure
- Too much need for recognition
- Too much running around like a mad thing

Warning Signs for the One-to-One Subtype
- Focus on wanting to prove that you are an intense, passionate person
- Too much focus on the partner: what they are doing, where they are, who they are meeting
- Too much focus on your own actions – not enough wider perspective

- Rivalry between your own goals and your partner's interest in other things

A ONE-TO-ONE THREE'S VIEW – CHARLOTTE

What I like about my Type

My ability to adapt; even when I was a child I had this ability to move from one situation to another without effort: changing class, moving house, landing up on holiday in a place I didn't know – all of this was no problem to me. Yes, I was a bit anxious, but somehow this anxiety stimulated me. As proof of that, I know that when I don't know in advance all the facts of a problem that I have to solve, that motivates me and spices up my life. I would say that I'm attracted to every new situation that comes up. It's the same thing with different cultures; I lick my lips at the thought of travelling to somewhere I've never been to. In terms of other qualities: I like my optimism, my powers of concentration on big goals, my organisational ability, my confidence in my ability to bring things to fruition and my tenacity to hang on in there. All that enables me to create harmony between what I want and the life I live.

In my former professional life as a manager when I was responsible for more than a hundred people, I could rely on my sense of what needed to be done to bring things to fruition and my effectiveness at doing that. I never had any problem motivating my teams to achieve or surpass their objectives, because I always led by example. These days, as a psychotherapist, I enjoy bringing that quality to my work, putting my will at the service of the client's success, following through, supporting them and imbuing them with my energy.

What I like about my Subtype

I feel a real pleasure when I have a face-to-face meeting with someone; whether it's in my private or professional life, I experience a really enjoyment when I meet them. I have an image to illustrate this: imagine two children playing tennis

THE THREE SUBTYPES OF TYPE 3

and having fun. They're not counting the points, no-one's going to "win", but it's playful and they are really present to each other – it's as though the two people are moving as one. In these face-to-face moments there's a different quality of contact; it's as though we were discovering an intensity between us and building the present moment together. And of course it's also seduction, a game of conquest with the aim of drawing the other person's attention towards you.

What I like about the Combination of my Type and Subtype

I feel as though I'm doubly talented when it comes to persuading and charming people. I know how to play on my femininity both to gain a position of trust and to make close connections with people. In my professional life as a psychotherapist this combination is really productive: active listening, conversations and dialogue, unconditional support for my client, ability to take new elements into account .... With the combination of my Type and Subtype I can guarantee that my client will feel well listened-to! In my private life, I have many friends that I love meeting one-to-one, for example for lunch. In both of these fields I really like the fact that I'm respected both as a good friend and as a true professional. I don't see any problem in being seen by my children as a loving mother, by my husband as a sexy partner and by my clients as a charming woman.

Film Reference – Gone with the Wind

We are in Georgia, USA, just before the American War of Independence. Scarlett O'Hara is celebrating her sixteenth birthday at her family's sumptuous home, Tara. I think that the enormous success of this film is in part due to the fact that it touches all three subtypes: self-preservation with the war, life and death, famine; social with the changing customs and costumes of the periods before and after the war and one-to-one with the relationship between Scarlett and Rhett Butler. The character of Scarlett is the epitome of a one-to-one Three, as she states continuously: "I know what I want and I'm going to put on my most beautiful clothes, play on my femininity and use my repertoire of glances to convince each person I meet to give me what I want." As her glances change from intense to charming to wheedling, Scarlett charms them all: her governess, her father and mother, her brother in law, her first and second husbands.

As I see it, Rhett Butler also shows a lot of one-to-one Three characteristics; he also has to know how to bounce back and adapt quickly in order to survive the radical world change that happened in the southern states during this five year period. But coming back to Scarlett, the end of the film is significant; she weeps with emotion as she realises that safeguarding Tara is probably the best thing that she has done. She stands alone in the immensity of nature and her mask has dropped. She is herself, truly, without needing to prove anything to anyone, authentic at last. She discovers another dimension to herself, beyond the facile successes which came from her charm and her sex-appeal.

THE SOCIAL TYPE THREE

> *Preoccupations of Type Three: action, success, image*
> *Preoccupations of the Social Subtype: focus on friends,*
> *associations and groups*
> *= PRESTIGE*

Two energy forces converge here: the Three preoccupation with image comes together with the subtype's concern for their image in the social arena. *"I need to present a good image of myself to others, and my points of reference are the things that matter in society: having been to the right school, living in a good suburb, belonging to a fashionable club. My self-esteem depends on my reputation with the groups I belong to."* So they have to be seen as a person to be admired, attract the attention of others, be one of the movers and shakers, if not *the* prime mover of the group. *"My success depends on the approval that my behaviour attracts from others."*

They are extremely conscious of status: the titles they can put on their business card, the range of their responsibilities, their brand. The good opinion of others is crucial. This type pays particular attention to the number and quality of potentially useful relationships they have. *"It's really important that I know someone who can get me top seats for prestigious events if I need them..."* The deceit comes from the fact that they distance themselves from their true feelings in order to align themselves with the values of the group. They get confused between who they are inside and the external role they are playing. So you can end up with either an authentic social leader or someone whose ego is inflated by propaganda and the need to fabricate a good image. For a historical example I think that the Field of the Cloth of Gold, organised by the French king Francis 1st for the Duke of Burgundy, illustrates this well. François wanted to impress his guest by displaying his wealth. He organised an amazing event lasting several days: a banquet, performances, all sorts of magnificence. Unfortunately the Duke of Burgundy mustn't have been a social subtype; he preferred the simple welcome without fuss that the King of England set up for him – warmth and conviviality without going over the top.

The Paradox

Gaining prestige won't necessarily lead me closer to my true self and may even lead to the failure that I am trying at all costs to avoid.

Metaphor[3] – The Politician

What matters is gaining public approval, knowing the right people, gaining power within social institutions: government, companies, their parish, their home town.

Warning Signs for Type Three

- Being too preoccupied with work
- Too much stress and tension
- Too great a need for recognition
- Too much running around all the time

Warning Signs for the Social Subtype

- Too much need to be recognised
- Too much time spent keeping up social relationships
- Being a member of too many clubs and societies
- Too much devotion to the causes they espouse

A SOCIAL THREE'S VIEW – PIERRE

What I like about my Type

In my professional life, I like the characteristics of my type; my drive for success and my ability to adapt have enabled me to be successful in a number of different professions with no difficulty. So I love bringing projects to successful conclusion in roles as diverse as being head of a company, a negotiator, a therapist and an artist. I feel that I'm carrying on several careers at the same time without ever getting bored. Deep down, I think that I love being stimulated by situations which need to be organised as well as possible within a limited time in order to obtain the best possible result.

In my private life I use my type characteristics to make better progress in my personal development and to seek out good results for other people and for myself. I help other people to grow and that helps me to grow by using the talents of my heart centre. Another advantage of my type is that all the energy I spend on my projects gets automatically recharged the more successful my action is.

What I like about my Subtype

My subtype helps me to build a good platform to bring my professional projects to fruition, because of my ability to build relationships and take an interest in who is doing what, who has talents for what, who is interested in different things and who could get me into a certain field or sector of business. My social subtype also shows up in a deep sense that because the group is "stronger than me", I need to be appreciated by the group.

What I like about the Combination of my Type and Subtype

It's the way all my capabilities come together to make contacts which can be light-hearted and respectful at the same time. I can take in and understand the group in its entirety, and even identify with the whole group; it's as though, when conditions are right, I can fuse with, become one with the group.

*The combination of my type Three and my social subtype also gives me an ability to show myself to the best advantage in a group, to shine in public situations. I would be lying if I said that I didn't enjoy this a lot of the time; I want a "good public image" in order to get the personal recognition and the public standing that comes from that. This idea is probably one of the possible interpretations of the word **prestige** that is associated with this type – for me it leads either to my ego being reassured or the fact that I can be the one to persuade the group of its best way forward. This ability is the most important component of my leadership ability – and it's also very reassuring, even vital, as a way of existing within a group.*

Film Reference – Wall Street 2 – Money Never Sleeps (2010)

We're in New York at the time of the stock market crash of 2008 – a young trader, Jacob Moore, is willing to do anything to avenge his mentor, who was driven to suicide by shady dealings. He goes for help to the financial wizard Gordon Gekko, who has just finished a prison term for insider trading.

The two financial giants who struggle against each other in this film are both Threes: hyperactive, focused on movement and success; they know how to persuade people, lead teams and have the Three failing of being able to shut their hearts to their own feelings if there is a risk that these will get in the way of achieving their goal – in Enneagram terms it's Deceit.

What struck me in this film is the paradox of Threes; they know how to play on the emotions of others in order to persuade them, while at the same time putting aside their own feelings – like actors who are playing a role. Except that most of the time Threes don't realise that they're in this state of hyper-adaptability; they are so afraid of losing their ability to impress other people that they are always in role and can't come out of it in order to recontact their true self. In their quest for success their pragmatism, organisational ability and conviction are formidable allies. There must be something very appealing about living in this whirlwind of activity; it must be a bit like the feeling a surfer gets as they ride a wave that's getting bigger and bigger and is making them go faster and faster – and that means that, completely engrossed in their wave, they can't let themselves be troubled by their own emotions.

The Wall Street setting suits this kind of energy. In this film we see two fairly extreme examples of this type, and the struggle between these two financial giants gives us a more detailed picture of some of the Three characteristics.

The key word for the Social Three archetype is "prestige." So what matters is being well known, having a good reputation, being someone who has power in society – and "society" can be a company, a community or a town. It's about having influence, being able to use your networks to get information and pass it to the people who matter. In this context, it's about influencing the markets by using pieces of news to make certain share prices go up or down. This can feel like a good thing to do, as though you were using your networks for the benefit of a charity, or as here, it can be about letting a rumour circulate in order to destroy someone's reputation. Being recognised socially and having a large network mean that you are all the more able to make things move in the direction you want, either to build your own prestige or your company's. Or you could use your network in a more charitable way, and this is even more prestigious because you're working for the good of humanity. In the struggle between these two men, it's interesting to notice that the "blows" they land on each other are designed to destroy their enemy's prestige by bringing over most of the powerful people to their side – and these blows seem to be at least as painful as the physical punches that a boxer would throw.

The road to personal growth involves sobering up and getting back in touch with real human values: moving beyond the vanity of the need to be loved for your social image, in order to dare to sit with the uncertainties of your internal life, your hesitations, vulnerability and depth. That's what the end of the film enables us to witness.

The film itself is Social; it helps us to see the possible end of the capitalist/financial era and that it might be replaced by a more human world which is less dependent on virtual elements. It's the era that we're living in, and it's changing. Although the two main characters don't seem very sympathetic, at least there are two of them, and they show us two different faces of the same type – it's a good film!

THE THREE SUBTYPES OF TYPE 4

Wound

One day, Type Four children had a very strong feeling of being abandoned, of loss; they felt not only bereft, but also completely disconnected from their "true me". From that point forward, they experience a longing for a time in the past when they felt connected to something greater than themselves – they feel that something very important is missing.

Passion: Envy

"*I feel often that I am lacking, deficient, not up to what is being asked of me – as if I were not ok just as I am. And I don't like putting out that image to others, so I wish that it could change and want passionately for it to be different. This struggle against feeling bad pushes me to go out and look for the good thing that is missing outside me rather than inside myself*". Thus envy is transformed into energy.

As with Threes, self-image is important, but Fours tend to compare the image they are projecting against the ideal image that they might put out. "*Based on that, my attention goes to noticing the worst in what is here now, and the best in what is not here now.*" It's as though their way of paying attention focuses naturally on what they don't have or what is not going right for them. But as they are driven primarily by their emotions and therefore other people's acknowledgement of them is very important, they have to find ways to gain other people's attention. To achieve this, they develop and show their refinement, cultivation, elegance and unusual style, or they show their intensity by dramatising good or bad events.

In various works on the Enneagram, two other characteristics of this type are rarely mentioned: a lively interest in intellectual things – philosophy, psychology etc. – and a great internal depth. *"I like introspection; going down inside myself to experience deep emotions is a much more interesting way to live than stagnating in the banality of everyday life."* You will notice that there is a certain similarity with Type Two: *"There is an exaggerated identification with the needs of others, which means that they can often be responsible parents, understanding social workers, attentive psychotherapists and warriors defending the rights of the oppressed."*[1] The good side of envy is that it is a driving force; being dissatisfied with what they have motivates them to get on in life; magnifying feelings gives spice to life. The downside is that this leads them to have great romantic or elitist expectations, which bring longing and melancholy in their wake.

Preferred Defence Mechanism: Introjection

Introjection is taking or being the idealised person or object inside yourself in order to avoid pain, loss or separation. Undesirable traits can also be internalised as well as desirable ones. Introjection is about transforming the emotional truth of the situation by comparing what you are experiencing in the present with some else in the past or future; Fours believe that *"the grass is always greener on the other side of the fence."* As children, Fours experienced moments of pure happiness, and in those moments they felt utterly loved. They keep the memory of those intense moments etched on their heart, totally complete. As an adult, each time that they meet someone they hope to relive a moment which will be as marvellous as the one in their memory. Introjection is comparing the intensity, authenticity and emotional depth of what they are experiencing in the present with the memory of what they experienced once in the past. *"If that person here today really loved me, then I could reconnect with that sublime feeling that I experienced in the past".*

THE SELF-PRESERVATION TYPE FOUR

> *Preoccupations of Type Four: search for meaning, intensity, authenticity*
> *Preoccupations of the Self-Preservation Subtype: focus on the home, safety and material comfort*
> *= RECKLESS/DAUNTLESS*

Two energy forces crash up against each other here. Fours want to be people who are different from others, who live life intensely, and their self-preservation side wants to be safe in a material sense. Putting these two drivers up against each other is difficult. The Four energy refuses to live a life which is comfortable and routine; it prefers to create the possibility of loss through living dangerously. If Fours have to earn money, they want to do it in a way which is different from everyone else; they will often choose careers which are risky, either working on contract or self-employed. *"I have always wanted to work in the humanitarian field, but there must surely be easier ways to do that than spending eighteen months with Mother Teresa, six months under the bombing in Bosnia and organising the first democratic elections in difficult countries."*

Even more, when envy arises they tend to act boldly, suddenly resigning from a fantastic contract on a whim "for reasons of authenticity" or more often putting themselves in danger. In fact, what is happening is that through these bold acts the self-preservation the Four is recreating the feeling they had when they felt abandoned. There is a certain excitement in playing with fire, in taking every possible risk in order to maximise the emotional intensity of the situation. *"I have spent my life making fortunes and going bankrupt. It's when I'm in the most precarious situation that I can access my greatest creativity."* Helen Palmer suggests in her book 'The

Enneagram': *"By dancing on the volcano they take themselves away from the banality of existence."* They often have a very strong need for independence, and in their emotional life their lover can often be seduced, then rejected and then reclaimed.

The Paradox

Creating risk situations one after the other will only make my need for intensity bigger.

Metaphor – The Reckless Person

There is a tension between wanting to get material security and wanting to be completely detached from it. It's about taking the biggest risk possible each time that their survival instinct is triggered; acting daringly in order to magnify their sense of creativity.

Warning Signs for Type Four
- Focusing too much on what is missing
- Too much self-reference
- Too much need for intensity
- Too much concern for and need to be different

Warning Signs for the Self-Preservation Subtype
- Too much focus on security
- Spending too much time at work
- Being too focused on material well-being
- Too many routine evenings at home

A SELF-PRESERVATION FOUR'S VIEW – PATRICK

What I like about my Type

Type Four is often called "the tragic romantic" and I have to admit that although when I first encountered it I didn't like this label, in the end it seems quite apt. When I started to use the Enneagram for my personal development, once I managed to get a bit of distance from my automatic behaviours and the aspects of them that I found rather pathetic, I got to the point where I could look at them without judgement and therefore without fear. When I wander off into my daily flights of fancy and deepest dark fantasies, I try to view them with less indulgence, but also give myself less of a hard time about them. And it works! Yes, sure, the prince is still not quite ready to plant a kiss on the forehead of the sleeping princess, but I'm hacking into the brambles around the castle!

One thing comes to mind as I write these lines: as I've become more at ease in my relationships with other people, have I perhaps become less isolated? Anyway, I'm tending to bring my extremes closer together, while not forgetting that the distance between my extremes is one of the defining aspects of my character and that what used to be a shackle and a hindrance to me can become a precious tool. My passion of envy is little by little being transformed into something more dynamic and less depressing. This is leading to more well thought-through actions and fewer reveries going round in my head which, although they didn't make me happy, used to content me but led me into a vicious circle of pain and unhappiness. What I like overall about my type is this great capacity for internal depth, the feeling that I can sometimes be in the centre of myself, and, if this doesn't sound paradoxical, this feeling helps me to continue to find the way even deeper into the centre of myself.

What I like about my Subtype

I experience my subtype as a tendency, as a place I like to be; I like the comfort and the sense of being safe that it brings. I feel I have a particular gift in most of the areas around survival, particularly for food and cooking. I think that my subtype accentuates the enjoyment that I can get from my senses. I have a great sensitivity to touch; I've studied shiatsu, which is a bodywork therapy based on meridians, and feeling the contact with someone's body is very precious for me. As for music, I love the way it helps to create atmosphere in a place. I love cooking and enjoying the flavours, colours and

106

textures that I experience when I'm preparing a dish. I love sharing a meal with a few friends, and I take great care to create a comfortable space.

I experience this self-preservation subtype, this proximity to the material world as a maternal, cuddly energy which reassures me. As I have a tendency to lose myself in my philosophical thoughts, this concreteness seems to give me a kind of anchor point. My subtype stops me from flying off; it connects me to the constraints of the material world without necessarily limiting me. It enables me to put down roots, to live my great spiritual flights in the here and now and not in the kind of virtual delirium that I used to experience. For me, my subtype is a sort of matrix, a crucible within which I can develop myself and where I can labour away contently on my inner work.

What I like about the Combination of my Type and Subtype

*As far as my personal development is concerned, this combination seems to me to be the best one possible. My type opens me up to immense spaces and my subtype helps me to get centred again. The combination of the two gives me strength and coherence. I can't see how by just using my understanding of my type Four alone, I would have been able to manage the extremes of my character. In the past I used to find myself in all sorts of incredible situations such as, for example, resigning from a very good job in France and giving up my accommodation in order to end up in a foreign country, only to find out that the contract I was counting on was no longer available. Is that **intrepid?** Anyway, these days, thanks to my understanding of my type and subtype I feel as though I am on a less chancy life path, which is no mean thing for a Four!*

Film Reference – Out of Africa

The film is set in Kenya at the beginning of the 20th century. It is based on the life of Karen Blixen (played by Meryl Streep), a Danish woman who did nothing in the same way as most people; she set up and ran a farm in Africa single-handed – just imagine it! The film shows several decisive and intrepid projects she undertook: deciding to plant coffee: "Nobody has ever planted coffee at this altitude? I'll do it!", crossing enemy lines without protection during the war and creating a school for children with no support. Her self-preservation side shows up in the way she shuns the usual social obligations between ex-patriates and takes refuge on her farm.

A handsome man (Robert Redford) passes through, and a love story is born. Even this idyllic story has a self-preservation aspect: heat, complicity, few words, long looks, fingers brushing each other – self-preservation types in love aren't talkative! It's all much more sober than the rapture you expect with one-to-ones. The love story is made even more intense by the fact that the Robert Redford character is a Seven, with their characteristic reluctance to commit, to be stable. The plot revolves around a series of partings and reunions – the Seven goes walkabout and the Four stays put at home, until the day when Meryl Streep's self-preservation subtype leads her to suggest to her beloved that he settle down and make the farm his base camp. Robert Redford baulks at this; his beloved liberty is threatened. And then the decisive moment arrives; one evening by the fireside, he catches her sewing a button on one of his shirts. An act that seems quite normal to a self-preservation subtype takes on another dimension; the Seven sees this act as evidence that she doesn't respect his freedom and is trying to get her claws into him – and immediately the relationship is over. Other self-preservation aspects are more clearly described in the book than in the film; the enormous energy spent on the plantation, the hours of hard labour, fatigue, illness, financial worries, anxiety and insecurity.

At the end of the film, the plantation is destroyed in a fire – "insurance is for pessimists". This time it is the end. Meryl Streep is worried about the fate of the native people who were working for her. In order to ensure that they will be looked after and found somewhere to live, she goes down on her knees to the new governor during the cocktail party celebrating his arrival. As a social subtype he tries to find a diplomatic way to put her off, but Meryl Streep won't budge; her determination keeps her on her knees regardless of social conventions. This causes stupefaction in the assembled company and absolute embarrassment until the governor's wife promises in her husband's name that the future of the former employees will be assured. The independent, individualistic side of this type can be seen again as she buries her lover, who was killed when his plane crashed; she is alone, and you feel that she has never been really close to any other people.

THE ONE-TO-ONE TYPE FOUR

Preoccupations of Type Four: search for meaning, intensity, authenticity
Preoccupation of the One-to-One Subtype: focusing on the partner
= COMPETITION/HATE

Two energy lines converge here; the Four's need for recognition joins forces with the one-to-one subtype's ability to make close connections. The Four's desire to be out of the ordinary comes together with the one-to-one subtype's need to experience intense moments of contact. One-to-one Fours are about "fascination squared". Here we're dealing with personalities which are all or nothing, passionate and easily carried away. They build their sense of self-worth through their rivalry with others and they build their self-respect by comparing themselves to others.

109

Competition makes them forget their sense of what's missing. Their determination can move mountains; *"Just you wait and see what I do!"* Tom Condon says in his book 'The Dynamic Enneagram': *"Competition can be expressed in two ways: either by looking for others' approval: "My value goes up when people appreciate me" or through rivalry: "My value goes up if yours goes down.""* They rarely go into competition with friends, but woe betide you if you become a professional or emotional rival; they will need to prove that they are the best. In an emotional relationship they feel that if they are successful in their "seduction" it means that their value is equal or superior to that of their lover. They want to become the central person in your life, and they can also be the first to break off the relationship: *"By being the first person to break it off, I diminish the value of the other person and avoid the possibility of them abandoning me."* The good side of this type is their fighting spirit: *"Competition stimulates me."*

The Paradox

Comparing myself to others doesn't provide a firm basis for stable and durable self-confidence.

Metaphor – The Drama King or Queen

Competition with others is used to mask a feeling of personal deficiency and it creates a drive to surpass themselves. Other people's qualities are seen as a personal challenge and generally provoke a strong reaction. The value that they place on their own qualities tends to go up and down as they compare themselves to others.

Warning Signs for Type Four

- Focusing too much on what is missing
- Too much self-reference
- Too much need for intensity
- Too much concern for and need to be different

Warning Signs for the One-to-One Subtype

- Focusing on wanting to prove that you are an intense, passionate person
- Too much focus on the partner: what they are doing, where they are, who they are meeting
- Too much focus on your own actions – not enough wider perspective
- Rivalry between your own goals and your partner's interest in other things

A ONE-TO-ONE FOUR'S VIEW – CLAIRE

What I like about my Type

As I got to know my type, what I really liked was realising the enormous inner freedom I possess. I love my ability to be me, without being afraid of it or wishing I were otherwise, and I love my quest for a more and more authentic me. I also loved realising that my rejection of ordinariness and the frequent feeling that I'm different from others are part of me and can be a source of energy. Once I discovered this I was able to move away from the belief that the only reason that I sometimes deliberately acted differently from others was because of the need to be noticed. I also realised that I was often overwhelmed by different emotions and that I could try to step back from them in order to experience them more peacefully.

Finding my type also provided the means to free myself from certain inhibitions, particularly about expressing my artistic side, and gave me more freedom and self-confidence. For me, belonging to Type Four is about daring to be free: above all about daring to be me. The things that I used to see as gaps in myself I now see as gifts: intuition, empathetic listening, understanding beyond words, the desire and searching for deep knowledge – I consider all these to be sources of true richness for me.

And finally, I'm happy to be a Four because I don't experience it like some of the caricatures that you can find in some books: an envious unsatisfied person who is always on the edge of depression and an airy-fairy romanticism with over the top reactions and emotions that are always getting out of control! I think that the people who have found out and accepted the characteristics of this type have taken steps to tame their excesses and developed a measured way of expressing their inner self, so that it no longer makes them (and other people!) suffer.

I've finally managed to accept my hypersensitivity and these days I can even let myself be overwhelmed by positive emotions, and use my reason to enable me to put distance between me and my negative emotions. I also try to put my sensitivity and the intuition that comes from it at the service of other people, while still making best use of my natural qualities: setting high standards in everything I do or experience, and a healthy dissatisfaction with anything routine or banal. I value the opposite; I put great value on depth and looking for moments of authentic contact with others so that I can help them make the most of it too. For example, I volunteer for a charity which offers support to people who are looking for work or who are in other uncertain positions in life. As I got involved in this activity I really became aware of my ability to listen and give the benefit of my empathy to these people in difficult situations. I'm good at hearing about suffering without running away, and I'm able to stand beside them in their suffering because I feel everything they're going through very strongly. If occasionally I find myself overwhelmed by all they're telling me, I find these days that I can stay grounded in spite of all these intense emotions. The stability that I have rediscovered gives me the ability to keep on hearing and experiencing other people's pain; I think that this ability to be open to another's suffering is a characteristic of Fours.

What I like about my Subtype

I love all the importance and space that I can give to the person I'm with, the pleasure of listening and taking time with people that I get out of one-to-one encounters. I feel that these are real intense moments because they are just between me and the other person:

- *They're good for the person I'm with, because sometimes it's good to have a person who knows how to listen and take time with you. For them it's a relief; it gives them back their energy and self-worth.*
- *They're good for me, because every person is unique and many people are fascinating, funny and full of different aspects – it's such a joy to get to know these personalities more deeply!*

I have fond memories of all those great moments when the conversation was a like a well of energy that refreshed me, when the meeting led to a feeling of true intimacy and trust. After an experience like that I feel complete, strong and enriched by my contact with the other person and what they said, for the doors that they opened for me and for themselves, and for the trust they placed in me. I can't imagine how I could live without meetings like that, or how I could stop continuing to seek them!

What I like about the Combination of my Type and Subtype

*This is harder to say, because I often have the illusion that it's only me that has these amazing encounters and that experiences them with such intensity and depth. Is this impression real or a fond illusion? I have no idea. I prefer to think that everyone experiences extraordinary things, extraordinary encounters and moments of grace with other people. In any case, I'm trying to move beyond my old failing of **competition** to be the most loved, the most noticed or the one who stands out from the crowd, and to transform it into requiring myself and others to be authentic. My aim is no*

113

longer to live by comparing myself to others, but in loving and accepting myself.

Film Reference – Lawrence of Arabia

The choice of this film to illustrate the one-to-one Four may seem surprising on two counts: the first is that there are quite a lot of survival themes and you could see this as evidence of an intrepid self-preservation Four. But I tend rather to see the passionate rapture of the one-to-one Four. The second surprise could come from the fact that the story is not about a love affair between a man and a woman, but between a man and his vocation. Let's be clear, the intensity that one-to-one subtypes are capable of generating can be focused on any close thing that fascinates them: a beloved person, but also work, reading or an artistic creation.

The scene is set in Cairo in 1915. At that time, the Arab peninsula was inhabited by nomadic tribes considered by westerners to be backward in every way. But in the war against Turkey, the area became strategically important. Lieutenant Lawrence is a King's officer but he's not the typical soldier; he's an individualist and anti-authoritarian; he doesn't know how to salute and he doesn't care. Mad about Themistocles and oriental languages, he is seen as a bit of a way-out poet in military circles. He is subject to highs and lows of emotion as well as to periods of philosophical musing.

One day, Lawrence is sent on a mission to King Faisal, chief of one of the largest tribes, with the objective of finding out Faisal's intentions and reporting back. From the first interview, Faisal is very taken with the unusual side of Lawrence. Asked to describe his country, Lawrence describes England and its customs but without eulogising about them, and finishes with the comment: "but I'm not like the others". In fact, he dares to give his personal opinion in answer to all the questions Faisal asks him, allowing himself to voice the emotions in his heart, against the advice of his superior officer, who looks daggers at him. He even goes to the point of describing the Arabs as an absurd, barbaric, cruel and rapacious people. But Faisal is touched by his authenticity, which is so different from the usual dry diplomatic way of communicating. There are a number of one-to-one conversations between Lawrence and other characters in the film. All of these show us characteristics of the one-to-one: intense looks, emotions and body language. The two people having the conversation are often filmed in a landscape in order to give the sense of the close connection between them. Nothing else exists except the rapport between them, however many people are in the room or however much noise is around them.

The question of authenticity comes up several times in the film: refusing to drink the slightest drop of water in the desert as long as his guide has drunk nothing; risking his life to go back alone in the hottest part of the day to find a nomad who has fallen off his camel. It's about your actions being congruent with the emotion of the present moment, whatever that is. Other Type Four characteristics come out; Lawrence's behaviour shows that he is unique, different, a man apart: "No-one has ever crossed the Nefud desert? I will!" Even better, he has the idea of uniting several tribes – which no-one thought possible, not even the tribes concerned – to attack the port of Aqaba from the rear by coming out of the desert – which also seems ludicrous. As an English officer, he asks Faisal whether he can say that he is "serving Faisal of Mecca". The king replies: "And who do you really serve?" – if the truth be told, Lawrence follows his heart.

This passionate man falls in love with the desert and seems more faithful to Arabia than to England. But contrary to the Arab culture that he so respects, he refuses to believe that everything is written or pre-determined. He decides that nothing is written – and that each person can write their own story. At the end of the film, the hero has realised his dream; the tribes of the Arab peninsula are united around a common goal. Then he can withdraw, making way for the social subtypes who will take on the political process. To sum up the story in subtype terms, a one-to-one gives his energy to the self-preservation tribes so that they can organise themselves socially.

THE SOCIAL TYPE FOUR

> *Preoccupations of Type Four: search for meaning, intensity, authenticity*
> *Preoccupations of the Social Subtype: focusing on friends, associations and groups*
> *= SHAME*

For the Social Four, Envy is directed towards the social status of others or the fact that they belong to groups from which the Four feels excluded – it's a sort of idealisation of superior classes of people and a strong motivation toward promotion in society. *"I don't feel that I have their qualities – the ones that gain them respect and admiration. I feel different from them and I don't feel as though I'm capable of aspiring to their level – I'm ashamed when I compare myself to them. It is as though the past experience of my life has a stain on it which would exclude me from the group if they ever found out about it. Because I'm afraid of being rejected I do everything I can to make myself attractive, different and unusual. I've become very sensitive to what others think of me. If someone refuses me something, it's as though my whole self as a human being has been rejected – and the feeling of shame floods through me."*

Here we see a great sensitivity: a terror of being rejected if their fatal flaw is discovered. Their image is sometimes used to protect them from this: being part of an elite club, being attractive, being different from the other members. The two energy lines in this subtype are sometimes contradictory; the Four's desire to be different comes up against the social desire to be good enough and to be acceptable to the group norms. In this respect social Fours can sometimes look like Ones; behaving very correctly and formally is a way in which they can compensate for their feelings of inadequacy.

The Paradox

How do I reconcile the quest for individual authenticity and my need to be part of the group?

Metaphor[2] – The Critical Commentator

These feelings of incompetence arise mostly in social situations. Social Fours often take on the role of *"keeper of the group's emotional truth"*.

Warning Signs for Type Four

- Focusing too much on what is missing
- Too much self-reference
- Too much need for intensity
- Too much concern for and need to be different

Warning Signs for the Social Subtype

- Too much need to be recognised
- Too much time spent keeping up social relationships
- Being a member of too many clubs
- Too much devotion to the causes they espouse

A SOCIAL FOUR'S VIEW – VALERIE

What I like about my Type

My desire for authenticity in everything I am and do. I'm totally frank and honest in the way I present myself to others; I show myself just as I am, whether people like it or not. I say what I think (although over time I've learned to say it more diplomatically) or I keep quiet. I find it really hard to lie; I can't see the point of making people believe that you are someone other than yourself. I tell myself that I would be found out sooner or later and that would get a relationship off to a bad start. It's beyond me why anyone would need to disguise reality; it's complicated enough as it is.

I love the intensity of my feelings; I experience things fully and try to communicate this completeness to others. I always speak and act with intensity; I don't know how to do things simply and even when they are simple I will always put intensity into them. For example, when I worked in an office not a day would pass without my having something exciting to talk about: my family, my work, my emotional relationships or even something that happened in the street. Life has no interest for me unless I have the feeling that I'm living it to the full. That's probably the reason why I travel a lot. Another aspect of me is that I love original and creative things: anything which is out of the ordinary.

I love my ability to listen; people have always told me that I have a great talent for listening because I can really put myself in the other person's shoes without judging them. I'm most interested in other people's lives when they have been long and rich. I can feel what others are feeling and understand their uniqueness. I don't judge them; they are as they are. I don't like all of them, but it doesn't matter; what interests me is how human beings operate. I'm curious about anything that's different, for others as well as for me.

What I like about my Subtype

My ability to adapt: I can operate in any social setting – I can take on the modus operandi of radically different professional worlds. Also, I really like my ability to try and find explanations and solutions to other people's problems. In my work I used to love being faced with an intractable situation; it was always me that people came to when that happened. It was very stressful, but finding the solution was always the most exciting part. It's the same with my friends; people often ring me to get my opinion when someone has a difficult choice to make or is going through a conflict situation. I try to analyse the situation objectively and to suggest solutions they could try. This active and dynamic side of me makes me feel alive; when it's in operation my own state of mind goes into the background.

I love my funny and merry-making side; when I'm on form

and at ease I'm the person who can create a good atmosphere in the group by my quirky remarks or unusual standpoints. I love celebrations and want everyone to have a good time. I love having people round and sharing the good things of life with others: dancing, meals, good wine, concerts, ballets …

I love my sociable side; I'm always curious to meet new people, experience different cultures and be surrounded by lots of friends from different worlds. I love surrounding myself with people who have strong interests, and sharing them with them. I'm happy to follow them around country walks, going to museums or discovering new artists in galleries.

I love fighting for big causes: being a volunteer for UNICEF, taking part in research to improve human well-being, belonging to a group to improve teamworking at work. Trying to improve well-being for myself and for others is important in every part of my life.

What I like about the Combination of my Type and Subtype

*You know, when I only knew about my Type, I didn't know what to do with this discovery. These days it's my subtype that pushes me to react when I'm going through a bad patch; if I take some social action I come out of my melancholy – it helps me forget my smaller side. When it comes to my talent for listening it's the same thing; when I listen to others and help them find solutions to their problems I get to a point where I can put my own problems aside. And it's the same when I get involved in social causes; it gives me the feeling that I exist, that I'm useful for something. It gives a sense of legitimacy to the fact that I'm different and to the feeling of **shame** that I feel when I don't feel recognised, understood or heard. When I do something for others I forget that I'm not good enough; I feel less guilty for being the way I am. I tell myself that when the chips are down there is still something good and useful inside me.*

Film Reference – Midnight in the Garden of Good and Evil

John Kelso, a young journalist from New York, is sent to Savannah, Georgia to cover the well-known annual Christmas party held every year by rich art collector Jim Williams. But the festivities have only just begun when we hear that Jim has been arrested for the murder of his partner, Jimmy Hanson, a low-down gigolo. John suspects a society scandal of epic proportions and decides to stay around to cover the court case. He gets to know the local people to try to get to the truth at the bottom of the story, which is complex and disturbing.

The setting for the film already has a kind of Four air about it – we're in the steamy, romantic atmosphere of Savannah, where eccentric characters meet out-of-date customs which remind you of the Georgia of "Gone with the Wind." Jim Williams has a number of Four traits; he is refined, he lives in an eighteenth century house where Hugh Mercer lived in 1860. He is an art dealer who also restores paintings. His collection is impressive, but he says "It's not a collection, it's where I live!" The place is full of antiques: clocks, Persian carpets, Fabergé eggs .... Some of them have exotic stories: "That's the dagger used by Yusupov to kill Rasputin and that piece there comes from the carriage used at Napoleon's coronation." Jim confesses to "having an eye for how to make things more beautiful" and that he is "interested in all the trappings of aristocracy which catch my eye; I love beautiful things." When John visits the house for the first time you can feel Jim's pride as he shows off the unusual objects in his collection.

What matters to Jim Williams is his quest for excellence (a Four quality which is often forgotten; it's comparable to but very different from a One's quest for perfection). He chooses his words carefully; he takes his time, which gives weight to each moment and allows each emotion to develop fully. In my book "Discovering the Enneagram" I make the point that: "The unconscious motivation of Fours is to be unique, to seek intensity in life, to bring their deep emotions to the forefront."

Jim Williams has these characteristics; if you want unique, he's your man! – or more exactly, he is deliberately way-out.

Jim's sophisticated annual party is not any old party; everyone who is anyone is there: senators, local celebrities … The social norms are important too: "Have you been introduced?" "This is absolutely not the done thing" "How should we react to this event?" – as though there were an instruction book on how to behave and that they were surprised that sometimes it didn't provide the answer to every situation.

The key word for social Fours is **shame**. Psychologically, the Fours' need to put themselves on the edge of the group could be seen as a way of dealing with their feeling of being deficient. Their need to be unique gets greater the more they feel ashamed at being outside social norms, and this takes the form of being noticed by the group because they are "different". However, because you have gone out of your way to be different, when things get difficult this makes your position even harder. When something bad happens to you, people don't take your side, and make you pay for the eccentricity that they might previously have admired.

There is another interesting side to this – the idea of "friends". Social subtypes often put everyone they know in the category of "friend". Once Jim is accused of murder he realises that most of his "friends" were in fact simply society acquaintances: "They fell over each other to be friends with me, hoping and praying to be invited to my parties; they weren't critical of me then!"

Another Social element is at play here: rumour and gossip: "I refuse to live in a world where rumours pass for facts – old women's gossip has too much sway in this town – all the upright people of this town are cursing because I'm living here."

Not all Enneagram Fours are flamboyant extraverts, as often described in the books. From experience I've noticed that at least 50% of Fours are introverts, living out their emotional fantasies in their dreams, like Jim. Among Social Fours there are also two general morphological types; some, like Jim are solidly built and expansive, hail-fellow-well-met types with speech that is a bit divorced from reality. The second classic type is more angular and withdrawn, quick to react and with a much more sensitive way of expressing themselves.

THE THREE SUBTYPES OF TYPE 5

Wound

One day in their childhood, Type Five children felt intruded upon and invaded, as though someone had illegally broken into their private space.

Passion: Avarice

Avarice needs to be understood here in the widest sense: it's about how Fives hoard their energy when spending time with others and experiencing their emotions. There is a tendency to withdraw, to expend the least amount of energy possible, to detach themselves from the outside world. *"I hold back, because if I give something of myself, I feel stripped bare and I have the feeling that I am no longer worth anything"*. There is a sort of recoil from human contact: *"I try to get through life on my own; in that way, no-one will own me. I am afraid of relationships because I'm afraid of having to give something in return. So I take refuge in my thoughts as long as possible, as if I were trying to get the last drop of meaning out of my ruminations. This means that I don't have to open myself to others. I need to be completely free, with no attachments, like a solitary squirrel that runs away from contact in order to concentrate better on protecting the nuts which are my store of energy."*

"If the price of keeping the little that I have is to distance myself from others, from their needs and demands, then that's what I'll do." You have to put distance between yourself and the

person you are talking to; in this respect Fives all say the same: *"It makes sense to me that just as I try to limit my interaction with others, I also keep my needs to the minimum so that I depend on the outside world as little as possible."*

There are therefore three major themes here: the fear of being *"swallowed up by other people"*, the emphasis placed on their intellectual life and the concern for self-sufficiency. When they are with other people, Fives hold back their spontaneity and needs. When they are in contact with the outside world their sensitivity to what is going on inside them is cut off – it's a way of protecting themselves from the need to take action or express themselves. From the outside, they may therefore seem indifferent, cold or apathetic, but inside, their mental function is operating at full tilt. They focus on trying to understand and acquire knowledge, even if it means that they put off action until later. *"The scoping phase of a project is much more interesting than the implementation phases. Taking action means laying yourself bare and risking the possibility of feeling your emotions."*

Preferred Defence Mechanism: Isolation of Affect

This is about detaching yourself in order to observe, cutting yourself off from too much feeling and emotional sensitivity, distancing yourself from other people and from the surrounding environment – this reduces the impact of others on you, as well as the impact of your own feelings and desires. Isolation of affect is about isolating yourself from feeling your own emotions, and Fives use a number of methods in order to achieve this. *"My instinct to isolate myself works fast and powerfully. If you compare it to the tide coming in at the Mont Saint-Michel with the speed and power of a galloping horse, my pulling back is strong as the ebb of that tide. Using my mental faculties I cut myself off from all sensation and emotion. I'm still physically there, but I am so afraid that I will be unable to control my great sensitivity that I prefer to cut myself off."*

When Fives feel threatened in relationships, they take themselves off mentally or leave completely. Isolation can take several forms; the most classic is to choose something to think about and focus on it mentally to the point where nothing else exists around them. *"What happened this morning? I was so busy with my research that I've completely forgotten ... hang on a minute, when was this morning?"* A second form of isolation is compartmentalisation. Just as in a submarine where the watertight bulkheads prevent the boat from sinking if one of them is breached, Fives separate their experiences, their friends, their professional life and their private life from each other, to protect themselves from being totally submerged if their external security wall is punctured.

THE SELF-PRESERVATION TYPE FIVE

Preoccupations of Type Five: protecting yourself from invasion, limiting your needs, learning
Preoccupations of the Self-Preservation Subtype: focus on the home, safety and material comfort
= CASTLE

Privacy is good and the world is invasive, so Fives tend to reduce both their contacts and their material possessions; even small pleasures seem like extravagances. Self-preservation Fives are the minimalists of the Enneagram; they're proud of being able to make do with very little. Fives' survival depends on having a private space that they can withdraw to on their own. When they spend time alone in their refuge they can recharge their batteries. Because their survival depends more on their knowledge than on their possessions, there is a real pleasure in abstinence, in being happy with little, because that limits their dependence on the outside world. Thrift is synonymous with freedom, and that means being free from the responsibility of having lots of possessions.

With Self-preservation Fives we're dealing with real observers, who watch the outside world going about its business from behind the protection of their thick castle walls.

Their main preoccupation is to keep control of their private space: *"Keeping time for me and having a space for myself are two things which are as vital as breathing oxygen."* There is also another archetype of the self-preservation Five: the "wanderer". Detached from any fixed abode, they keep their "home" in their rucksack, in their campervan or their boat. They find great pleasure in being happy with little and they also experience their emotions better when they are alone.

The Paradox

Reducing my material needs to the minimum doesn't stop me being dependent on the outside world. As a self-preservation Five it's even more true; even if I want to cut myself off from the outside world I will still end up being dependent on it one day.

Companies know that there are two ways to develop: invest or reduce your costs. Always choosing "reducing costs" isn't a solution; one day you will still have to invest – and the longer you've been pulling back, the greater the investment will need to be.

Metaphor – The Hermit

Your home or refuge is like the keep of a castle; it's a place to withdraw from the world so that you can feel safe, you can think and recharge your batteries – it's about putting thick walls between you and the cacophony of the outside world.

Warning Signs for Type Five
- Wanting to make do with what you already have
- Putting too much distance between you and the world
- Too much withdrawal into the world of the intellect
- Not expressing your emotions

Warning Signs for the Self-Preservation Subtype

- Too much focus on security
- Spending too much time at work
- Being too focused on material well-being
- Too many routine evenings at home

A SELF-PRESERVATION FIVE'S VIEW – DANIEL

What I like about my Type

Being appreciated by others for being reliable, someone you can count on. I love being available to offer service by giving information or advice. When things get difficult you can turn to me; my calm unflappable nature is reassuring. I also like my intellectual talents. I know how to stand back from a situation, to detach myself from it and get an overview.

For example, if we were talking about the Middle Ages in France, my mind would immediately go digging around in my memory to dredge up everything I know about this period in other parts of the world. I'll place the Middle Ages in their correct place in the timeline between the Palaeolithic and the twentieth century, and if you're interested in a discovery that happened at a certain point in time, I will put it in the context of other discoveries that happened before and afterwards. I don't consider myself a mine of information, but I do think I have a certain talent for sorting and knowing where to find all sorts of information.

What I like about my Subtype

I've a particular attraction to material things; I like knowing how practical things work. For example, not only can I tell you how the TV works, but I also get great pleasure from opening it up to see the connections, its structure and how it's set out. I also like my minimalism; I'm very happy to live with little. I rarely envy what I haven't got; I'm quite happy finding a solution with what's already there. When I was young, I used to say to myself that if I were well organised I could live with just one pair of jeans and one shirt, as long as I could wash and dry them in less than an hour. But on the other hand, I think I'm quite generous towards other people. They may sometimes have the impression that the present I've given them isn't expensive, but I will have spent much more on them than I would on myself.

What I like about the Combination of my Type and Subtype

My tendency to withdraw makes me a good listener. Because I find it very easy to detach myself from my own emotions, I can follow the other person's line of reasoning and guide their reflective process, whether it's adults or my grandchildren. I also like my ability to be alone; it's wonderful to be able to take the time to experience some things without being disturbed. For example, one very special time for me is the evening after a lovely summer's day. The sun is setting, the temperature is dropping and the birds are taking advantage of the gentle warmth. If there is someone with me to share the moment, that's ok, but if I'm alone that's good too. It gives me independence and enormous freedom. People often say that Fives find it difficult to share; as far as I'm concerned I don't think I'm like that. Most of the time I wouldn't go looking for someone else, but if someone comes into my space, as long as their intentions are peaceful and they respect my temperament I have no problem welcoming them in – as long as they ring me first to let me know they're coming. Well, ok, it's true that I do have a bit of a gruff side. **Castle?** *I don't know, but I certainly relate to the word "refuge".*

Film Reference – Finding Forrester

We're in the Bronx with Jamal, a young black man, who has two passions, basketball and writing. Just as he's got a place at the prestigious Mailor school he meets a gruff, mysterious, reclusive, misanthropic writer – William Forrester. Although once Forrester wrote a bestseller, he hasn't written anything for thirty years and has slipped back into

128

anonymity. There's no reason why these two should become friends; their age, their education, their culture and even the colour of their skin separate them – but they do, and the film tells that story.

I have always thought that the subtypes and defence mechanisms are two of the most important aspects of the Enneagram. Here, William shows us the defence mechanism of isolation. Wounded by life, his Five instinct is to withdraw, to turn in on himself, to hunker down in his head, cut himself off from his emotions and his physical sensations. Sometimes, particularly for self-preservation Fives, the isolation is also physical. William has lived in the same apartment for decades, and never goes out. He gets his books and food delivered and spends a lot of time looking out at the neighbourhood through his binoculars. Nobody sees him; when he sits at the window he is hidden by his net curtains, to the point where the young people who play basketball under his windows call him "Window". No-one has ever seen him and a flutter of the curtains is the only proof of his existence – this is the epitome of isolation.

Later in the film we see another part of the Five: minimalism. It's about being happy with as little as possible, limiting your energy expenditure and your emotional contacts. In speech you use the minimum number of words to say what you have to say – you come across as very serious. The first two meetings between the main characters are non-verbal; the next ones take place on either side of a closed door, with William looking through the spyhole. His invitation to come in is made simply by opening the door; not a word is spoken.

Self-preservation subtypes focus principally on themselves, their body, safety, territory and possessions. The royalties from William's books seem to bring in enough for him to live on, so his physical welfare is taken care of. His territory extends to everything that he can see from behind his curtains with his binoculars. What he's interested in is the life of the neighbourhood; this is very characteristic of self-preservation subtypes, who focus firstly on what is closest to them before (possibly) taking an interest in what is further afield.

With self-preservation Fives the energy of the type and the subtype go in the same direction: material independence, taking refuge at home and minimising contact with the outside world. The word associated with this type is **castle**. William's flat is a storehouse where he can protect himself from the rest of the world and ensure his safety. Whereas one-to-one and social Fives simply isolate themselves mentally, for self-preservation Fives the isolation is physical and territorial as well.

I am moved by Fives' sensitivity; their isolation is actually just a way to protect themselves from their acute sensitivity. This film pays homage to the courage of a Five who takes the risk to come out of his castle, rediscovering his vulnerability and daring to step out into the realities of the external world. His journey to achieving this means moving beyond old fears and healing old wounds – once he has made contact, his manner is simple and direct.

I was struck by the delicacy, almost prudery of this type; they can convey emotions without necessarily saying anything at all. Other things William shows us are that he has a rich intellectual life and at the same time a gentle humanity with no condescension. And he is capable of a searing expression of the anger of the Eight, which stands out because of how far removed it is from his normal type behaviour.

Jamal shows us how to make contact with this type: slowly, with great intellectual honesty. And in the last part of the film William shows his generosity when he saves his friend, to whom he is deeply committed, with a great example of Five non-attachment.

THE ONE-TO-ONE TYPE FIVE

Preoccupations of Type Five: protecting yourself from invasion, limiting your needs, learning
Preoccupations of the One-to-One Subtype: focusing on the partner
= CONFIDENCES/SECRETS

Two contradictory energies are in play here: the Five's desire to withdraw is in opposition to the one-to-one's desire to create a relationship. This creates a lot of tension: *"I want an intense connection with the other person, but I need to keep my independence. I have emotions, but I don't want them to overwhelm me."* So Fives can put relationships in compartments; this enables them to have intense encounters with people which will be special moments for sharing confidences that are "outside time" – well separated from their emotions before and after the meeting. While they're in contact with someone, there is an atmosphere of secrecy; their tone of voice is discreet and their gestures are restrained, but the quality of their presence is strong. With this in place they can lay themselves bare to the person they confide in: *"You're the only person that I can reveal so much of myself to, but I trust you."* However, these partners in conversation need to be at the same intellectual level as them.

In affairs of the heart, they don't necessarily ask for great demonstrations of concern; it's more about small gestures: a look, a flower, a brush of the hand, a kind word... At work, one-to-one Fives have strong powers of concentration; they can get so carried away by their job that they almost become a bit compulsive and might start looking like Ones or Threes. On the outside, they don't necessarily give the impression of being distant; the one-to-one flame makes them easier to make contact with than self-preservation Fives.

The Paradox

Compartmentalising my emotional life to separate it from the rest of my life will end up making me uncomfortable.

Metaphor – The Secret Agent

It's about sharing confidences within a limited circle, in the privacy of one-to-one conversations. You choose carefully who you want to make a relationship with.

Warning Signs for Type Five

- Wanting to make do with what you already have
- Putting too much distance between you and the world
- Too much withdrawal into the world of the intellect
- Not expressing your emotions

Warning Signs for the One-to-One Subtype

- Focus on wanting to prove that you are an intense, passionate person
- Too much focus on the partner: what they are doing, where they are, who they are meeting
- Too much focus on your own actions – not enough wider perspective
- Rivalry between your own goals and your partner's interest in other things

A ONE-TO-ONE FIVE'S VIEW – ERIC

What I like about my Type

I love the delicacy of Fives. During Enneagram workshops I've attended, Fives often come and ask me for information. I've noticed then their respect as they ask whether I'm available for a conversation; it's a sort of apprehension lest they invade my space or show indiscretion. I recognise that I feel like this myself when I'm with other people; it's the way I like to be approached. But when it's me that's going towards the other person, my contact with them can sometimes be a bit rough, because I often launch straight in to what interests me without first taking care to build a friendly relationship. I am trying to be delicate, but the enacting of it sometimes produces the opposite effect!

I love my desire to get to the bottom of things. This means that answering a question while respecting the length of answer the other person is expecting is a real sacrifice for me. Each time I explain something I want to point out why I'm putting forward that point of view, why I think it comes from there, why I think this truth might be different according to different people or circumstances, why there are often confusions between what you see and what's actually happening, why...... When I'm explaining something I feel that I have to give the whole picture, and missing out certain parts would make it seem as though my thinking were confused.

I love my trustworthiness. As I'm used to being happy with very little, it's easy for me to know what's important to me. So when I give my word, not only is it something I've thought through, but I reorganise my priorities so that I can honour what I've promised. One of the things that surprise me most in life is the lack of prioritising that I come across in other people. Based on their mood, someone they've just met or a sudden whim, they will put off something that they had promised to do for someone. For me, respecting the person you've made the promise to is an indispensable part of that promise.

What I like about my Subtype

One-to-one encounters give me energy and pleasure; it's as though I'm extending the present boundaries of the relationship, so that I can move towards something that is even better. It's an opportunity to give an extra impulse to the relationship. Wanting to be important or unique in the eyes of the other person is also a driver that pushes me to go beyond the way I normally do things. What I'm starting to enjoy more and more is being in contact with other one-to-one types; it's probably with them that I experience the most intimate and deep connection. I don't find it easy to meet people socially, in the middle of a group. Often I don't dare to open up much if the movement and noise around me give me the feeling that people aren't really listening.

What I like about the Combination of my Type and Subtype

*It's true that in general I'm a bit stingy with my time, my thoughts, expressing my emotions and touching people. But when a relationship really interests me I can become generous and I want intense communication; I let myself express my sensitivity, particularly if I feel that it will be well received. In an atmosphere like that I also manage to block off my reflex to move away when I'm touched. It's a bit like in the Asterix cartoons; there are magic potions and antidotes! The intensity, depth and trust of a one-to-one relationship are the clear antidote to my natural Five withdrawal. That's what I understand by the key word **confidences.***

My subtype also helps me make contact with others. Although most of the time I tend to have a distant, observing attitude, as soon as an interesting one-to-one relationship is on the horizon, any blockage I feel just disappears. Then I can be welcoming, friendly and convivial in my relationships. I also think that the delicacy of my Five sometimes enhances my one-to-one ability to focus on the other person. The desire to get to the bottom of things really comes into its own here. I want to understand the other person, our relationship and myself. My subtype takes me beyond wanting to understand how things work, into how human beings work.

And finally I want to come back to my trustworthiness; for me, a relationship that has been deep is never forgotten and will always retain a flavour of what was wonderful about it. The relationship can end, but there will always be a memory of its most strongly experienced moments, the moments that enabled me to express my humanity, which is the best of me.

Film Reference – Sex, Lies and Videotape

Graham Dalton videos and collects interviews with women talking about their sex life. When he returns to his home town he catches up with an old university friend who has become very successful, and his wife. This meeting will have surprising consequences for all of them.

Type Five shows up here in that Graham is an introvert who keeps himself a bit apart from the world in order to analyse it better: "I watched you eat, talk and move and I saw a whole person..." He doesn't want a phone because he finds it intrusive; his house is minimalist in style; he needs solitude, but at the same time he is courteous and "normal" when you meet him.

The One-to-One Five comes out in that the first time Graham meets Ann, his friend's wife, on her own they immediately get into quite an intimate conversation: "People say that men learn to love women they fancy, whereas women fancy people they like." All one-to-one subtypes have this competence, but particularly Fives; they don't waste time with preliminaries, they get straight into the conversation they really want to have. This is where the key word **"confidence"** comes from – it's about being interested in the other person's life, soul, desires and feelings in the present moment. Why waste time skirting round the heart of the subject? Every piece of information about the other person is interesting and emotions are separated from thoughts.

Another aspect that doesn't often get talked about with one-to-one Fives is time – they need time to think, analyse and reflect. They have a short communication window and so social chit-chat is superfluous – and you find this also at the end of the interaction; once the intense conversation is finished, Fives can close things off in a very abrupt way. So this word "confidence" can also be applied to the process: keeping your distance before and after the one-to-one contact, and an intense intimacy while you are having your tête-à-tête.

In this film, Graham very quickly gets to know all the intimate details of his friends' sex life – it's as though he wants the other person to give him the most intimate details of their life as quickly as possible – he wants to create a strong, rapid connection with them.

Through the medium of a delicate subject, this film gives us a very accurate portrait of Graham's character. It hangs together; the Five's sensitivity and his way of living in his head rather than in the world are obvious and important. The dilemma of the Five is beautifully illustrated: how do you become real and take action rather than living your life through fantasy?

THE SOCIAL TYPE FIVE

Preoccupations of Type Five: protecting yourself from invasion, limiting your needs, learning
Preoccupations of the Social Subtype: focusing on friends, associations and groups
= SOCIAL TOTEMS / PROFESSOR

There are two contradictory energy lines here: not wanting to be invaded and wanting to play a role within the group. In the olden days the totem was a carved tree trunk that summed up the history and culture of the tribe. What matters for social Fives is places where people get together and important events in society. For example, in the UK it might be Cup Final day and the last night of the Proms; in the USA it might be Thanksgiving and the 4th of July, in Australia, Australia Day and Anzac day and so on.

Social Fives are fascinated by the ideas and people that influence the culture and history of a country. They are interested in national gatherings and social landmarks and want to play a role in them. The want to develop a specialist expertise, be a model, be a source of knowledge. They feel the need to be one of the people at the head of the tribe, perhaps as their adviser. They want to be inside the circle of initiates; they love titles and degrees. They are particularly attracted by research systems about social trends: research polls or political forecasting institutes. Turning all these things into concepts and theories will enable them to predict future events through their expertise. We are a long way here from the stereotypical Five who is the *"hermit in the depths of the wood"*. Social Fives go eagerly towards others, or at least towards the people who attract them intellectually. They may even be in at the beginning of certain sorts of clubs, particularly networks where experts exchange information. When the circumstances are favourable they can be garrulous to the point of over-loquaciousness. In that context you would really have to look hard to find a hint of the holding back which is characteristic of their type.

The Paradox

Too much emphasis on analysis can make my "expert teacher" explanations so abstruse that no-one can understand them.

Metaphor – Elite Think-Tank Member

It's about a thirst for knowledge, a desire to master the symbols and language of society (totems) – and there is the need to disseminate them by teaching or writing.

Warning Signs for Type Five
- Wanting to make do with what you already have
- Putting too much distance between you and the world
- Too much withdrawal into the world of the intellect
- Not expressing your emotions

Warning Signs for the Social Subtype
- Too much need to be recognised
- Too much time spent keeping up social relationships
- Being a member of too many clubs and societies
- Too much devotion to the causes they espouse

A SOCIAL FIVE'S VIEW – ERICA

What I like about my Type

I love collecting, sorting and analysing information – and I mean large amounts of information – my memory banks have lots of storage space! There's something very satisfying in thinking, analysing, using my intelligence to move things forward. I can easily see the overview of a situation and I like creating models to help others to find their way in the world. Other people tell me that I have a real talent for words, for giving explanations that help to clarify things. Another aspect is that I like to live simply; I don't need to own a lot of stuff in order to be happy.

What I like about my Subtype

I relate more easily to the word **professor** *than* **totems**. *I've got a sort of compulsion to teach, to share my knowledge with others, to the point where I can spend all day thinking about "how could I make this idea understandable to others?" Fives are often described as not taking up much room, and that's true of me most of the time. I do tend to withdraw; I tend to think that others won't be interested in my life or my opinions. But when I'm being a "teacher" I'm completely different. I feel big and powerful, as if the role of teacher gives me permission to be centre stage. Being in the role of professor enables me to be in control, and I can become a bit of a control-freak, wanting to organise every aspect of the class – I've had to learn to restrain this impulse because I was becoming too directive. Learning to facilitate rather than lead has been both a challenge and a joy.*

What I like about the Combination of my Type and Subtype

I have to say first that it's not always easy to manage these two contradictory forces. As I cross the threshold of the classroom I'm sandwiched between my Five instinct to run away and hide and my social impulse which wants to go into the classroom to play a role. Once I'm in the classroom the tension disappears and I'm fine, but the moment before that when the two impulses are clashing is really difficult. Being a teacher allows me to share my ideas, to get feedback, to put my ideas forward and to have a role in the world. My other role as a facilitator also enables me to get in contact with people in a safe way, because the boundaries of the relationship are clear. I don't have to give away too much of my privacy, I can just play a role, as though I were an actor!

My need to have intellectual control over the situation means that I'm good at organising things and I often find myself in a leadership position in the group, without having asked for it. Over time I've learned to hide myself less; I'm starting to speak my truth and use more personal examples rather than telling an emotionally neutral story. Understanding my subtype has really helped me to notice the moment when my defences kick in, and since I recognised that I'm getting much better at gradually asking them to calm down so that I can stay present and open my heart.

Film Reference – The Social Network

The film is set in October 2003, when Mark Zuckerberg, a Harvard student who gets drunk because he's just been dumped by his girlfriend, hacks into the Harvard database to get data on all the female students. He then creates an on-campus website for rating them – it's about putting two photos side by side and asking viewers to vote for the most attractive. He calls the site Facemash and it's an instant success; the site goes viral, crashing the Harvard system and starting a campus scandal. Mark is accused of having wilfully breached security systems, privacy and copyright laws. And of course this is the moment in which Facebook is born.

Some time later, Mark creates facebook.com, which spreads like wildfire round Harvard and then other US universities, before going world-wide. This invention sets up fierce conflicts; what were the real facts about its invention; who can really claim to be the inventor of this worldwide social network?

Something that will become a pivotal concept of the 21st century destroys the friendships of its pioneers and sets in place confrontations with enormous consequences at stake.

This is not a sympathetic portrayal of a Five – on the contrary. There is a side to Mark that is intellectually pleased with himself, even condescending; there seems to be a total lack of kindness or human warmth. If you see this in Enneagram terms, his head centre is so over-prized that he's not really living in his body. When you compare him with the twins who sue Mark because they say he stole their idea, the contrast is striking – the twins are rowing champions and are completely at ease in their bodies, whereas Mark seems to see his body only as an object. He has no physical rhythm; he sleeps irregularly and food is simply fuel. The way he speaks is also interesting; his voice is monotonous with no hint of compassion. I need to emphasise that not all Fives are like this! – the way this character is portrayed is a caricature.

Mark is also a stereotype of a social subtype – he is only interested in society: how others live, what motivates them, what brings them together, how they interact. He can divide them into subgroups, for example couples versus singles, well-off people as opposed to less well-off people, students from the best universities versus the others. We find this characteristic in most social subtypes; they have a sort of meta-view of any group; they are interested in how it works as a whole, whether it's a social group, a country or the whole world.

The key word for the social Five is "**totems**" – in Enneagram terms this is about crossroads, support systems, places where people come together, whether it's a society gathering around the national news bulletin or people with the same interest gathering at a national sports stadium. If you add to this the social subtype's concern for social or intellectual prestige, you can see why creating Facebook would be a totem par excellence. Although colossal amounts of money are talked of in the film, that's not what motivates Mark; he wants to create a social revolution. From a social Five perspective, Facebook would be the crossroads of the 21st century: the place where you exchange information on who's where, who's doing what, who's going out with whom etc., etc.

This particular film shows a fairly rare type – a social who is anti-social – a person who is fascinated by society and yet runs away from it. His only interest is relationships between others; he doesn't like to spend time with people like himself. He likes understanding patterns, the energy lines that underpin society, and he even becomes the instigator of sites that help them to communicate, get together and exchange information – but he is too caught up in his own excellence to actually interact with his peers. This film leaves a bitter taste in the mouth; our illusions are shattered – but it is a fascinating portrait of the type.

THE THREE SUBTYPES OF TYPE 6

Wound

One day the Type Six child felt betrayed; authority wounded them or they felt that they were under surprise attack. Whatever happened, the child came to believe that the world is potentially hostile and unpredictable; safety only exists if they can foresee what other people intend to do.

Passion: Doubt/Fear

Sixes are afraid of their own impulses or of acting spontaneously. Stopping their own first impulse themselves is better than being in confrontation with the outside world. It is a fear of being, but the meaning of the word "fear" covers many things. You could call it "timidity" because it implies two poles: inhibition, but also courage – a sort of anxious hesitation in action. It is as though Sixes are in a constant state of anxiety and underlying disquiet even though there is no apparent external danger. *"It feels like a frozen fear, an alarm which is still switched on even after the danger has ceased to be a threat. But you never know when danger will arrive; you have to be constantly on the lookout for clues which will show that something is out of the ordinary."*

Claudio Naranjo says[1]: *"Most of the time this fear is not necessarily apparent. It's more a question of a psychological fear: fear of changing, fear of the unknown, fear of hostility, fear of pitfalls, fear of being alone in a threatening world, fear of being betrayed or fear of loving. These different forms of worry lead to behaviours such as insecurity, hesitation, risk aversion, being paralysed by doubt, lack of drive, a tendency to double-check, lack of self-confidence and difficulties with unstructured situations."*

Fear makes Sixes uncertain about action. Thus they rarely feel certain enough and often need lots of information before taking action. In order to achieve this they will arm themselves with intellectual and logical arguments that will keep them safe. They become devotees of reason: asking good questions, imagining the unexpected, thinking things through and finally making a decision. They don't just look for solutions to the concrete problems they can see, they anticipate and even go looking for solutions to problems that might arise at some point. Faced with their fear of taking action, they develop a very effective strategy: postponement – it's a reflex response to put things off until later.

But let's come back to the two poles of timidity: inhibition and courage. For example, if you're in great danger you only have two options: flee or plunge straight into the danger. If you are timid or a Six you always have these two options available and you don't know, even one second in advance, which one you will use. This tends to make Sixes the most ambivalent and unpredictable of all the Enneagram types; from one moment to the next they can go from submission to rebellion or from kindness to violence.

Preferred Defence Mechanism: Projection

When you believe and can see that the outside world is very powerful and so much bigger than you, a feeling of insecurity is bound to follow. *"My feelings are affected by the external environment, which is powerful and threatening. My imagined fears become realities which I have to either avoid or fight."* Projection therefore comes from the fear of insecurity and it can confuse doubts and real facts: *"You are 15 minutes late, so you are being unfaithful to me!"* With practice it becomes possible to separate reality – *"My partner is 15 minutes late"* – from mental projection – *"My greatest fear is that you will be unfaithful to me."* Peter O'Hanrahan says that projections can also be positive: *"Positive projection happens when Sixes give up their own authority and positive qualities in order to attribute them to others, which for the person they're projecting onto can be just as unsettling as a negative projection would be. It gives them the impression that they're not being recognised for who they really are, but are being used as a coat-hanger to hang projections on. Also, the positive projection can rapidly morph into hostility if the person concerned turns out not to be worthy of it."*

THE SELF-PRESERVATION TYPE SIX

Preoccupations of Type Six: trusting, doubting, worrying about the consequences
Preoccupations of the Self-Preservation Subtype: focus on home, security and material comfort
= WARMTH

Being nice to people is a good survival strategy. If people like you, you don't have to be afraid: *"If I don't know you, I don't know if I can trust you. So I'll be warm towards you so that I can protect myself against unexpected reactions."* If I look for and give warmth and am a welcoming and generous host, it lessens the risk of my being attacked.

Self-preservation Sixes can relax when they are with someone who knows them and who they can trust. When they are at home with their friends they know what to expect and they can allow themselves to let down their guard. *"I use my ingenuity to make and keep up relationships. In this way I have a circle of close friends that I could use as a circle of bodyguards if I were attacked, just like Napoleon had his guard, who would have sacrificed themselves to protect him."* Because they carry this loyalty through into their actions, they are a great support to each of the members of this guard and will take their side in any argument. *"Of course I'll be there when they need me – we're all in the same boat. Life is hard and you have to help each other."*

Self-preservation Sixes often enjoy team sports where they can get to know the other team members well and can feel that they are protected by the group. They also have a strategic reflex to use humour, charm and even self-deprecation to bring possible enemies round to their side. *"Sometimes I even find myself playing the role of victim, exposing my vulnerability, in order to lessen someone's possible hostility towards me."*

The Paradox

Hoping that being nice to people will make the world a safer and more predictable place is a delusion.

Metaphor – The Loyalist

Because they don't want to find themselves all on their own and out in the cold, making relationships with people is an absolute necessity. In addition, living in a neighbourhood or area that they know adds to their feeling of security.

Warning Signs for Type Six

- Being worried all the time
- Spending too much time thinking about safety
- Thinking too much about the possible consequences of an action
- Too much projection and thinking about the worst case scenario

Warning Signs for Self-Preservation Type Six

- Too much focus on security
- Spending too much time at work
- Being too focused on material well-being
- Too many routine evenings at home

A SELF-PRESERVATION SIX'S VIEW – CLAUDE

What I like about my Type

When I realised I was a Six, the great thing was that it explained all my doubts and fears – just knowing that helped to solve some of them! I also gained a deeper understanding of myself, not only because I realised my failings, but also because I became aware of the good things that I could offer to the world. It was probably the first time in my life that I clearly saw that I had lots of good qualities and that I could do something with them. Being the person who always sees the possible elephant traps in a situation can be an impossible way to live if you let it dominate you, but it can be transformed into a weapon for peace when you know how to train it.

In the same way I realised much more acutely how ambivalent I can be; I can be soft and submissive in some situations, aggressive in others, trust someone in the morning and distrust them the same evening. Once I understood this important fact I managed to move from doubt to faith and started to use my fears as a motivator. Life is no longer an unwinnable fight; it has become a challenge that enables me to move forward!

I love my sensitivity, my gifts of anticipation and my practical intelligence. I also love my connection to nature; I find that forests are a lot less dangerous than towns. Out in the natural world I feel protected, as though I'm part of a unifying whole. I also like my relationship with my body. I'm really in touch with my body and I know when it's the beginning of my sleep cycle, when my body wants to eat and how long it wants to walk for.

What I like about my Subtype

As I gain self-awareness I'm more able to realise quickly that some of my worries are completely unjustified – and then I can laugh at myself! I'm sure that no-one could make more fun of me than I do of myself. Self-preservation subtypes are particularly aware of material things; I am always checking

146

that the train is on time, that the storm hasn't destroyed everything, that the car hasn't broken down. So my subtype enables me quickly to compare my fears with reality. Another good side of my subtype is preparing in advance; when I'm leading a workshop you can be sure that the participants will have everything they need, because I have thought of everything: from soap to towels, from crockery to biscuits, white and brown sugar, normal and soya milk, teaspoons, felt-tipped pens, pencil sharpeners (just in case!) bus and train time tables. And of course I've asked whether there are vegetarians or people with allergies – but I've learned to stop myself asking in advance how many people prefer tea or coffee!

In my class at the nursery school where I teach, everything is prepared so that nothing could happen which would disturb the smooth running of my teaching. Once I'm reassured by all my preventative preparation I can let myself go to live in the present and the children have a great time with me! I'm also a therapist for adults and there too, I make sure that my workplace is organised; I've set everything up to create an atmosphere of calm, serenity and trust in order to ensure the best possible relationship with the client.

What I like about the Combination of my Type and Subtype

*Finding my subtype made me realise how much I set things up so that people who get close to me can't attack me. This is what gentleness and **warmth** is about; I smile, prepare myself, organise everything to give the impression that I'm gentle and not aggressive. Since I realised this, I've been able to develop my inner observer to notice the moment when fear and suspicion get hidden behind my defensive smile. These days, practising this self-observation enables me to experience the present moment much more calmly; I've become lighter and more spontaneous. I've improved my ability to forward plan in order to avoid potential risks – and I get less anxious about possible dangers. Doing this means that I can move* *beyond negative projections, let go and give more weight to my intuition. I always knew that I had this natural intuition – now I've learned to make it more conscious and use it more in everyday life.*

Film Reference – The Third Man

It's Vienna in 1949. The American writer Holly Martins lands in Vienna, summoned by his friend Harry Lime, who has offered him work. Hardly has Holly arrived when he discovers that Harry has been killed in a road accident – he arrives just in time to attend his funeral.

Six energy is all around in the film itself and in the role of Holly, the main character. The surroundings are worrying; the town is divided into five zones, four of which are controlled by the American, Russian, English and French armies of occupation. The centre of town is international. The Austrian police seem powerless and the inhabitants prefer to keep quiet most of the time rather than engaging with the international authorities. From a Six point of view, the position of the authorities is therefore not clear, and it's certainly a long way from being transparent and trustworthy. Holly is not taken in; hearing the account of the accident given by the British Major Calloway, he starts to have doubts. Even though the police have interrogated witnesses and drawn up a statement about the accident that seems to hang together, Holly smells a rat.

Although Holly knows that his friend is dead and nothing will bring him back, he takes up the case on his behalf rather than just leaving on the first available plane. He wants to know and understand everything: "I can't believe that's all there is to it – will you help me?" When asked the question "Have you got reasons for being suspicious?" Holly can't give a reply except to say that his Six intuition tells him that someone is hiding something from him and that appearances are not necessarily the same as what's hidden behind them. Little by little, clues appear which justify his suspicion. Information is difficult to get hold of and the different stories of the witnesses don't tally. The official version isn't implausible, but the list of worrying facts gets longer: "It's really strange that Harry's two best friends were there at his side, but that it was Harry's chauffeur who was driving at the time of the accident..." "Why did they take the body to the other side of the road when it would have been easier to take it into his house?" Holly becomes certain that he has raised a hare when the concierge tells him about a third man who helped to carry the body: " ... a third man who kept his head down, who looked like Mr Lime but who didn't give evidence at the inquest." From that point on, the Six is on the trail: "I'm going to get to the bottom of this story!" The fact that people warn him about his safety several times doesn't weaken his determination: "I need to have the final word on this story."

The film accelerates; it's full of unexpected surprises, false accusations and traps, fog and twilight. The suspense and anxiety build – Holly is in danger, hunted down and accused of murder. As we watch this we think we have seen something, but we're not sure whether we have. Shadows are thrown up on to walls; even the ground doesn't always seem flat; it's full of slopes, steps and mounds of rock joining different levels. Questions get mixed up with each other and we don't know what we can trust any more – any more than Holly does: "What sort of spy are you? Why are you following me? Will you show yourself? Will you come out into the light?"

Friendship and betrayal are set against each other – another type Six theme. Having discovered that his former friend was a criminal, Holly finally decides to walk away from this friendship, although Harry's former partner prefers to remain faithful to the relationship she had with him: "Why do I have to betray him? I loved what we had together." The last scene of the film is just as telling about Type Six. The executioner has become the victim; he is face to face with the mob, all alone; you almost feel you want to protect him. We see him being chased and in all kinds of danger. Full of sideways looks, he has become the target and as soon as he shows himself he will be gunned down. At the end we seem him standing, completely alone, listening to the noise of his pursuers' footsteps approaching, with the look of a hunted beast in his eyes, trying to decide which passage might offer him a chance to escape. This feeling of being the victim alone in the face of a hostile world is so common for Sixes. As for the self-preservation theme, it's there all the time as well. Holly is alone and even his surroundings suggest the need for self-preservation: the town is ruined; there is no food and no way of keeping warm.

THE ONE-TO-ONE TYPE SIX

Preoccupations of Type Six: trusting, doubting, worrying about the consequences
Preoccupations of the One-to-One Subtype: focusing on the partner
= STRENGTH/BEAUTY

It's in one-to-one relationships that fear comes up most strongly, but it's also one-to-one relationships which are the most important for this subtype. So one-to-one Sixes use strength and beauty as ways to build their self-confidence: *"If the other person thinks I'm strong, intelligent and sexy, not only will they be less likely to attack me, but I will also have more self-confidence."* Underneath, they worry about not being loved, about whether they are attractive. Almost without realising it they exaggerate their strength (mostly men) or their sex-appeal (mostly women) in order to hide both their immense desire for and terror of being in a relationship.

Focusing on bodily beauty means that you don't have to look closely at the other person and this enables you to behave more calmly in relation to your fear. Some one-to-one Sixes are avid customers of gyms or beauty salons; for others, practising martial arts keeps the body fit and also reassures them that they could stand up to an attacker in the woods. Others will behave like kamikazes in various ways: being insolent to people in authority, taking stupid risks such as riding a motorbike very fast without a helmet, doing dangerous sports such as bungee jumping or skydiving ... *"Through these bravura actions I get face-to-face with my fear, I defy my doubts and I come out of it with more self-confidence. There was a time in my life when if you had said "Are you game?" about anything, I would have been up for it".*

The ambivalence that was mentioned earlier turns up at three levels:
- Moving from the desire to charm the other person to wanting to test yourself against them
- Sudden movement from admiring yourself or the other person, to denigration
- Moving from obedience to rebellion, particularly in relation to authority.

The Paradox
Making the outside world responsible for your internal fear and your impulses won't improve your self-confidence in the long term.

Metaphor – Charmer/Warrior
People who are more inclined to be sweet, muzzle their fear by turning it into creativity and by creating harmony or beauty in their surroundings. People who are more warrior-like muzzle their doubt by self-hypnosis, rash acts of bravery, a lively intelligence, hitting back through repartee and holding strong ideological positions.

Warning Signs for Type Six
- Being worried all the time
- Spending too much time thinking about safety
- Thinking too much about the possible consequences of an action
- Too much projection and thinking about the worst case scenario

Warning Signs for the One-to-One Subtype

- Focus on wanting to prove that you are an intense, passionate person
- Too much focus on the partner: what they are doing, where they are, who they are meeting
- Too much focus on your own actions – not enough wider perspective
- Rivalry between your own goals and your partner's interest in other things

A ONE-TO-ONE SIX'S VIEW – SAMMY

What I like about my Type

Being loyal to my nearest and dearest. When I like someone they can count on me; I give love and friendship without asking for anything in return. Moreover, in daily life, I like the side of me that is "feel the fear and do it anyway" which leads me to go forward and carry through anything I take on. This can sometimes take some extreme forms, for example when I was younger I tried skydiving, bungee-jumping, firewalking and any number of difficult mountain climbs. Once I get started I don't give up easily. In my work I also enjoy the side of me that checks every detail so that I can be sure that everything has been done properly and made safe.

What I like about my Subtype

My ability to make the most of each moment, fully and completely. For me true life is in those moments when I'm in an intense one-to-one conversation, whether it's professional or personal. In order to be successful, these moments need two ingredients; we need to have created a climate where we can listen to each other in confidence, and the person I'm talking with must be prepared for a fair amount of intensity in our conversation or exchange of views. If that's in place, I feel reassured; I feel that within this framework I'm not at risk, I can trust the other person and move towards them. When it comes to work situations, I really like my ability to forget everything that's going on around me in order to have a one-to-one relationship with a particular project; in that situation, as long as I'm not disturbed, I can bring an enormous amount of concentration to my work.

What I like about the Combination of my Type and Subtype

My Six gives me the courage to take on the challenges of being alive and my one-to-one subtype gives me the concentration and intensity to push through to the end in situations where I might otherwise have been afraid. When these two work well together, my self-confidence goes up exponentially. In my social and personal relationships, friends tell me that they love the sparkling side of my personality; it's as though the Head focus of my Six joined with my one-to-one energy gives me a particular sense of humour that is lively and witty. Moreover, my friends know that my friendship with them is for ever, sustained by the intensity of each of our meetings.

Film Reference – The Messenger: The Story of Joan of Arc

If you're of a sensitive disposition, stay away from this film; it's pretty violent. A lot of the violence could probably have been omitted without reducing the interest of the film. The panel of Sixes who looked at it decided to retain it in order to illustrate the one-to-one Six, because it shows a number of Six characteristics that you don't find elsewhere, particularly the duality between Strength and Beauty which I've never seen demonstrated elsewhere with the intensity that you see here.

It's 1420 and Henry V, king of England and Charles VI, king of France, have signed the Treaty of Troyes, which stipulates that the kingdom of France will belong to England when the king dies. But the two kings die within a few months of each other and Henry VI, the new king of England, is only a few months old. Charles VII, the Dauphin of France, has no desire to give up his kingdom to a child. A bloody war breaks out and the English and their Burgundian allies invade France.

The beginning of the film sets up the contrast between the natural carefree nature of Joan at the age of about 7 or 8, and the sudden unpredictable violence of the outside world. At this time, life was harsh; your village might be calm in the morning, you go out for a little walk in the forest and when you come back the village has been sacked, pillaged and the inhabitants killed. This sudden violence, which breeds insecurity, is a true Six characteristic. Sixes might not have experienced it in such dramatic circumstances as in the film, but it's a constant feeling for them; the outside world is inherently dangerous. This belief gives Sixes a certain internal violence; they can be a sort of sensitive cat on a hot tin roof, ready to do battle.

Joan has visions; she receives messages from God. The film questions whether Joan is an inspired saint or just a little girl who conjures up pictures in her head. Here we have another Six characteristic – because the outside world isn't stable or trustworthy, you have to be on the alert and develop intuitive antennae to suss out danger before you are attacked. Joan has her spiritual antennae, but all Sixes have more or less developed their own particular warning signs. The film emphasises this characteristic when Joan comes for her first interview with the Dauphin in the great hall of the castle. He hides to test her gifts and see whether she can recognise the Dauphin among all the people present – and Joan finds him. We have all heard this story at school, but this scene in the film emphasises it well.

Joan is pious; she has faith in God and in her mission, and this faith is galvanised and multiplied by her one-to-one subtype, which enables her to become the single source of support for others. And with Joan of Arc, this ability becomes a laser beam – even the word charisma is an understatement in this context. Joan is luminous; her faith transfigures her. In this badly-led country, which is mostly under the heel of the invader, most of the population is submissive and worn out by incessant unhappiness. Joan gives them back their hope; her charisma works miracles for the troops' morale and shows in the risks they take for her on the battlefield.

Joan has a mission to boot the English out of France and crown Charles VII at Rheims – in other words, to work to bring peace and security back to the kingdom – it's Six territory again. Another Six indicator is the fact that when they put themselves in danger, it's rarely for themselves. You can argue about Joan of Arc, but everyone seems to agree that she never acted out of the desire for personal glory. Sixes fight for a cause, for a project; Joan fights for the cross and for her standard.

Joan has a sense of repartee – this is also part of the story. The reports of the trial support this – extraordinary for someone who couldn't read or write. At the trial, the judges ask her how she can prove that she is really the envoy of God as she claims: "I didn't come to do tricks. You are all more intelligent than me. How can you doubt that it is He who guides my steps – almost 500 leagues through enemy territory to bring you His support. Isn't this proof enough?" And later: "Swear on the Gospel that I will tell the truth? – No. I don't know what you're going to ask me. You might ask me questions that I couldn't answer." We're in Six heartland here: Belief? Proof? Trust?

Joan is betrayed ignominiously by the person she helped to crown king, Charles VII. Depending on which version you read, either he just dumps her, or at the worst he contrives to have her captured by the enemy. It goes without saying that actions like this magnify Six's uncertainty – this just serves to confirm their belief that you can't trust anyone. The last sequence of the film shows us Joan in prison, face-to-face with her conscience. The setting is a bit overblown, but it is a good expression of the internal dialogue of the Six: "Were my voices true sources of information or were they projections of my mind? Did I act out of loyalty or fear?"

Even if you close your eyes during the worst scenes of violence, the film is still worth seeing. Milla Jovovich gives an unforgettable performance as she shows her ambivalence between courage and fear, between trust and suspicion, between leading and following, between intuition and projection – and the image of the Six comes out of it enhanced.

THE SOCIAL TYPE SIX

> *Preoccupations of Type Six: trusting, doubting, worrying about the consequences*
> *Preoccupations of the Social Subtype: focusing on friends, associations and groups*
> *= DUTY*

Two complementary energy lines come together here. For social Sixes, doubt about trustworthiness focuses on the group or workplace. In an emergency if you're part of a group you're less vulnerable than if you are alone, but belonging to a group leads to obligations and duties. From this comes a ferocious intolerance for cheats, a respect for law, devotion to carrying out responsibilities required by authority and a tendency to follow the rules. Having these priorities means that being well-informed, responsible and hard-working are natural ways to operate. At work the organisation chart needs to be transparent, with clear divisions of labour and regular checks that people are doing what they are supposed to be doing. *"When I apply for a job, I just have to ask to see the company's organisation chart so that I can understand how things work and see whether it's well put together or a dog's breakfast. Once I take up my post I ask people what they do, what it's for and who checks it – I'll even ask those questions of people who are much further up the hierarchy than me."* Social Sixes are very sensitive to little deviations from the rules, because that weakens the system. Moreover, taking on the role of guardian of the rules inevitably guarantees them a place at the centre of the organisation.

In family life they place great importance on remembering birthdays, everyone turning up, and organising the annual reunion with the rest of the family tribe. They also place great importance on respecting social norms such as voting – on one hand because it's the duty of every citizen but also because it makes you responsible for the authority you elect. They therefore spend an enormous amount of energy *on "doing their duty"*, with the consequence that *"doing your duty"* can be both reassuring and a heavy burden. *"Because I really liked the company where I worked and I had a job with a lot of responsibility, it was important to do my duty and I worked ten times harder than other people would have done in my place."*

The Paradox

Being above reproach in the way you do your duty is not necessarily the best way to build your self-confidence.

Metaphor[2] – The Lookout

Being clear about your role within the group is an obsession. Knowing the rules and setting up clear contracts with friends and colleagues is vital in order to conquer your fear and avoid being excluded.

Warning Signs for Type Six
- Being worried all the time
- Spending too much time thinking about safety
- Thinking too much about the possible consequences of an action
- Too much projection and thinking about the worst case scenario

Warning Signs for the Social Subtype
- Too much need to be recognised
- Too much time spent keeping up social relationships
- Being a member of too many clubs and societies
- Too much devotion to the causes they espouse

A SOCIAL SIX'S VIEW – HENRI

What I like about my Type

My attraction to analysing complex situations, which includes an attraction to identifying all sorts of problems. I value my refusal to accept things or events as they first appear; it enables me to discover what is really at the heart of things. If I add to these two characteristics the fact that I'm a good listener and my goodwill towards others, I think all this makes me especially gifted for working with other people as they look inside themselves. I like the fact that what I do is serious and important, even if my concentration fails now and again. I tend to be vigilant and careful, but I can be very reckless sometimes. In my job as a consultant I can be zany and provocative in order to induce changes in the frames of reference of the situation. I'm well organised and honest, and respecting values is important to me, because I'm very concerned for the well-being of others.

What I like about my Subtype

My tendency to be aware of the social, collective, community aspects of situations. I see the big picture and I want great things for humanity. My values continuously push me towards wanting to improve the way the world works. I'm very aware of situations where the human aspect isn't given its proper importance – in workplaces, groups or the world in general. My work as a consultant aims to put humanity at the heart of organisations and I'm able to take account of the whole complexity of organisations. I'm very concerned for the needs of people who are weak or marginalised. My work enables people to work with what they are feeling; I bring a way of looking at things that helps people make sense of situations.

Friendship is important, and when I get too taken up with my causes in the world, it hurts me to feel that I don't have my friends around me. My work as consultant, coach and trainer is my most important commitment. When I'm out in the world

*I encourage people to ask themselves deep questions about their life so that they can live better. I have a **duty** to get involved in social causes; I really enjoy deep work on the meaning of actions, life and the world. Spirituality, philosophy, psychology, personal development and sociology are some of the fields I like best – but not politics; because of my honesty and a sense of my powerlessness to change the world through political action I can't get involved in a system which I see as corrupt.*

What I like about the Combination of my Type and Subtype

My ability to envisage and explore the future sometimes gives me premonitions about what will happen in society, organisations or for humanity. I value the things I believe are important: looking after the weak, integrity, faithfulness and taking care that everyone should have their just place without being crushed by people who are stronger or by organisational forces. Put this together with my concern for the group, and it all enables me to get involved in the world in order to help the common good: through trade union activities, working with human beings toward being able to live better, speaking out for what is good in humankind and helping people's hearts to be transformed.

The acuteness of my analysis almost always shakes people up, and makes those I work with ask themselves fundamental and radical questions. When I have decided to take on the defence of a position my lines of argument can be implacable, almost like a steamroller. I have an immense fluency of speech; I have no problem finding the right lines of reasoning and taking the time to develop them. I can bring an enormous amount of energy to bear in order to take action to make the world a better place; I'm always prepared to go and meet MPs or ministers to move things forward in the right direction. On the other hand, like Cassandra, even though I have a visionary gift I can sometimes find it difficult to stand up and be visible in order to take action.

Film Reference – Towering Inferno

This film pays homage to firefighters the world over: "Those who dedicate their lives so that others may live" – i.e. in Six terms those who do their duty in order to keep their fellow citizens safe.

The film takes place in San Francisco in 1947, at the opening of the tallest sky-scraper ever built. All the top people in town are there: the mayor, senators and celebrities. The film's theme is about foreseeing the worst in order to prevent catastrophes that are caused by an accumulation of unfortunate circumstances. Little by little we find out that the builders haven't finished installing the security system, that cheap grade electric cables have been used instead of the more reliable ones which had been agreed upon, and that the fire doors haven't arrived. Who is responsible for all this? – the son-in-law of the property developer, who is in charge of logistics for the build. Was he trying to save money or was he simply incompetent? Was he bribed? – It doesn't matter because the harm is done. Hundreds of people contributed to this enormous project and because of one man who didn't do his duty, not only is the whole project doomed to failure but it will endanger the lives of innocent people. The film also points the finger at the other person responsible – the property developer.

Here is an extract from a conversation between the architect (Paul Newman) and the property developer:

Architect: "I thought we were building a building that we could live and work in safely. If you had to cut costs, why didn't you simply build fewer storeys?"

Developer: "You know perfectly well that I kept to building regulations."

Architect: "Yes, but I've seen the other side of it: none of the air conditioning ducts are fireproofed, the corridors don't have fire doors ...." (and the subtext is "You're not a Six, so you've been happy to give instructions and not take the time to check that they've been followed.")

The film is Social in two ways. At a general level, the storyline is about the town, the people who run it and the people who live in it; more specifically, it shows how three hundred people organise themselves to work together to deal with a crisis situation. The main character in the film, a Social Six, is Mike the fire chief, played by Steve McQueen. When he arrives, he doesn't back down before the ranks of celebrities or the loud-voiced developer who is concerned with his social image. Even though the fire doesn't seem serious at that stage, he foresees the worst case scenario and demands the immediate cancellation of the opening celebration. Then he demonstrates the character traits of a true Six: he takes account of multiple factors, anticipates all the possible consequences such as broken glass falling all over the neighbourhood and moves immediately to mobilise the forces needed such as helicopters.

Through the reactions of the other characters, this film also shows us the two extremes of Six behaviour: panic and loss of lucidity on the one hand, and courage and risk taking on the other. The concept of responsibility comes up many times, for example when the son-in-law berates his wife: "You never leave me alone, always talking about responsibility – the Duncans do nothing but go on about responsibility and duty all the time!" His wife replies "I don't see what's wrong with having a sense of duty!"

The fire chief shows us just how far this sense of **duty** can go. He gets himself flown by helicopter to the roof of an external lift that is stuck at the seventieth floor because of a power cut. There he has to cut a cable with a blowtorch, attach the lift to the helicopter and bring the twelve passengers inside safely to the ground. Later in the film he again risks his life from a sense of duty, to blow up the water tanks at the top of the building in order to drown the flames. With no way of getting down, he risks being carried away by the torrents of water unleashed by the explosion. The message at the end of the film shows us a social Six perspective par excellence; he says to the architect: "We were lucky that time, but this sort of disaster will happen again unless one of you comes and asks me how to build these things properly." The Six atmosphere is threaded throughout this film: danger, insecurity, doubt, suspense – you're guaranteed to be trembling in your seat!

THE THREE SUBTYPES OF TYPE 7

Wound

One day, Type Seven children were stopped as they were in full flow, and it felt as though someone had cut their wings off. They were made to follow the instructions inflicted on them by authority, and as a result, they experience any sort of confinement as pain.

Passion: Gluttony/Greediness

The fear of confinement and boredom leads to Sevens' desire to experience as much as they can while they are free – as long as the experiences are varied and fun. This leads them to be greedy for as many different experiences as possible, and because they might get tired of what they're doing right now, it's a good idea to keep an eye on what might be over the horizon – they've always got some plan of what they might be doing somewhere else or in the future. Two things are going on here: fleeing suffering and taking as much advantage as possible of what is on offer here and now.

In order to achieve this, Sevens have antennae that are tuned to take in multiple pieces of information simultaneously; using this they can choose the project which is most exciting right now. Their senses take in and deal with facts very rapidly and their brain is taken up with processing information at top speed as soon as it arrives. They are unconventional and interested in anything, which is at the edge of their cultural experience – they're like Christopher Columbus. They rebel against constraints, structures and heavy organisation, but it's a rebellion that avoids rather than confronts. They would prefer to come up with a new idea rather than attack the status quo – they are adventurers more than fighters. Sevens don't like hierarchies; they're seeking an egalitarian world. Liberty and equality are tightly linked for them; no-one can hope to be free while hierarchy persists. Their indiscipline is therefore the expression of their need to be free.

However, they can be considerate and obliging when they are helping others to have fun. In return, they believe that they are entitled to the affection and attention of people around them. They use charm, seduction and intellectual vivacity to persuade others to be their playmates. They are totally lost if they are turned down. *"I spend a lot of time trying to fill up my sense of emptiness; I think of ways to have fun and I am completely thrown when other people don't join in my plans. When that happens, I have to fill my sense of emptiness on my own, and the only way I can do it is to keep moving, either physically or mentally."*

Preferred Defence Mechanism: Rationalisation

This means reframing experiences in order to find their positive side; finding an explanation for the bad things that happen so that they have less impact on you. How you deal with suffering seems to depend on your state of mind and your mental processing; the more activity there is, the less sadness and suffering will get through to you. *"I didn't really lose that job; it gave me the opportunity to change it for another one – and I'm sure I'll find one next week."* Concentrating on positive things in the future enables them not to have to feel their emotions. They must not let themselves be pierced to the heart; that would be devastating. *"It's nothing; I've only broken my leg."* They have to find an explanation for every accident, keep detached from it, bounce back and keep moving.

THE SELF-PRESERVATION TYPE SEVEN

> *Preoccupations of Type Seven: being free, having fun, keeping moving*
> *Preoccupations of the Self-Preservation Subtype: focus on home, security and material comfort*
> *= CLAN*

The Seven energy needs to have fun, and self-preservation subtypes want to place great emphasis on time spent at home with their nearest and dearest. So self-preservation Sevens want to organise as much fun as possible, particularly with their family and close friends – their clan. They want to share projects, have great meals, enjoy themselves and split their sides laughing with their clan members, even if it means they have to be the organiser, cook and life and soul of the party. This subtype can sometimes be confusing because although they are self-preservation, they need an audience in order to perform, so there may be quite a few friends in their life. However, although the clan may vary in size, most of the relationships stay quite superficial and there are only a few people to whom they have a close, real emotional attachment.

The second idea around clan is about ensuring your survival by staying in a gang. You need to have a network to ensure your survival, if possible a network of friends who share your projects: buying a shared bungalow in Tahiti, taking a gap year to go round the world or *"sharing TV dinners at Paul's place when there's an important match on".* Self-preservation subtypes are reassured when there are plenty of other people involved in their projects. When you're having a thousand ideas a minute, it's reassuring to know that others have validated your proposal; it means that at least one of your ideas has become more than a solitary fantasy. If you want to make sure that your network of friends gives you the reassurance you seek, you need to hear their latest news quickly – it's nice to know everything that's going on, and it's nice to be the first to know. Moreover, as soon as you know the latest you can put it to use to help your projects come to fruition.

The Paradox
Wanting to be reassured by having your clan around you doesn't actually banish your fear of being empty inside.

Metaphor – The Holiday Camp Organiser
Your fellow-organisers are your family, you're operating within a secure boundary, the food has plenty of variety and your salary comes in without fail at the end of the month – so your Seven energy can play!

Warning Signs for Sevens
- Too many projects
- Too much movement
- Too much head activity
- Too much optimism

Warning Signs for the Self-Preservation Subtype
- Too much focus on security
- Spending too much time at work
- Being too focused on material well-being
- Too many routine evenings at home

A SELF-PRESERVATION SEVEN'S VIEW – SEBASTIEN

What I like about my Type
My vivacity! I think quickly, I sometimes feel as though I can think about several things at the same time. One day in a panel someone asked me to say more about this – the image that came to me was that my mind works like a cooker with several dishes cooking away at the same time. In the same way, I like to make connections between ideas that don't seem initially to have anything to do with each other. And because I like to keep things light and optimistic I often get a great deal

of fun out of pursuing surprising intellectual trains of thought. Coming back to the image of the cooker again, it's as though a drop of one dish jumped out of its saucepan and dropped into another one – the flavours mix and create a new taste!

I can't work in a linear fashion, finishing one project before going on to the next one. I will open several folders and move from one to the other continuously. My office is covered with a mountain of files that have nothing to do with each other. One day two folders fell on the floor and the contents got mixed up. I happened to glance at two sheets of paper that had landed together and they gave me the inspiration for a new idea. That night as I went to sleep I wondered whether I unconsciously set things up so as to provoke these incongruous comings-together. My children say that I'm a naughty-funny father, a sort of mischievous funny imp with zany ideas.

I also love my joie de vivre. In the worst moments of my life I always have a little voice deep inside that says: "This isn't serious; it will pass." One of my favourite proverbs is: "Every cloud has a silver lining."

What I like about my Subtype

My ability to work fast. I know how to organise my practical life so that I can do what I want when I want. When I'm fixing things around the house, nothing gets in my way; my work may not be of the highest quality, but in a flash lightbulbs are replaced, shelves are put up and doors are planed down. In my job as a wine merchant it's the same; I organise myself so that everything happens fast. Mostly I prefer to work alone; deep down I'm pretty much of an individualist and I'm quite happy to be self-employed. I work sixty hours a week, but as it's my choice it doesn't weigh me down – but I do have someone who helps me out.

I need to be organised so that I can move from desire to action very quickly, for example when the weather's good and I feel like going and playing tennis. While we're on the subject of sport, my relationship with my body is very important and I've found that this is true for most self-preservation subtypes.

I even ran a marathon just to explore that side of myself – it was exhilarating to find that after "the wall" you get to what they call "intoxication", an amazing feeling of physical well-being. I also love saunas and ayurvedic massages. When it comes to food, I'm quite a gourmet; I love good things, but I pay attention and listen to my body's signals to find out when to stop.

What I like about the Combination of my Type and Subtype

I think that my self-preservation subtype moderates my Seven energy. As a Seven I want everything to happen quickly: thinking, reading, taking action and moving on to the next thing. My self-preservation subtype brings me back to the rhythm of the earth, of the peasant in the fields. My relationship with my body that I referred to earlier is a good example of this; paying attention to my body slows me down. I probably eat more slowly than other people because the time I spend at table is important – it's a key part of the planning of my day.

*I have no problem being alone. Once when I was younger I found myself spending a week's holiday on my own and that suited me very well; I just slipped naturally between reading, going for a walk and cooking – there was plenty to do. I love being out in the countryside; I feel free and joyful there. These days it's different; I've got a wife and two children and so of course I go on holiday with them, but we tend to choose a simple holiday format, in the country. I think being with my **clan** is the important thing; we're together, there may not be a lot of things to do but we make our own amusement.*

Film Reference – The Best Exotic Marigold Hotel

A young Indian from Jaipur has inherited a dilapidated old hotel from his father, and he comes up with the idea of creating an old people's home for out-of-pocket

Europeans. He sets up a website where he attracts clients with wonderful pictures showing what the hotel could be – a sort of bucolic palace, rather than what it is – a ruin which he wants to restore.

The Indian hero, Sonny (played by Dev Patel, the star of Slumdog Millionaire) shows us the good sides of Type Seven: boundless enthusiasm and spontaneity, but also the down-sides – a rather childish side, denial of what isn't working and rationalisation of everything that happens. Rationalisation is the principal defence mechanism of the Seven – it's about reframing reality in a positive way: – so your room is dirty? – not really, if you imagine how it will soon be in the future. No money? – it's all relative – just think of what you're going to earn in the future.

When the first guests arrive, Sonny's in the middle of painting a wall and the rooms aren't ready, but his enthusiasm and good humour lessen at least in part the shock experienced by the new arrivals, who are completely thrown by the gap between what they were expecting and the harsh reality. Some rooms have no doors, the internal telephones don't work – but these are just minor details for Sonny. He only sees the exotic historic palace, which will be a splendid place to live in. It's a typical example of the Seven's ability only to see the best in the situation and to ignore everything that's not working or which could derail the project. His watchword is "Everything will be all right in the end – and if it's not all right, it means it's not yet the end."

The self-preservation subtype shows up when we consider where the majority of the film's time is spent: it's definitely self-preservation because we're preoccupied with survival – money, the house (sorry, palace!) and all the practical aspects of life – phones, painting the walls, food: everything to do with comfort and well-being. We're in a world of the senses – noise, heat, streets teeming with people. Sonny tires himself out in order to keep his guests comfortable, balance the books and ensure the survival of his hotel. We see the importance of **clan** in the fact that he has no friends or relations – he's determined to make this work on his own. A clan is often a small circle of close friends or relatives that you can count on. Here, at least at first, there is no-one – and later, it's the guests who help him out and who become his clan.

There's no single star of the film. The six retired British people who decide to head off to India because they're broke, are a collection of eccentric characters. The culture shock they experience forces them to rediscover their true selves in order to survive in their new environment. The characters are well-written and we get to care about each of them as their masks fall away and they recount their stories, fears and frailties.

The self-preservation subtype is gently exaggerated, caricatured and challenged until we arrive eventually at its most lovely manifestation – the realisation that welcoming emotions enables us to arrive at a balance between life's light and shade. This includes the way the film portrays India, where life, death and suffering bump against each other round every corner. This simple and moving story shows us several wonderful ways in which the human spirit can be transformed – it's a great film.

THE ONE-TO-ONE TYPE SEVEN

Preoccupations of Type Seven: being free, having fun, keeping moving
Preoccupations of the One-to-One Subtype: focusing on the partner
= FASCINATION/SUGGESTION

Two energy lines converge here: the desire to have fun combines with the ability to create one-to-one contact. The thirst for intensity is doubled because the desire to do the maximum number of things in the minimum time comes together with the desire to experience intense one-to-one encounters. One-to-one Sevens tend to jump into every new project they come across, and be strongly attracted to every new person they meet. This is **fascination**: being strongly and rapidly influenced by everything new, and therefore very quickly pulled out of their centre towards things which are external. They live in an amusement park full of attractions; getting to know other people gives them intense pleasure. And the fascination works both ways; their aim is to charm every new person they meet, to become part of their story, to work with them to imagine the future. They apply their considerable talents of thoughtfulness, vivacity and gaiety to creating the closest connection they can – "epicurean" is exactly the right word to use here.

This ability to dream and paint vivid pictures of possibilities can sometimes make the person they are with feel that promises have been made, whereas the Seven only sees it as a shared dream or a moment's fantasy – and this can sometimes lead to misunderstandings and disappointments. Sevens don't necessarily realise that this marvellous conversation might just be their way of escaping from the harsh reality of everyday life. Or perhaps they simply don't notice that their attention for any particular topic tends to tire very quickly and move off towards another, equally fascinating, source of energy. In their emotional life they therefore often find it difficult to commit for the long term. Success in relationships needs to come through the realisation that they have a butterfly tendency and that they need a framework to live within – they need to discover that in the end, limitless freedom is actually a constraint.

The Paradox

Knowing how to make your partner dream may not be what they are most looking for in daily life.

Metaphor – Don Juan

It's about fascinating the other person to the point of hypnotising them and leading them into your dreams of adventure. They tell tales like Cyrano de Bergerac did, to bring freshness and lightness into this brutish world.

Warning Signs for Sevens
- Too many projects
- Too much movement
- Too much head activity
- Too much optimism

Warning Signs for the One-to-One Subtype
- Focus on wanting to prove that you are an intense, passionate person
- Too much focus on the partner: what they are doing, where they are, who they are meeting
- Too much focus on your own actions – not enough wider perspective
- Rivalry between your own goals and your partner's interest in other things

A ONE-TO-ONE SEVEN'S VIEW – VANESSA

What I like about my Type
I love novelty – one of my childhood heroes was Christopher Columbus – it's about setting off on an adventure to discover new horizons. One day I happened to be in the Place du Trocadero in Paris on the first of January – and it was the day of the start of the Paris-Beijing rally. I was full of the excitement of the adventure, the speed, unknown routes, exotic smells, the faces of people from different races. And of course it's all connected: the new, adventure and excitement. As soon as I got my school leaving-certificate I gave up studying; I had several jobs and ended up organising sporting trips to Asia for people who wanted to climb mountains or go diving.

Another of my character traits that I really like is my curiosity. I'm curious about everything; anybody or any book is likely to catch my interest. The worst thing is the TV; in fact I don't watch it any more because I end up being seduced by every channel, whether it's the news, cartoons or game shows! The good side of that is that I get fun out of trying new activities without necessarily feeling that I have to be good at them – it's all about fun. When it comes to sports, I must have tried nearly all of them in the water, in the air and on land: from kite surfing to polo, not forgetting skydiving, tennis and aikido! And it's the same with people; if we've never met before, so much the better – whoever you are, whatever life you've led, come on in, you're welcome, and thanks for being in my life!

What I like about my Subtype

My ability to focus on what I'm doing – nothing else exists in the world when I'm concentrating on something – like a book for example. A bomb could go off ten metres away and I believe I wouldn't hear it, because I'm so absorbed in what I'm doing, whether it's a book, a film, a game or my work. That might seem difficult to explain, particularly because I'm a Seven and they like changing activities frequently. But this is how it works: one second I'm working and the next second I've finished; in an instant my attention moves on to something else, let's say a musical tune – and in the twinkling of an eye I'm 200% in the music; I am the music, I become the music, completely and exclusively. It's so strong that it can't last; it's like a laser that is of such incredible intensity that it has to change direction because otherwise it would burn the thing up if it stayed focused in the same direction. So I change the subject or my attention goes somewhere else. The good side of this is that I love the intensity that comes from this ability to concentrate. The downside is the feeling of being superficial, of lacking the constancy I need in order to get a wider view of the world – which would then enable me to be more constant!

What I like about the Combination of my Type and Subtype

*The Enneagram talks about **fascination/suggestion**; this type and subtype combination is about the same capacity for concentration, but this time focused on a person. I've even had bets with friends about whether I could get someone with their* *back to me to turn round, simply by fixing them with my laser look. Friends looking at me while I was doing this thought I looked mad, but it worked; after a few seconds the person turned round – they seemed to feel a presence behind them. Being a bit more serious, because of my type I'm curious about very new contact I make, and because of my subtype I want to charm them or be charmed. So when I'm with someone I'm interested in, I bring to bear the Seven's mental agility and the one-to-one's warm intensity to create a strong link and keep the other person's attention on me. I know how to make the other person share my enthusiasm for a project and I get caught up very easily in the ideas that they share with me. In these intense one-to-one moments it's as though every day is Christmas day; it feels as though I have champagne running in my veins, fireworks going off over our heads and confetti falling out of the sky.*

Film Reference – Dead Poet's Society

It's 1959 and the austere and conservative Welton College is one of the most famous schools in the USA. Its values are tradition, honour, discipline and excellence. Into this world at the beginning of a new year comes John Keating (Robin Williams) – a most unusual teacher. He tries to instil in his students the love of life and freedom and awaken them to what they really are: "Find your own way, set yourself free, dare to go off to conquer unknown worlds." Totally out of place in this formal setting, John Keating teaches the danger of conformity and the challenge to hold on to your own beliefs: "Find your own rhythm, act as seems right to you, be yourselves." He finds support for his ideas in literature:

"Gather ye rosebuds while ye may,

Old Time is still a-flying:

And this same flower that smiles today

Tomorrow will be dying"

He pushes his students to "make your lives extraordinary". He takes them out of the classroom and runs his classes in the open air, even finding a way to mix football and poetry. He pushes them to be creative, inventive and innovative: "Be the master of your life, not the slave. The amazing spectacle rolls on and you can bring your poem to it – what will your poem be?" He gives them his passion, his joie de vivre and his confidence: "I think you have great things in your belly"; "You will learn how to savour words; this is important, because the language of words and ideas can change the world". He dreams of creating free spirits because he believes that it is in their dreams that people find freedom.

We see the classic shape of type Seven: pranks, puns and the association of disparate ideas join with ideas of adventure, freedom, anti-conformism, spontaneity, innovation and idealism. Added to this we see the passion of the one-to-one subtype – "We read and write poetry because human beings are made of passion" – sometimes to an extreme extent: "Poetry spread its nectar on our tongues, our souls rose up, women fainted and gods were born from our work". The natural seduction of the one-to-one joined with the verbal agility of the Seven epitomises the key word for this type; John Keating is **fascinating** in his devotion and his motto Carpe Diem, which in his terms means: "live intensely and drink life to the lees, so that in old age we don't suddenly discover that we haven't lived".

THE SOCIAL TYPE SEVEN

> *Preoccupations of Type Seven: being free, having fun, keeping moving*
> *Preoccupations of the Social Subtype: focusing on friends, associations and groups*
> *= SACRIFICE*

Two contradictory energy lines come into play here: the Seven need to satisfy your own desire for pleasure, set against the Social need to give up your individualism for the benefit of the group. So there is tension between your duty to other people and your desire to run away to something new. Social Sevens feel responsible for others and resent what feels like a burden, but their subtype forces them to respect certain social conventions. *"I hate wearing a tie; they strangle me, but socially I have to wear one when I go to the office."* This is the price they have to pay for having a network of friends.

Personal freedom is sacrificed for the benefit of social ideals; their deep sense of obligation to others requires them to sacrifice themselves in order to carry out their social duty. *"I like to contribute to making things happen. Right now I'm involved in a voluntary organisation which offers disadvantaged children tennis and football clubs during the holidays. It takes an enormous amount of time and I don't expect to get any social recognition for it but it's my way of contributing to making the world more fun. The worst part of it is the committee meetings every fortnight, where I get so impatient waiting while everyone has their say – it's such a drag!"* They try to find a social role which enables them still to be themselves. They see the benefits of playing the "group" game while still recognising the limitations of a group – in this situation they're prepared to sacrifice present pleasure for the greater good of realising a future dream. It's also true that working in a group increases the project's likelihood of success: *"And if the others are on the same wavelength as me, we can have fun while we work."*

The Paradox

The paradox is that you want to be part of a group even though you know that this same group will limit your freedom to do as you like.

Metaphor[1] – The Idealistic Visionary

It's about having a vision that they believe is right and finding the courage to bring a group together to bring the project to fruition. As Idealists, Social Sevens try to make the world a better place, or at least a happier place which it's more fun to live in. The danger is "Peter Pan syndrome", where idealism gets confused with utopia.

Warning Signs for Sevens
- Too many projects
- Too much movement
- Too much head activity
- Too much optimism

Warning Signs for the Social Subtype
- Too much need to be recognised
- Too much time spent keeping up social relationships
- Being a member of too many clubs and societies
- Too much devotion to the causes they espouse

A SOCIAL SEVEN'S VIEW – PHILIPPE

What I like about my Type

My ability to gather in and pull the essentials out of an enormous amount of information in a very short time. This enables me to cut down my preparation time for meetings to the minimum, while still giving the impression that I'm perfectly up to speed with the situation. This "conjuror" side to me always surprises other people, and the facility and confidence with which I can talk about subjects I actually know relatively little about often surprises me too! I feel that my type characteristics make life easy because they bring obstacles down to size; I only remember the positive side of things. For the people around me I think I'm a fun person to be with, because when you're with me we don't take ourselves too seriously. Most of the time I'm in a good mood; I'm always making jokes and I'm a creative sort of person – I love lightening the atmosphere with my puns, whether or not people get them. People don't always understand my associations of ideas because I often bring together several elements that don't appear to be connected.

What I like about my Subtype

I like the fact that I'm prepared to put in effort which I certainly wouldn't make if I wasn't motivated by the role I want to play in the community. My social subtype enables me to do things for the common good or take part in community initiatives. It's a good subtype for me to have because it gives me patience, connection to others and a sense of duty. It leads me to continuously improve myself and be curious about everything to do with other people. I feel connected to the different organisations I belong to, as long as I've chosen them myself. I'm not going to carry the world on my shoulders, but I'm open to what's going on around me.

What I like about the Combination of my Type and Subtype

I get the impression that my social subtype balances some of the possible excesses of my Seven type. My social subtype leads me to be drawn into the need to work with others, and my sense of sacrifice certainly helps me to be less self-centred. However, there are limits beyond which I'm not prepared to go; some meetings are just unbearable because they're so long. For me personally, the combination of my type and subtype has given me the ability to become a valued leader of the group; I know how to bring a bit of lightness to meetings, balancing rigour and jokes. In fact, I don't think I ever take myself completely seriously. I've got a sort of vivacity that enlivens the meetings I run, but at the same time my sense of sacrifice makes me a credible voice for the common cause, and my views are taken seriously.

In my profile there is however one stumbling-block that gets in my way: the difference between the way other people see me from the outside (always positive) and the way I see myself, which is that I often feel that I'm not "serious" enough to take on big responsibilities. In the past this made me turn down some exciting proposals in my professional life, but once I got over this, I am now valued as a leader who is seriously capable of disarming detractors without seeming to, and who can take other people's criticisms with a certain amount of self-deprecation. As well as that, my unbounded imagination and the way I associate ideas enable me to nudge groups in the right direction and improve the way they operate.

Film Reference – Charlie Wilson's War

Based on a true story, the film starts with a congratulatory statement addressed to Charlie Wilson, US Representative for part of Texas; "the defeat and dismantling of the Soviet Union and the fall of the Berlin wall are major events in history. This battle has many heroes, but Charlie Wilson is chief among them. Less than thirteen years ago the Soviet Union seemed invincible, but Charlie, against all the odds, dealt the fatal blow – without Charlie, history would have been profoundly and painfully different." The whole film has a social feel.

Back to the beginning of the story – in April 1980 Charlie hears a report on Afghanistan where the reporter states that the USA seems not to realise that if Afghanistan falls and the Russians get to the Gulf oil-fields, the USA will fall soon afterwards.

Charlie's journey brings him into contact with two truculent characters: Joan Herring (social 8) a rich Texan heiress, who has decided to make things change in Afghanistan – and a CIA agent, Gus (self-preservation 8) who wants to get even with the Russians. Between the three of them, in a few years they manage to get millions of dollars of secret funds voted by Congress to supply the Afghan resistance fighters with the arms to get the Russians out of their country.

Charlie has an immature, rather light-weight side. He describes himself as a "skirt-chasing whisky drinker". Getting the best out of life seems more important to him than being taken seriously as a politician. He gets into sleazy situations in a Jacuzzi with call girls, and deals with multiple concurrent projects at breakneck speed. As you would expect of a Seven, he belongs to several committees "where the State Department, the Pentagon and the CIA meet".

The whole film has a Social feel; it's about networks and relationships: "I've a friend who has made a wonderful film about why the Americans have to help the Afghans, and I'm showing this film at my home in Houston, to raise funds." (with all the Texan jet-set present of course!) Or: "I've managed to arrange for you to meet the Pakistani President, and I've set up another meeting in Israel with ..."

It's clear that being a Social is partly about exchanging favours. For example, Charlie agrees to be on the ethics committee, and in return demands a seat on the board of the Kennedy Cultural Centre: "I really want to be on it; women love to get invited to it and I don't have the money ..." Once he's in, Charlie pulls in favours that people owe him; a key example is when he convinces the Chair of the budget sub-committee to influence his group to give their support, and before you know it 40 million dollars of secret funds have been sent to the Afghan rebels. We can see how social subtypes use committees and meetings to make sure their point of view is heard. Whereas charisma is more associated with the one-to-one subtype, socials often have a gift for public speaking that sometimes carries them away.

Social subtypes are also good at alliances and political games – they have a social intuition that is almost like the 6 intuition, which can foresee the consequences of each twist of the plot. "In Congress I support Israel; I owe my seat to Jewish donors and I don't know what they will think if I start supporting a Muslim cause". Charlie's like a snooker player who before every shot weighs up the consequences of his actions on the rest of the balls. Socials know the people who matter in any community; they give and receive little favours, they get invited to the parties that matter, they know how the other neighbourhoods operate. One of the keys to their social success is their network; they need to be in touch with the people who have the power so they know the right person who can help at any particular moment.

I never thought I would use a war film to illustrate the Enneagram, but fortunately this terrifying subject is treated with an odd-ball humour which brings lightness to the plot.

THE THREE SUBTYPES OF TYPE 8

Wound

One day, Type Eight children felt humiliated or powerless in a situation which they experienced as unfair. They came out of this with anger against the world, and in particular against parental power.

The Passion: Lust

Lust is the absence of control over the instinctive drivers: a rush of energy to bite into life with all your strength. The excess of intensity is very powerful: spicy food, speed, music at full volume, a tendency to want to stimulate the senses – as much as possible and right now! There may be a tendency to aggression in the sense of *"jumping in to help myself to everything around me, to take from it what I want"*. Classic qualities of this energy are enthusiasm, generosity, enjoyment of relationships – to the maximum every time. As Claudio Naranjo says *"It's the pleasure of lots of everything, of going to the limit of their flights of fancy, of what's not allowed, of fighting to get pleasure. There is no enjoyment when there is no obstacle on the road to satisfaction. Pleasure is not just satisfying your instincts, it's having to fight to satisfy them."* There is a propensity to sudden strong anger that passes quickly. Eights are strong, impulsive characters with a tough spirit; they are often considered the most anti-social type on the Enneagram with a taste for conflict, intimidation, living life aggressively and a disdain for weakness, sensitivity and fear.

Taking risks enables them to deny their own fears, feel strong and speak their mind; they have a tendency to intimidate those around them, while seeming to be afraid of nothing themselves. When discussing this type we often talk about the temptation to dominate; however I would describe it as a fierce hostility towards the authority in power rather than the desire to take power themselves. Eights are harsh because they have blinkered themselves against anxiety. First and foremost they tend to trust their senses, the tangible, the here and now; therefore they tend to be suspicious of high-flown ideas, the abstract and the spiritual. What they are seeking above all is the feeling of being alive.

Preferred Defence Mechanism: Denial

Denial – it's about not seeing danger, not feeling fear, not being in contact with their vulnerability – minimising the impact and importance of these things. Parts of reality are treated as though they simply don't exist: "*There is simply nothing there.*" It's a classic way of refusing to face suffering – you look at something and don't see it. You do everything to ensure that reality and the seriousness of the situation don't affect you – it doesn't exist; it never happened. They have a breastplate that stops them feeling emotion, an armouring of the heart, which prevents implosion: "*I'm like the commander-in-chief who must forget the number of soldiers who will die if I'm going to win the battle. In order to remain strong, I need to annihilate my tenderness. I'm happy that that is part of my automatic behaviour.*" Another example – "*People have often admired my courage, but I have never recognised myself as courageous. I wade in without seeing the consequences; I act impulsively before the slightest emotion has time to take hold.*"

THE SELF-PRESERVATION TYPE EIGHT

> *Preoccupations of Type Eight: living intensely, getting what you want*
> *Preoccupations of the Self-Preservation Subtype: focus on the home, security and material goods*
> *= SELF-SUFFICIENCY*

It is as though when they were young, self-preservation Eights had to fight to survive or conquer a territory. They developed a strong urge to satisfy their primary needs: eating, drinking, earning money, having a roof over their head, protecting their tribe. Their insecurity about survival leads them to control the environment: *"I need to know who is where and who is doing what. Life is like a jungle where the strong take advantage of the weak. I behave like a detective because I want to better protect the people who matter to me, so I want to know their comings and goings. On the other hand, I can't stand people trying to control me. If that happens there'll be trouble – I will fight in order to stay independent. "* Like the other self-preservation types, they tend to be stay-at–homes. *"I don't need luxuries, just minimum comfort. If I had to, a cold shower wouldn't be a problem."* A Spartan way of life and routines are reassuring.

There is a great tendency for them to feel attacked. It's a bit as though they add together the characteristics of the types that precede them on the Enneagram diagram: the castle defender of the 5, the problem of trusting people of the 6 and the thirst for freedom of the 7. But unlike the 5, they are not high up in the keep of their castle observing everything, they are down in the castle courtyard gathering information and giving orders. In their professional life, they are one of the best types at delegating; they assign responsibilities, define the mission, insist on regular reports and can be contacted in case of emergency. Within the castle, the king is on his throne, you know where to find him and you know he'll be there.

The Paradox

Grabbing every situation energetically risks of lessening my chances of being able to experience and show tenderness and subtlety.

Metaphor – The Justice

They work off their pent-up aggression through physical challenges and material security. As soon as they sense an injustice they go into battle. They are ferociously protective of the members of their tribe; woe betide you if you touch a hair on the head of their child!

Warning Signs for Eights

- Too much power
- Reacting too quickly
- Too much aggression
- Too big a presence

Warning Signs for Self-Preservation Eights

- Too much attending to security
- Too much time spent at work
- Being too pre-occupied with material things
- Too many "routine" evenings at home

A SELF-PRESERVATION EIGHT'S VIEW – CLAIRE

What I like about my Type

I have very high expectations when it comes to the consistency and truth of what I do. I say what I think and I believe what I say – except when I'm overcome by anger or when I exaggerate now and then. You can trust me; I am trustworthy and if you are in trouble, I'll come running! I am not afraid; I am sheltered by my warrior's armour. For me life is a struggle, where my role is to defend what is right. Sometimes I feel like a bull in a china shop; I express myself badly or act clumsily, just when I want to be tactful or diplomatic, empathic or kind – but I find it hard to be other than a rather gruff bear. I can see straight away what is wrong with a situation, a thing or a person. Without being pessimistic, I can instinctively see the weak point in the situation. I can see problems coming as clear as day and I'm rarely surprised by what happens. I love taking up challenges and showing what I can do, particularly when others doubt me. But if I don't believe in something, I can't make myself put energy into it. I prefer to wait until the situation becomes more favourable, or hope not to have to do something I don't believe in.

What I like about my Subtype

I tend to be solitary and independent. When I'm alone with myself I can feel that I'm not out of line with everyone else. I love drawing, reading a wide range of books and doing DIY projects around the house. I've redone everything from floor to ceiling to ensure that it's all solid, clean and healthy. I love matching colours and decorations. Of the three little pigs, I'm the last, the one who hasn't yet finished his house because he wants it to be solid and safe, but who will be ready when the wolf comes. On the TV, I like watching cookery and interior design programmes. At home I feel light and free, snuggled up in my little cosy nest. It's probably about the **satisfaction** *of knowing how to enjoy material well-being in a simple way. I like it when things are just so; then it's as though time stops in a state of balance and nothing can come to overturn the established order. That doesn't mean that I can't enjoy change – as long as it brings more solidity and balance. In fact, although I don't really want to admit it, I do have a big need for stability and reassurance. I sometimes think (I know it's an illusion!) that I don't need anyone. In the end, I usually prefer to get on with things on my own and be able to do what I like, rather than getting mixed up with a group where you have to reach consensus and make concessions, with the risk that nothing will get done.*

What I like about the Combination of my Type and Subtype

Just like the other areas of my life, my love life is like a battlefield – I expect a lot of my partner. I need to feel that he is someone solid that I can count on and that he will be there for me if I ever need to lean on him. But I also need softness and laughter. If something is wrong between us I feel a vague unease and I have to keep looking until I discover the cause. I'm talking about my emotional life because it's part of the territory I need in order to survive, as are the few friends who make up my clan. As I'm very demanding in my relationships, I have few friends. When I'm sad or angry and I need to express my emotions, I can frighten people with the intensity of my words. The next day I generally feel better and move on to other things, but my friends are still affected by what I said the day before. I hate having to ask for help or a favour; I try to sort everything out myself without having to depend on others. But when I can delegate and everything goes well, I really love being able to let go and hand over responsibility to others.

Film Reference – Million Dollar Baby

The film is set in a boxing ring in downtown Los Angeles. We know we're dealing with an Eight because it's about combat. This is a survival film in the sense that it's about physical sensations, exhaustion, physical effort, sweat and blood, life and death. Hilary Swank won a best actress Oscar in 2006 for her performance. Her character is about 30, down on her luck, employed as a waitress in a neighbourhood restaurant, who suddenly decides she want to be a boxer. Her key characteristic is that she's a fighter: "I was born like that. I only weighed five pounds when I was born and I had to fight just to get into the world." Her trainer teaches her how to really inhabit her body: how to move properly, dodge, keep in balance, flex her knees, fight her way forward, fight while retreating, cope with pain, breathe, transcend her exhaustion. During the training sessions, the shots of legs moving look like a ballet.

When it comes to relationships there are few words; being in relationship with other people is experienced bodily. When things get tricky there is no intellectual refinement; words are few and come straight to the point: "If you're pretending that you wandered into this restaurant by chance, in order to persuade me to leave my trainer, don't give yourself the trouble; I will never leave him." She turns on her heel and walks out; the other character hasn't even had the time to say hello or anything. Her fights are the same – direct, blows coming thick and fast. She wins her fights by first round knock-outs.

In her bodily reactions we can see the impulsive immediacy of the Eight. And on the other hand, we also see the human warmth under her modesty, the feelings behind what is not said. We can also see the clan here; there are just three people: the boxer, the trainer and the janitor. The end of the film is about life and death, about the battle between life and death. This film shows an extreme view of the self-preservation subtype – someone who is completely focused on their body and their job. It's about the simplicity that this sort of life creates; there are no social niceties or games of seduction. Symbolically this film shows us how important it is for Eights to be able to express their aggression. You can see how this aggression could have destroyed this young woman from the inside out if she hadn't discovered boxing, which enabled her to externalise it.

THE ONE-TO-ONE TYPE EIGHT

> *Preoccupations of Type Eight: living intensely, getting what you want*
> *Preoccupations of the One-to-One Subtype: focusing on the partner*
> *= POSSESSION/SURRENDER*

As they don't do anything by halves, one-to-one relationships for Eights are going to be full on. Wanting to avoid hesitation or wasting time, relationships are going to be conducted in an all or nothing way: *"Either I'm in charge of the evening and my husband gives over complete responsibility to me, or he takes charge and I completely give in to him. It's either complete possession or complete surrender. This also happens in household responsibilities; I'm in charge of everything to do with the children and holidays; he does the accounts and looks after household arrangements. We are each totally responsible for our sphere and we don't waste time consulting each other before making decisions."* It's like the passionate abandonment of a lover: *"I give myself up completely to you; I control nothing in our relationship."* But don't be fooled; in order for this relationship to remain alive there still need to be times when you can have confrontation – conquest, passion, raised voices and then conquest again.

Assigning clear responsibility for jobs doesn't stop Eights needing to have an argument now and again. Sometimes things are a bit unclear: *"On the one hand I want each of us to be free, and on the other I'm a "one gal guy" and I want to know where she is and what she's doing at any moment. I want each of us to have our secret garden, but at the same time I want her to share all her secrets with me!"* This complete trust is tinged with uncertainty: *"Because I'm looking for stability in my emotional life, I feel as though I have the right to know everything about her, and on the other hand I'm really attracted by the idea of abandoning myself totally to her."* If they don't find a way to live this with awareness, one-to-one Eights can get very possessive. When it comes to friendships things are much simpler; if you trust each other, then you can share everything about your lives – no wasting time or formality, you go straight to the heart of what is important to you. At work it's the same pattern; some one-to-one Eights are OK with 100% delegation, but for others, delegation conditions have to be screwed down tight.

The Paradox

Wanting completely to abandon myself to the other person or wanting completely to control them are actually two extremes of the same excessive behaviour.

Metaphor – The "All or Nothing" Partner

It's about using your strong presence to possess or control people close to you who are worth the trouble, without realising that your domination can feel crushing to them.

Warning Signs for Eights

- Too much power
- Reacting too quickly
- Too much aggression
- Too big a presence

Warning Signs for the One-to-One Subtype

- Focus on wanting to prove that you are an intense, passionate person
- Too much focus on the partner: what they are doing, where they are, who they are meeting
- Too much focus on your own actions – not enough wider perspective
- Rivalry between your own goals and your partner's interest in other things.

A ONE-TO-ONE EIGHT'S VIEW – ELISABETH

What I like about my Type

What comes to me straight away is my honesty, the side of me that is clear, simple and direct. In my relationships with others I don't cheat; what you see is what you get. For example I just don't know how to sit back and think about a course of action – I say what is true for me, just as I experience it. I can take on a leadership role, but equally I can be quite happy for someone else to take charge of the group, if I know

190

that this person is just and fair. You can really count on me if I agree to do something. I need a certain amount of freedom to operate well. The most important thing for me is that people respect others, particularly those who are most vulnerable. I won't defend an intellectual theory that is based on reason, if I can see that people are suffering because of it. I've got a strong instinctive nose for abuses of power and false justifications for action. I often feel strong and fragile at the same time. I'm not always looking for confrontation, but if the cause is just, I'll take it on.

What I like about my Subtype

One-to-one relationships are like sweet moments in a hard world; when I'm in a one-to-one with someone I can speak my truth and go deep. I can have really rich encounters, whether they are regular or even daily, like those I have with my husband for example, or "one-offs" with people that I won't see again. I have lots of friends, but with each of them I will have a relationship, which is unique to them, strong and specific. In the course of a day, having a one-to-one moment, even if it's very brief, gives me joy and strength.

What I like about the Combination of my Type and Subtype

As you might expect, I put a good deal of energy into each one-to-one encounter, and that gives me the ability to understand and help the other person. Through this one-to-one closeness I can bring a certain quality of presence that enables the other person to speak freely about themselves. Because they feel that I'm really listening to them, they can take the risk of telling me what is in the depths of their heart if they want to. Moreover because my Eight gives me a strong base, the other person feels that they can lean on me and that I'm with them as they go through whatever trials they are facing. My Eight characteristics mean that I avoid theoretical discussions and that I occupy a space that is practical and

191

almost physical; it's as though the other person can take strength simply from the fact that I'm there.

And finally, I think that my impulsive Eight temperament is softened by my subtype – it's as though my desire for an intense and beautiful connection with the other person rounds the corners off the excesses of my whole-type energy.

Film Reference – Casablanca

The film is set in Morocco in December 1941. One of the possible escape routes from the German occupation goes through Marseilles, Oran and Casablanca, which at this period is controlled by the Vichy government. Once in Casablanca, refugees can try to get a visa to fly to Lisbon, which is neutral territory. If they can't, they remain stuck (often for a long time) in Casablanca, where thieves and smugglers also congregate. Rick (Humphrey Bogart) is the owner of a fashionable café. In the past, he had been wanted by the Germans, but he wasn't the type to give in easily. The Eight shows up clearly; he's the boss. His speech is cool but authoritative; his orders and his convictions are clear and direct and his decisions are quick, almost instantaneous. He doesn't drink with his clients; his café is not for sale. He protects his employees and ensures they get paid, even when the café is closed down by the authorities. He has no diplomatic skills and his readiness to fight is up front, even if it is tempered a bit by his subtype.

One day Viktor Lazlo arrives; he's a resistance chief who needs to flee to Lisbon – and he's with his wife Ilsa (Ingrid Bergman) who used to be Rick's lover. The film turns around the characters' meeting; the one-to-one encounters are intense and passionate. The power of the way they look at each other is almost bewitching. At first Rick is brusque towards Ilsa; he has never forgotten their previous relationship and is angry with her because she broke it off. The contrast between the love he still has for her and the stern tone in which he speaks to her is striking. Then gradually the defences break down – and we learn how sensitive Eights are, under their armour. Rick, the impulsive unpredictable one who hasn't a sentimental bone in his body, becomes aware of his feelings and in a split second his heart does a somersault. A moment before, he loved her passionately but would do nothing for her; now he loves her just as much and will do everything to protect her. We're right in one-to-one Eight territory here; they give themselves completely or not at all. At various moments in the film we see the instinctive intuition of the Eight and the sensitive intuition of the one-to-one subtype come together: "You know that one day you'll have to choose and you'll come back to me"; "Don't tell me lies; I know you're prepared to say anything" he replies, although she hasn't opened her mouth.

This film is strongly emotional; each of the three protagonists is prepared to give their life or their freedom for the one they love. And the film hinges on one of those rare moments in life when a crucial decision offers the possibility for transcendence. Your ego and pride push you in one direction and yet on the other hand you have an opportunity to do something that takes account of the more subtle, higher aspects of being. In this film it plays out in a real practical decision – three people and two tickets for Lisbon – which way will Rick jump?

THE SOCIAL TYPE EIGHT

Preoccupations of Type Eight: living intensely, getting what you want
Preoccupations of the Social Subtype: focusing on friends, associations and groups
= FRIENDSHIP

For Social Eights, the Eight excess shows up in their life with other people. The well-being of the group is their top priority; the Protector side of the Eight shows up as the patriarch/matriarch: *"Family gatherings are essential. Every year I move heaven and earth to get the whole family together;*

it's absolutely crucial that we continue to meet up regularly." Their tendency to want to repair injustices often plays out through membership of a structured group: "You have no idea of the number of networks I belong to: sports clubs, old boys' associations, parent-teacher associations, groups to do with local government. I wonder how I still find the time to see my wife and children. On the other hand, they come to these gatherings with me as often as possible, and I'm happy for them because they have the opportunity to meet people."

Friendship becomes a strong bond: "One for all; all for one". Their aggressiveness lessens when they are with a group that shares a common goal: "With my friends I can let myself go. It's as though my usual aggressiveness gets transformed into generosity towards the group; I find it reassuring to be in the middle of the group and it's a sensual pleasure to feel part of the whole. When that happens I can let my guard down, open up to my feelings but also let my hair down, drink and sing. I put my big energy out into the group in order to ensure that every celebration will be memorable." When they are less well-balanced, Social Eights can unconsciously create sub-groups within the group and provoke confrontations between them.

The Paradox

Gaining more and more friends is not the best way to face up to and deal with my insecurity.

Metaphor[1] – The Patriarch/Matriarch

Anger and aggression are channelled into the needs of the group and pressed into service of the common goal. Loyalty to the cause takes precedence over personal feelings and needs.

Warning Signs for Eights
- Too much power
- Reacting too quickly
- Too much aggression
- Too big a presence

Warning Signs for the Social Subtype

- Too much need to be recognised
- Too much time spent keeping up social relationships
- Being a member of too many clubs and societies
- Too much devotion to the causes they espouse

A SOCIAL EIGHT'S VIEW – ARTHUR

What I like about my Type

I love my energy; it can move mountains. I also like my ability to cut through a situation and make a quick decision, particularly when I feel that it's the fairest decision. I love living life to the full. I see myself as a generous person who loves enthusing other people – when you're with me it's never depressing! Even at work there's always a good atmosphere; team members often get in a bit early and leave late so that they can enjoy the good-humoured atmosphere that I try to engender around me. In the Enneagram I recognise that I have a lot of Eight qualities, but I also recognise a lot of Two in myself; I love helping others to move their projects forward. When I have to lose a good team member because they are leaving to pursue their life's dream, I'm the first person to encourage them to live their life to the full.

What I like about my Subtype

I love most of the people I meet; I want to have real contact with them. When you meet me you don't need to circle round me carefully; you can say things honestly, directly, no matter how many other people are in the room. I encourage everyone to speak their truth and in that way relationships are more honest. I love it when people talk about their passions in life; it doesn't matter what they're talking about, what interests me is hearing that people are fascinated by something which hooks them, which makes them really happy – what's important is that they're living life to the full! On another front, it's true that I very quickly get a sense of the sub-groups within the group; I can feel who's on whose side,

195

who is against them and how the clans relate to each other within the group. I'm less interested in the actual organisation chart than in the feelings that I get about the ties that bind people together.

What I like about the Combination of my Type and Subtype

I think that my social qualities add value to my Eight qualities. I find it easy to start relationships with people quickly. For example, I love building relationships with the business people where I live: the butcher, the baker and the postman. I like talking to them, finding out about their lives; I like to know that they are my friends. I'll ask them out for a drink and they will often invite me to their family celebrations: a child's wedding, a christening or a wedding anniversary. I really love those moments when different parts of society come together – I also love introducing people to each other. I know how to help them understand that I know them as real people, that I know who they are inside and that I like them just as they are. It wouldn't occur to me to ask someone to become a different person from who they are.

Moreover, I know all the birthdays and saints days of the people I know, and I take the time to congratulate them on the right day, whether it's one of my close friends and family, one of my staff or a shopkeeper. It's also important to me to attend important social events; I always manage to get tickets for the international rugby tournaments and in an ideal world I'll go with a group of at least ten people. When I play tennis, I love arranging to meet lots of friends, and once we see how many turn up, organising ourselves so that we play several games on several courts, depending on how many of us there are. What matters is friendship, by which I mean getting together, conviviality and having a drink together after the game.

Film Reference – The Godfather

It's difficult to find a film that illustrates the strength of the Eight and at the same time their easy-going directness. Most films we looked at leaned to one side or the other, but the people who viewed them came down in favour of the Godfather, which demonstrates many of the social Eight characteristics, with a couple of caveats:

- Marlon Brando is too passive to provide a true illustration of the type. He shows a slow, deep energy and takes time to listen impassively. Normally social Eights have a more dynamic and active energy.
- The gangsters' world doesn't show this type up in a good light.
- There's a bit too much violence, murder and bloodshed.

The film is set in Chicago in 1946, where various gangs are fighting to control the criminal world. Don Corleone is the patriarch of the Sicilian clan. The lead role and the film itself are in Eight territory because it's about strength; you have to be strong and recognised as strong, otherwise others will gang up on you, their organisation will take you over and you will find yourself a vassal to a lord who is more powerful than you. In order to survive, you have to have a well-structured organisation and a simple hierarchy with a clear leader who doesn't need to control everything but who has to co-ordinate and be in charge of information. The film is full of scenes where people come to report to Don Corleone – he is not just the chief; he's the Godfather, the patriarch.

The social subtype also shows up in family events: marriages, christenings and burials. In life, these moments matter to all of us, but for a social Eight, they are crucially important. The wedding scene that opens the film sums this up; everyone is there, family, cousins, friends, business colleagues and local shopkeepers. This moment illustrates the meaning of the word friendship: the importance that social Eights attach to relationships that have ritual communion attached to them. Social Eights want you to be present at big events in their life and will make great efforts to be present at yours, if you invite them. On the other hand, they will be very annoyed if you forget them: "I can't remember the last time I had coffee at your house!"

The social Eight also shows in the fact that Don Corleone knows the heads of the other tribes; he knows who has power and compares them to each other: "I respect you and I'm very pleased that your interests don't conflict with mine." He has a large address book of contacts and is happy to do favours for people, in anticipation of the favours they may one day do for him. Social subtypes usually prefer to base their alliances on information rather than force; it's in their social relationships that they need to show their strength. So they need to have a network of influential relationships: "I need people who have friends in high places."

The social subtype is also demonstrated by the knowledge of and respect for customs and ways of doing things. There are correct ways to greet someone, and it is impolite not to say a formal goodbye: "I'll speak to Mother for you; I'll explain to her why you couldn't say goodbye to her." "Excuse me, I'll have to speak Italian to Mike" (in your presence, and I know you don't speak Italian.)

Vengeance is another theme that comes up here. At one point in the film Don Corleone gets his clan chiefs together, thanks them for coming, carefully says each individual's name and the territory they represent, and says clearly that he is not going to take vengeance for the harm that has been done to him; this is admitting that revenge would be the most natural recourse for an Eight. This moment shows the sometimes difficult alliance between the spontaneous aggression of the Eight and the relative moderation of the Social subtype. By his approach Don Corleone manages to save face socially and also show the power he still holds. But he's not taken in by the situation; he has sensed, viscerally rather than intellectually, that the others see him as weak and that they're getting ready to move against him. He even warns his son about how they are going to do it. Just like the dominant male that knows that his tribe is threatened, his Eight gut instinct has sniffed out a plot. His social subtype, which knows how groups work, lets him know what method they will probably use.

Another sense of the word friendship is the life and death loyalty between him and the other group members. Several scenes illustrate this, particularly the fact that you never take a stranger's side against a family member. When the social Eight is dominant, as he is here, group cohesion is the most important thing – and here also we see their principal failing. It's not that he doesn't love his wife and children, it's that he doesn't have time for them because his first responsibility is to his social role. We don't always see it clearly in this film, but one of the most important aspects of the social Eight is their firm but jovial authority, which sometimes reminds us of Twos as they have this dynamic but not directly confrontational energy.

THE THREE SUBTYPES OF TYPE 9

Wound
One day, Type Nine children felt deserted and that no-one was taking their needs into consideration. They felt that there was a total lack of love and that no-one was paying attention to them. To calm their pain, they decided to live by proxy, melting into the background, into habits or into not expressing their needs.

Passion: Inertia
This is about forgetting yourself, not taking your own needs into account; it's a laziness about loving yourself appropriately. It is as though there is a lack of ability to look inside yourself. Nines lack goals, reasons for living; they're just like someone who lets themselves be carried along by the current of life. What they're trying to do above all is not to rock the boat; they're not bothered about where they are actually going. Claudio Naranjo talks of a lack of fire and passion. By being phlegmatic they manage to desensitise themselves, not only to their physical sensations but also to their emotions. It is as though there were an airbag between them and the stimuli of the outside world: a shock-absorbing cushion that protects them but which also lessens their reactiveness to situations; all their impulses are suppressed.

Preferred Defence Mechanism: Narcotisation
This is about becoming numb, forgetting yourself by dispersing your energy into the comfort of your external

surroundings, staying asleep. There are two classic forms of narcotisation. The first consists in dozing off into your habits – timetables, routines, daily rituals and material comfort – cushions, your garden, TV, reading. The rhythms of life become sacred, life purrs along contentedly and what is important is dissolved into what is not. The boundaries between the self and the outside world become fuzzy; by turning any work into robot-like activity you avoid getting emotionally involved. Aggression is numbed and with it self-esteem; you prefer to stay at this stage of your evolution rather than taking the risk to change. You don't consciously choose to ignore the stimuli of the outside world, but that is in fact just what you do.

The other form of narcotisation is just as common, but rarely talked about in Enneagram books: activity. You forget yourself, you camouflage your priorities by generating a cloud of busyness: *"It's not that I'm doing nothing, it's that I keep finding so many things to do."* In fact, Nines have gone to sleep on their priorities. For example, in order to avoid the discomfort of getting involved in a conversation about a topic which is damaging a relationship (which is what they had agreed they needed to do), they get involved in a succession of little unimportant activities: repairing the bumper on the car, putting up a fence at the bottom of the garden, going to the swimming pool... Things of secondary importance take so much space and time that important things are simply numbed out of existence.

THE SELF-PRESERVATION TYPE NINE

Preoccupations of Type Nine: fleeing from conflict,
avoiding stating their truth and taking their space
Preoccupations of the Self-Preservation Subtype: focus on
the home, security and material goods
= APPETITE

Often, the self-preservation Nine just gets described as a stay-at-home: *"I ask as little as possible from life. I have my routines and habits, I don't go out much, I've made my home comfortable and yes, I suppose it's true that I hum along gently in the routine of my life."* But this is not the most common pattern. Self-preservation Nines can summon lots of energy, usually for improving their material comfort and looking after the basic needs of their tribe – to the point where they forget themselves. They play down their personal needs; their real emotional needs are replaced by thinking about practical things: food, the jobs that need doing at home, shopping, being a couch-potato, doing the garden. *"It's true that when I do the shopping, I always buy twice as much as I need. For example, one day when I got home I realised that I had bought thirty rolls of toilet paper although there are only three of us at home. When I get to our holiday home, the first thing I do is go shopping; I need to know that the fridge and the cupboards are full – it's vital – then I can feel safe."* It's as though what their inner self really needs is replaced by the non-essential.

What is really important at any particular moment gets hidden under the energy they put into practical tasks: *"Knowing what I really want requires time. When my husband suggests something to me, I think I'm ashamed to tell him that I don't know or that I need time to give him a true answer. So I buy myself time by telling him that we'll talk about it later and I work off my frustration at my lack of self-esteem by doing the vacuuming, although the house might actually be quite clean."* Focussing on practical things serves the purpose of releasing their pent-up feelings of internal anger. They tend to amass too much stuff: furniture, knick-knacks and clothes. Usually their cellars are full of all sorts of things; it's as though their fear of not getting enough love has been turned into a fear of not having enough comfort. *"When I say I'm OK, I'm not so much tuning in to a feeling inside myself; rather it's about feeling in harmony with the place where I happen to be at the time."*

The Paradox

Raising my level of comfort won't give me back my identity.

Metaphor – The Comfort Seeker

They excel at organising their home and daily life into rhythms that suit them – sometimes at the risk of spending too much time and energy amassing material goods in order to make themselves more comfortable.

Warning Signs for Nines

- Too much comfort
- Too much kindness to others
- Too much self-effacement
- Too much indolence

Warning Signs for the Self-Preservation Subtype

- Too much focus on security
- Spending too much time at work
- Being too focused on material well-being
- Too many routine evenings at home

A SELF-PRESERVATION NINE'S VIEW – OLIVIER

What I like about my Type

I love my calm side; it's not that I'm necessarily slow or that I don't care, but I like to take the time to live and I like things to get done in their own good time. In today's world, I have the feeling that I'm living in a society that values speed above everything else. That doesn't suit me; the seasons have a rhythm; the day has a rhythm; my body has a rhythm. This is universal and built into our biology. In order to grow, fruit needs the right amount of time. Personally, I feel that I know how to listen both to my internal clock and to the great clock of the universe and I will try as much as possible to align the two. That's probably why I like gardening; it puts me back in harmony with the rhythm of the earth. Also, I'm aware of the lunar cycles and I take them into account when I'm planting. But when I have to speed up, most of the time I don't have a problem doing that. For example, when I'm playing tennis I can launch myself across the court to get a shot, but when the point is finished I take the time to breathe and go back to my place without hurrying. In the same way, during the course of a day I alternate lively periods with slower periods, and I find that this balance is healthy. I find it hard to understand people who live at a hundred miles an hour all day long.

What I like about my Subtype

I like the atmosphere in my home. Everything has its place, but it's OK for everyone to mess things up in their own way and then put them back together as they see fit. People tell me that it's good to come to my place; it's comfortable and calm – in fact most of the time I prefer to invite people to my house rather than going to theirs. I suppose I am a bit of a stay-at-home; my friends know that I'm always welcoming, they come over when they want and I'm very happy to invite them in. Moreover, in contrast to most of the stereotypes about Nines, my self-preservation subtype gives me an appetite for work. I'm the head of a large communications company and I like that; I like bringing projects to fruition, motivating people, earning money and also taking the time to enjoy it. On holiday I'm attracted to sunny places where I can let my body have fun swimming, playing tennis and spending time on the beach.

What I like about the Combination of my Type and Subtype

I think that my talent for listening to others (which I attribute to my Nine) and the instinct for creating comfortable surroundings, which comes from my self-preservation subtype, come together in two places. At work if I want to find a publicity slogan that will work, I'm very good at taking on board the opinions of everyone around me, and then my subtype gives me the ability to imagine what it will look like in

204

*practical terms, which brings the idea to life; such and such a fruit, with this colour, photographed from that angle with this exposure will make you think of that taste. I see that as a sort of practical, down to earth intelligence, which I think is the special gift of the self-preservation subtypes. Following the same line of thought, I'm quite good at DIY. So for example, on holiday one year I realised what was wrong with my car's engine and that I knew how to fix it. From that moment I lost track of time; I took the time that was needed to make the repair. I'm not necessarily impatient to finish the job as quickly as possible; I know my goal, I know how to get there and I prefer to work at my own pace rather than forcing myself to do it more quickly. It's as though I have a strong **appetite** for life but it's an **appetite** to live at my own speed.*

Film Reference – The Constant Gardener

A young English diplomat, played by Ralph Fiennes, is leading a quiet life as an expatriate in Kenya. He lives alone, cut off from the busy cacophony of Nairobi; he spends a lot of time watering the house plants in his office (whence the title of the film) and is very conservative and politically correct in all his business meetings. One day a young woman falls in love with him and marries him. She is passionately devoted to humanitarian causes, is doing research about the underhand practices of pharmaceutical multinationals and ends up being killed.

From that moment he changes radically. This is where the Nine qualities really start to come out; an unsuspected internal strength springs up, together with determination, self-confidence and ability to stand up for himself. He finds a meaning for his life; he has a goal and no-one's going to stop him. He's still the same man, but everything has changed. He lives his life differently and his priorities are clear. He has got back in touch with his life force and the animal strength that he had been cut off from. Now there is a consistency and coherence about him. This is a self-preservation film because it's about illness, caring, life and death. This film shows us two extreme examples of self-preservation Nine and during the course of the film we witness the transformation of someone who rediscovers his true self.

THE ONE-TO-ONE TYPE NINE

Preoccupations of Type Nine: fleeing from conflict, avoiding stating their truth and taking their space
Preoccupations of the One-to-One Subtype: focusing on the partner
= UNION/FUSION

There are two contradictory energies here: self-forgetting and the desire for an intense one-to-one relationship. Often this leads to fusion with the partner. *"I forgot myself to the point where I completely identified with their needs and desires. I felt that my life was happy because there was no conflict. I was a windsurfer for 17 years; I was even French champion. And suddenly one morning on holiday when I was getting my board out, I realised that deep down I didn't like the sea or the wind. For 17 years I had believed that I liked windsurfing because my partner did. Realising that I didn't was a heavy blow."* Union is living a joint existence rather than an association of two individuals; this is the old-fashioned fantasy of marriage; one plus one equals one. *"For a long time I believed that merging totally with my husband was the most wonderful proof of my love for him and of the success of us as a couple."* In fact this is the heart of the problem – self-forgetting.

Looking at this more deeply, you could say that it's about making your life together as comfortable as possible in order to avoid asking yourself whether you're really happy. *"You know, it's exhilarating to forget yourself to the point where you merge completely with the other person. It's as though I were a sponge absorbing my partner. This osmosis is so nice; it's like a cocoon which is all curves and no corners."* At work, these same characteristics show up; *but* in the end an excellent ability to adapt to the boss' priorities can get in the way of fulfilling your true potential.

The Paradox

Merging with my partner's wishes makes it less easy to express my own needs.

Metaphor – The One who Merges

Researchers, composers or artists often have the feeling that they have totally become one with what they are working on. They are so absorbed, so fused to their work that they are unaware of their tiredness or hunger.

Warning Signs for Nines

- Too much comfort
- Too much kindness to other people
- Too much self-effacement
- Too much indolence

Warning Signs for the One-to-One Subtype

- Focus on wanting to prove that you are an intense, passionate person
- Too much focus on the partner: what they are doing, where they are, who they are meeting
- Too much focus on your own actions – not enough wider perspective
- Rivalry between your own goals and your partner's interest in other things.

A ONE-TO-ONE NINE'S VIEW – CLAIRE

What I like about my Type

My ability to exude a sort of peacefulness; I feel that I've got a collection of qualities that help me create harmony. For example, it's not that I've got a particular gift for choosing furniture, but I manage to arrange things in a room in a way that creates a pleasant sense of things fitting together – and a sense that in these surroundings people can live in peace. People tell me that I give off an energy that is both powerful and calming. I think I've got a really subtle ability to understand the desires, needs and suffering of people around me.

I like listening and I like the fact that other people feel free to tell me what they want. If necessary, I think I'm a good support for other people; I'm someone who's available, who is prepared to take the time to sit with words or silence, to help the other person find solutions to their problems or suggest what they might to do sort out their difficulties. I also like to be aware of the different viewpoints in a group and play a role in creating harmony in the midst of differences. I'm very sensitive to what the Christians call the communion of saints; this principle holds that everything in the universe is connected and that each person's actions impact on the rest of the world. I would really love everyone to feel more responsible for the well-being of all the people on earth.

What I like about my Subtype

The opportunity to experience really high-quality one-to-one relationships. In my work as an osteopath, when I'm treating a baby, it's quite magical to be able quickly, without using words, to establish a connection with the essence of this little human becoming, which all of a sudden calms down and becomes peaceful. It's about communicating easily, being able to make an exceptional connection with someone, being able to get straight into a deep conversation where you dare to reveal yourself because of this immensely strong contact, even if it's very short-lived. It's a sort of very brief total fusion. A simple look can be the catalyst that someone needs and the quality of my one-to-one contact enables me to express to someone that I care about them, just by a look.

What I like about the Combination of my Type and Subtype

Again, in my work as an osteopath, I think that the combination of my Nine and my one-to-one subtype gives me qualities that enable me to help people find new balance in their life. I think that Nines' talent for welcoming and listening to people combines with the one-to-one subtype's dynamism and drive to make contact. I feel as though I've got these two dynamics within me; one is the receiver – a cup you can pour something out into which is patient and has all the time in the world, and the other is more assertive in relation to the outside world – it dares to express what it feels and take action. These two parts of me rejoice when I witness another person open up to and understand things for the first time.

To take another example, I've got twins who are very different: a boy and a girl. I'm very at ease with them when they're together, or when I'm with each one of them separately. In both situations I know how to listen to them and to try to give them ways of understanding and accepting themselves.

Film Reference – The English Patient

It's 1945, near the end of the war. Torn apart by the terrible conflict she has lived through, Hana, a young nurse, hides herself away in an abandoned monastery in Tuscany. She brings into her hideaway a pilot with amnesia, who has been terribly disfigured by a plane crash. The three main roles in this film are great examples of one-to-one profiles. The love story between Count Almasy and Katherine Clifton is an object lesson in the kind of passion which can unite two people of this subtype. However, for an example of a one-to-one Nine we need to turn to Hana.

The first characteristic of the Nine is the ability to listen. This film is Hana's story, but she's not the main character – it's through her listening that the story is told. You often find this with Nines; they can be the central character in a story without standing out at the front of the stage. Other clues that we're dealing with a Nine: Hana has a gentle presence that can't stand conflict, she finds it hard to say no and she is looking for peace and quiet. Several times during the film she finds herself listening to stories of great pain. She receives these stories of suffering with calm and consideration and gives them the time they need, which is so characteristic of this type. Nines know more than others how to take time to truly take in what the other person is saying, to give their thoughts time to sink in rather than jumping straight in with their own opinion. When Hana speaks it's mostly to say things that are simple, sober and gentle. During the time-span of the film (several months) she lets things evolve in their own time. Hana forgets herself; when she's keeping watch over her patient late at night, he asks her "Why do you stay so late?"

As for the one-to-one subtype, it's everywhere in the film. Every time Hana looks at someone you can see the fire in her look. A Nine's look is probably the least piercing of all the one-to-one subtypes, but it's very sustained. Often, this look is accompanied by silence: "I want to create a strong bond with you" says the one-to-one by their look; the Nine doesn't say anything, because they don't know what to say. In Hana's character you can find a charming side that is able to create one-to-one closeness very quickly. The relationship she develops with her patient very clearly goes beyond the normal nurse/patient relationship. She's not in love with him but she has an intense one-to-one connection with him.

The ambivalence between the one-to-one's need to move towards and the Nine's instinct to do nothing shows up on several occasions, as well as the contradiction between finding it hard to say no and expressing what you want. For example, in the very first scene we see Hana in a train, easily looking after several patients on her own, but unable to say no to one of them when he asks her for a kiss. Later, she is equally unable to say no to her friend who asks her for money so that she can go and buy lace in the next village. But on the other hand, she has no difficulty in making a rapid decision to demand to be left alone to look after her dying patient. One day, Caravaggio, an

Italian who claims to know the identity of the mysterious "English patient", interferes in the life of the two recluses; yet again, she can't manage to say no. Later, she regrets it "I preferred the time when there were just the two of us" she says to her patient. When Caravaggio and her patient tell each other their troubles she listens, without intervening or judging.

This kind of one-to-one Nine character, which combines softness, firmness and charm in a "starring role that doesn't take all the space for themselves", comes up often in films, particularly in some of Catherine Deneuve's roles ("Indochina" for example) or Grace Kelly's ("Rear Window"). A male equivalent might be James Stewart in Alfred Hitchcock's "The Man who Knew too Much".

THE SOCIAL TYPE NINE

> *Preoccupations of Type Nine: fleeing from conflict, avoiding stating their truth and taking their space*
> *Preoccupations of the Social Subtype: focusing on friends, associations and groups*
> *= SOCIAL PARTICIPATION*

Self-forgetting can happen in groups too; it's a reassuring way of experiencing belonging. You feel loved: *"By devoting myself to the group I have an excuse to defer my own needs. Belonging to the group leaves me free to speak or not, to state my truth or not. I can start by listening to others, hearing the different points of view, taking the time to see how things are working. I enjoy taking part, being there, without necessarily getting involved."* Sometimes social Nines stay on the edge of the group, not really knowing how to get more involved – they sort of melt into the group. They often ask themselves the question: *"Do I really have a place in this group?"* when actually they are not taking any action to take up their place.

They often end up with responsibilities within charity organisations because other people think that they will be good at it. *"I ended up being president, treasurer or secretary of five different organisations without ever having applied for the roles. I'm not even sure that I ever actually said yes; I simply didn't say no and somehow it was all agreed. But hey, it was great to meet all these people, listen to them and eventually make decisions together. And then one fine day I woke up to myself and asked what I was really doing there, because I hadn't consciously volunteered to do it."* This is all about comfort; regular meeting dates in the same venue and committee members that you know well limit the unexpected and the potential for worry. *"It's reassuring to keep meeting up with the same people; it gives me confidence. I even think that it's the context where I feel most comfortable to really talk about myself."*

At work, people often say that Nines would be the ideal people to chair a management committee. There's probably a lot of sense in this idea for the social subtype, although it may be less true for the other subtypes.

The Paradox
A group is not necessarily the easiest context to learn how to state my own point of view.

Metaphor[1] – The Bringer-Together
They go along easily with the wishes of the group, to the point where they give up a lot of themselves for the common good.

Warning Signs for Nines
- Too much comfort
- Too much kindness towards other people
- Too much self-effacement
- Too much indolence

Warning Signs for the Social Subtype
- Too much need to be recognised
- Too much time spent keeping up social relationships

- Being a member of too many clubs and societies
- Too much devotion to the causes they espouse

A SOCIAL NINE'S VIEW – FLORENCE

What I like about my Type

As a good representative of my type I found this question easy at first, but on reflection it was mostly the negative aspects that came to mind. After I'd got rid of these I managed to identify what I like about my Type. I feel that I'm good at managing my emotions. On the one hand I've got a kind of bumper that absorbs shocks that come from the outside world, but on the other hand I only very rarely show my own emotions to the outside world. I think I'm open-minded and tolerant, and I don't make great play of my ideas, opinions and feelings. This talent means that others can express themselves freely, knowing that they won't be judged. I've also got the gift of often being able to find the idea that will enable people to understand each other or come to an agreement. And lastly, when I live in a flat or house, I just inevitably seem to create a living space which is pleasing to everyone, with a lovely warm atmosphere.

What I like about my Subtype

*I'm completely in my element in a group. I speak easily, I organise the debate and I make sure everyone gets to speak – I just seem to set up these sorts of situations. Professionally, as soon as I get a new job, I organise work groups. It seems completely obvious to me that people need a place where they can express their goals, their objectives and their difficulties within a group. The time taken for these work meetings is absolutely crucial to building the team. Both the big picture and the small practical concerns are discussed and debated by the whole group. This is my **participative** management style; it's tried and tested and it seems to work for me and for everyone's benefit. But let's be clear; it doesn't get in the way of productivity. My teams are like bee-hives; they are warm*

213

and convivial – but that doesn't prevent everyone meeting their targets. And what's more, on a daily basis I encourage the general sense of group cohesion by hosting lunches and coffee-breaks. In my personal life I hardly ever just invite one or two people to my house. I would rather have ten or a dozen people around and prepare a meal for everyone. My relaxed presence in the group means that I can unite people around a cause that I can then defend vigorously.

What I like about the Combination of my Type and Subtype

The alchemy of my Nine and my social subtype means that people often describe me as having "quiet strength", or as "the iron fist in a velvet glove". In a group I never feel alone; my energy merges with everyone there and I identify with them. This means that I can then guide, organise, stop and decide both for myself and for the others. It's as though I become the spokesperson for the group and the more identified with them I am, the more easily I can speak for them. The bits of my type which I consider negative then seem to disappear; being in a group puts me more at ease than being in one-to-one situations.

Film Reference – The Russia House

When Katy, a Russian editor, tries to get a manuscript written by a Russian engineer to the British publisher Barley Blair, she unwittingly draws them into the world of international espionage. When the manuscript, which contains sensitive military information, is intercepted by British counter-espionage, Blair is sent rather against his will to Russia, in order to find out more about the document.

Blair's style is rather laid-back; the contrast between his gangling form and the military style of the counter-espionage men is amusing. We see here someone who lives by his own rhythm and won't let anyone else impose theirs on him. When counter-espionage try to get him involved in their work, we see that he needs time to digest the information and decide what he wants to do. In the end, he goes unwillingly, against his better judgement, without ever having said "yes" and having even said "no". He feels that he can't stand up to them so he prefers to go with the flow, wait and see.

We can also see the laid-back side to Barley in the fact that for the whole film his life hangs by a thread and he knows it, but he still stays calm. We see him fishing while people a few feet away are deciding his fate. When he takes a lie detector test with several witnesses, he seems as though he's somewhere else, detached from what's happening. It's the defence mechanism of the Nine to "narcotise" – to numb themselves so that they don't feel stress or the difficulties of the situation.

This film shows us the passive/active polarity of the Nine. The passive side is that Nines don't decide straightaway what they're going to do; they are followers rather than deciders, they sniff the wind and take a position that will keep them away from conflict. In this film, it's probably thanks to this temperament that Barley survives as long as he does. This apparent lack of harshness makes him non-threatening; people are less suspicious of him. He puts you to sleep in the sense that he seems innocent and leads you to drop your guard. And then there is this strange time management where he never seems to be in a hurry and trusts that things will get done in their own time, if at all.

He does have an active side, because Nines do decide in the end: often on the basis of what they don't want. And when they're sure that they've taken the right path, their Enneagram arrows kick in; at point Three they find efficiency and practicality and at Six they suss out the ebb and flow of the situation, its consequences and different scenarios.

Peter O'Hanrahan says: "This subtype merges easily with the desires of their friends and the groups around them." In this film, Barley doesn't really merge but he does drop into the role of spy that he's been given so well that you sometimes ask yourself whether he actually is a spy. And you ask yourself whether he hasn't, like a Three, immersed himself so well in the role that he's lost himself.

SUBTYPES: THE KEY TO THE ENNEAGRAM

There is also a "community benefactor" side to his character; in the midst of his busy life (which could almost make him look like Seven) he is a stalwart member of his orchestra and his Anglo-Russian association. He has loads of friends and knows lots of people. With his "hail fellow well met" energy he plays music for a dozen guests on spoons, glasses, the table and cigarette papers – all without raising his voice. Everything around him is harmony – both the Nine and the social energies.

He's also interested in culture and other countries: "I love the USA, but I also love Russia and England." He also talks about Czechs, Vietnamese, Koreans and Afghans in great depth. He is also capable of delivering brilliant speeches in company, for example the day when he held forth on: "How to save the world between lunch and dinner – I believe in the new Russia. Twenty years ago it was a nightmare project; now it's our only hope. We think we can ruin you with the arms race, playing with the destiny of the human race." And when he's interrogated by MI6, they cynically ask him "Do you believe this?" He replies "I don't know; I believe it when I say it, but you have to be in Russia." He merges with the situation he finds himself in, to the point where even his beliefs seem to change in order to fit in. Anyway, it's his social viewpoint, his awareness of which groups matter, of sub-groups within groups that enables him to find a solution to get out of this mess. For example, he has to deal with both Americans and English people; he knows how their mind-sets are different, he sees how they operate separately and together and he can take advantage of that. It is the competences of his subtype and his type that enable him to get out of the situation alive.

It's fairly rare in cinema for a Nine to be shown sympathetically and even heroically. This role shows us a typical Nine and also shows us how they can be people of action and decision. Just because you are laid-back doesn't mean that you can't take strong action or risks when you need to. You find this quality in some tennis champions; they seem like sleepy teddy-bears when they get on to the court, often lose the first set but then, when the diesel has warmed up, they run, fight and win with an energy which is diametrically opposed to the one they started the match with. In fact it's quite difficult to caricature this type because they vary so much according to the circumstances. Once they have decided what they want or where they want to get to, nothing stops a Nine; their stubbornness takes them forward with the energy of a rhinoceros.

References for Part 2

SUBTYPES OF TYPE 1

1. Whatever your memories of the films which are used as references, you are strongly recommended to see them again so that you can really experiences the energy of the character as well as their behaviour. The 27 films are all available on DVD.
2. Claudio Naranjo (1991) *Ennea-Type Structures; Self-Analysis for the Seeker*, Gateway
3. Ibid
4. Peter O'Hanrahan *Enneagram Work* (unpublished article; see www.enneagramwork.com)
5. Sandra Maitri (2001) *The Spiritual Dimension of the Enneagram – Nine Faces of the Soul.* Putnam/Penguin, New York

SUBTYPES OF TYPE 2

1. Claudio Naranjo (1991) *Ennea-Type Structures; Self-Analysis for the Seeker*, Gateway
2. Peter O'Hanrahan *Enneagram Work* (unpublished article; see www.enneagramwork.com)

SUBTYPES OF TYPE 3

1. Claudio Naranjo (1991) *Ennea-Type Structures; Self-Analysis for the Seeker*, Gateway
2. Peter O'Hanrahan *Enneagram Work* (unpublished article; see www.enneagramwork.com)
3. Peter O'Hanrahan *Enneagram Work* (unpublished article; see www.enneagramwork.com)

SUBTYPES OF TYPE 4

1. Claudio Naranjo (1991) *Ennea-Type Structures; Self-Analysis for the Seeker*, Gateway
2. Peter O'Hanrahan *Enneagram Work* (unpublished article; see www.enneagramwork.com)

SUBTYPES OF TYPE 6
1. Claudio Naranjo (1991) *Ennea-Type Structures; Self-Analysis for the Seeker*, Gateway
2. Peter O'Hanrahan *Enneagram Work* (unpublished article; see www.enneagramwork.com)

SUBTYPES OF TYPE 7
1. Peter O'Hanrahan *Enneagram Work* (unpublished article; see www.enneagramwork.com)

SUBTYPES OF TYPE 8
1. Peter O'Hanrahan *Enneagram Work* (unpublished article; see www.enneagramwork.com)

SUBTYPES OF TYPE 9
1. Peter O'Hanrahan *Enneagram Work,* www.enneagramwork.com

PART 3: WAKING UP TO YOURSELF, USING YOUR SUBTYPES

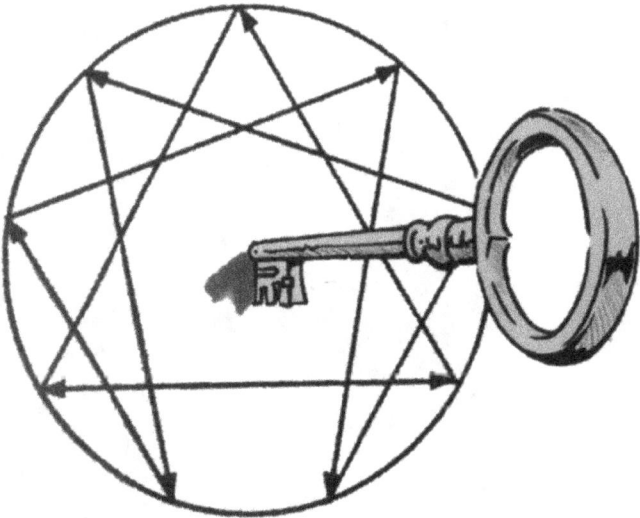

CLEARING THE WAY FOR TRANSFORMATION

Making use of twentieth century developments

The journey towards being fully ourselves is not easy, so let's get some help from some of the travellers who have already opened up the path towards the Self. In the hundred years since Carl G. Jung first used the word *ueberpersoenlich* in 1916, the transpersonal movement has developed considerably.

The transpersonal movement is a community of thinkers from different disciplines, whose aim is the expansion of consciousness. Michel Random[1] explains in more detail *"The transpersonal is characterised by listening, opening and questioning. Transpersonal thought establishes the relationship between terms like conscious and unconscious in a more global and subtle vision – that consciousness is Oneness"*.

Since Jung, this message has been taken up by many authors. Some of the classics are *Psychosynthesis* by the Italian Roberto Assagioli, *Conversations on Waking Dreams* by Robert Desoille, and *Existential Pyschotherapy* by the Austrian Viktor Frankl. But there are also more accessible works such as *Hara, the Vital Centre of Man* by Karlfried Graf von Duerckheim, *Spiritual Communion of Mankind* by Rudolf Steiner, *Flesh and Soul* by Boris Cyrulnik, *Peace is the Way* by Deepak Chopra – and a few more scientific ones such as *Chronicles of Heaven and Life* by Hubert Reeves, *The Soul of Nature* by Rupert Sheldrake and *The Limits of Thought* by David Bohm.

They all put forward the same message, which is the same as that of the Enneagram: *"We are all so much more beautiful than we think we are; we all have unsuspected resources within us. They are there, inside us; it's simply that we're not in touch with them. We're off-balance because we're looking at the world from a limited viewpoint."*

The Frenchman Michel Random was largely responsible for making this transpersonal view available to a wider public through his various works[2], and through the Tokyo International Forum of 1995, organised by UNESCO and the USA.

The transpersonal movement is interesting because of its interdisciplinary nature; in its research it brings together scientists like Matthieu Ricard, religious people of various beliefs, philosophers, doctors and psychotherapists. We can't separate the renaissance of the Enneagram from the psycho-spiritual context of the time; and it's crucial to remember that Claudio Naranjo was the successor of Fritz Perls at Esalen. The transpersonal movement sits clearly at the crossroads between science, psychology and spirituality. All these have one point in common; they are convinced that meditation, in whatever form, is an essential practice in order to achieve relaxation of the ego and expansion of consciousness.

Understanding the particular contribution of the Enneagram

Since the beginning the Enneagram has had a spiritual purpose, and this means that it will never be simply a base-level development tool. So at this point it is useful to remember some of the key elements that make the Enneagram different from other models.

The Enneagram is a symbol

It is a metaphor which can be interpreted at different levels of consciousness[3]. The Dictionary of Symbols states: *"The Enneagram diagram has the property of being able to bring together in a single model all the influences of the unconscious and the conscious, as well as the instinctive and spiritual forces which exist inside everyone."*[4]   Authors like Boris Mouravieff have further explored this symbolic dimension[5]. This is both the strength and the weakness of the Enneagram; some people admire it for the fact that it can be interpreted at different levels; others demonise it for the same reason, considering that any tool that is not scientific is not reliable and may even be corrupting.

The basis of the model is a circle

The circle is the most inclusive model we can possibly imagine. If we suppose that the circle represents the whole of the potential that exists inside us, the Enneagram offers us a complete map of signposts to help us grow and bring ourselves to unity. In this system, the circle represents the infinite grandeur of our potential and expresses something like: *"Our possibilities are much greater than we have ever imagined. In the circle, just look at the tiny part around which our consciousness oscillates, and compare it with the space that we have not yet explored."*

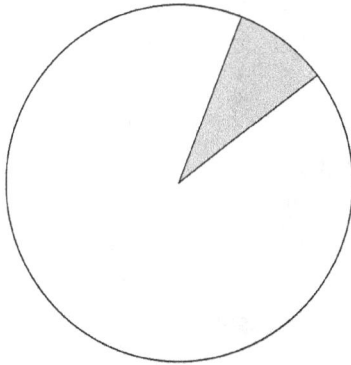

Figure 19 – My self, in relation to the potential to be discovered

From another point of view, if we consider the circle as portraying the sum total of points of view of all the men and women in the world around a single truth that is in the centre of the circle, we realise that in an argument no-one is ever right or wrong – there are only different points of view. If we start from this mindset, every person who has a different point of view from mine becomes enriching, because they open me up to a perspective that is not the one I normally hold. This way of expressing things may seem abstract, but with the map that the Enneagram provides, it becomes both concrete and powerful.

Anyone who has taken part in an Enneagram workshop lasting at least three days will bear witness to that.

But let's come back to the circle as a way of symbolising different points of view – this brings us straight away into a spiritual way of looking at things. We can only bring ourselves to our full potential by recognising how we are different from others and by being in contact with others. This is the key philosophy of Martin Buber: "*I am a person if I am linked to another person. When I detach myself from the other, I cease to exist.*" When the Enneagram is taught in the narrative tradition, it gives us the map we need to recognise the limitations of our own point of view, the key to be more accepting of how we are different from others and the desire to truly meet other people in their deepest self.

Type is considered to be an agent of change[6]

Working with your type is the tipping point which enables transformation, the means whereby ordinary consciousness evolves towards the dimensions of higher being. The act of accepting which one of the nine archetypes we habitually live in is to accept that, for reasons which go back to our childhood, we have made the choice all our life to give one of our facets precedence over the others. In recognising this we also acknowledge our principal shortcoming and take it on board as the starting point for our development. Helen Palmer says "*Seen from the spiritual point of view, type is the shell which supports the essence of the core being. This type is a conditioned structure which works on auto-pilot, but in as much as it is a shell, a container, we must respect it – it gives us security, an identity, and it increases our sense of our self-esteem. On the other hand, type is also what keeps in place the source of our suffering. Effectively, there is a difference between the objective reality of an event and our experience of it, which has already been filtered by our type.*" For example, when we feel stress, (i.e. a disagreeable tension), most of the time we have in fact generated this suffering ourselves, through the bias of our type.

As soon as we start paying close attention to ourselves, type gives us useful insights

The Enneagram names the central preoccupation of each type; the subtypes help us to notice more quickly when we're (yet again!) reacting according to one of our conditioned patterns. This tool therefore has immediate value because if we know what we're looking for, after a relatively short period of training we can learn a lot about ourselves and begin to notice our behaviour.

Type is useful in everyday situations

In particular, subtypes describe the precise shape of our recurring behaviours in everyday life. Whereas just knowing our type can leave us in a state of uncertainty, wondering what on earth to do with this discovery, recognising our subtype gives us nowhere to hide; dozens of times a day we all have to face up to it: *"Silly idiot, there's your automatic pattern again!"*

Type comes out of a deep historical tradition

Type is based on the key tendencies that people succumb to when they are not centred in their Self. Whether there are seven, eight or nine of them, we can find them in many traditions and cultures going right back to the Desert Fathers, the first Christian monks of the 4th century, who identified nine passions (which are the ancestors of the seven deadly sins): anger, pride, vanity, envy, sadness, avarice, gluttony, lust and self-forgetting. We can see that this list is almost exactly the same as the list of Enneagram passions, except that sadness appears instead of fear.

Managing the mid-life crisis

The mid-life crisis is a universal experience. Most civilisations have a term that describes it. C. G. Jung was the first to introduce the concept into psychology, calling it "the tipping point of life". Since then, a number of authors including the monk Anselm Gruen have written books about it[7]. Often, this crisis comes to light after a shock: bereavement, redundancy, divorce, an accident ... It can also hit us the day that our last child leaves home, or come on slowly as a kind of underlying depression with no apparent cause.   This crisis has three characteristics:

- It is existential – it questions the meaning of life.
- It happens in the middle of life, when part of us realises that there is less time left to live than we have lived already.
- It is deep and life-changing. Things can never be the same once it has appeared.

Abraham Maslow and the transpersonal movement say that we all come to a point where we realise that we have fulfilled most of our material, emotional and social goals. This is the characteristic of the "wealthy discontented" generation we talked about earlier. Humanistic psychologists describe the four existential pressures that form the basis of this crisis:

- *The search for meaning.* Why does life exist? Why are we on the earth? Do we have a mission?
- *The finite nature of life: death and rebirth.* All living beings are mortal. All relationships will end one way or another. Throughout our lives, we must undergo bereavement.
- *Loneliness: basically, we are alone.* We are born alone and we die alone. Between the two, we spend a lot of time trying to avoid loneliness.
- *Limitation: we are only human.* We are not all-powerful, in fact we're extremely limited. We are not as strong as we would like to be, and sometimes that gets us down.

This realisation tends to generate two possible calls to action. The first is that we're fed up; we've run out of energy. We're physically tired of living out of kilter with our true self. Other emotional and psychological factors make this lassitude even more acute; our neurons have had enough of being continuously under tension; our emotions have had enough of being our bodyguards. The other impulse we experience is a longing; it is as though we feel a call, a hunger to be ourselves – a part of us is not complete; we long for fulfilment. We want to get back in contact with the amazing sensations we have all experienced in those rare moments when we glimpse what it is like to be a fully enlightened being. In short, we want to rediscover ourselves, fully and freely; we need to reconnect deeply with the essence of ourselves. And then one day, somewhere within the chaos of our mid-life crisis, a desire appears which gives us the impetus to transform ourselves. Annick de Souzenelle encourages us to take the initiative ourselves: *"Why should we have to wait for an external trauma to show up in order to learn who we are? Why should we have to wait for great misfortune to happen, in order to learn that it is time to walk away from the person that we are not, the person that we appear to be?"*

REDISCOVERING UNITY – THE PATH TO AWARENESS

So, coming back to unity with ourselves is the aim, but how do we do it? By relaxing our defences in order to find moments of completeness.

Moving towards the Self

Essence and personality are two aspects of the same self. Essence represents the true Self, what we were before we discovered as tiny children that we couldn't sustain this way of living, this total innocence, this spontaneous reaction to the environment. Rediscovering this way of being requires us to deconstruct our defence mechanisms, with help from others, over time, taking it gently. This approach is different from the classic psychological approach that says that we need to maintain a solid defence mechanism. Humanistic psychology thinks differently; from its point of view, the more we can relax our defence mechanism the more balanced we will be. The more powerful the defence mechanism is, the more we are sick: that is, cut off from our true Self.

If we live totally within our personality we are not completely authentic; the original meaning of "persona" was "mask". Within our personality, nothing within us works normally and effortlessly; we force ourselves, we play a role. The personality is therefore present in everything we do; the type pattern always finds a way to get itself out of trouble in almost any situation ... The only problem with this is that every form of suffering reactivates the fear, tension and workings of the type, which separates us a little bit more from our Self, which raises the level of suffering ... It's a vicious circle which continues until, eventually, life calls us back to ourselves ...

Relaxing our defences

Humanistic psychology suggests that we should relax our defences and stop the automatic activation of the type – so far, so good. But in order to do that we have to work on our unconscious. Most of the time, type behaviour unconsciously blocks suffering so that we can't even feel it. Dr Janov says: *"In general we don't feel primal suffering directly, but we experience it in the form of tension. Therefore therapy consists in bringing the patient to the point where they no longer avoid what is hurting them, helping them progressively to feel this suffering in order to free themselves from it and stop the symbolic behaviours which come from it, together with the tension which it produces."*

Getting back in touch with repressed feelings

Personality develops as a response to the impossibility of experiencing a painful feeling. At its centre is the repression of the feeling and its transmutation into "type" behaviour. Although the nine types give us nine different points of view, the work to free ourselves is the same for all types; we need to dismantle the stressors of the original wound, by dismantling the tensions and the defence mechanisms. If we don't do this and let the type continue to run things, the defence mechanism reinforces itself; this gives the impression that we're functioning well, but in fact we're being ruled by a deep-seated internal tension.

Some people run away from this challenge, thinking that, as we live in stressful times, it is normal to put your armour on and accept that living under tension is inevitable. Moving towards essence means daring to imagine that we can aspire to something beyond better social functioning or relief of our symptoms; we have to start looking at our motivations. Moving towards essence also means imagining that it might just be possible to reach a state of being which is different from the one we experience normally: a life without tension, free of defences, where we can be completely ourselves, welcome each feeling as it arrives and experience an internal unity. This doesn't mean that we will never be worried or unhappy again; rather it means that, whatever we have to deal with, we will react to the situation by seeing things as they actually are, living each moment in the present with no expectations, and noticing any possible distortions caused by our type.

Re-centring ourselves on a regular basis

An old belief says that the journey from personality to essence happens in a straight line – don't count on it! The journey of evolution is anything but a long tranquil river and it certainly isn't straight. The development work to loosen conditioned behaviours really does yield accelerating results in the medium term, but the anchors of personality still assert themselves on a regular basis: less and less violently certainly, but they still keep coming back. The goal we are aiming for is not to eliminate the ego or to hope that it will stop its attacks. Rather, the goal is to notice earlier and earlier that the ego has taken charge and to re-centre ourselves before we get too far away from our balanced self. As Robert Assagioli says in his book 'Psychosynthesis': *"You will never kill the ego; you can only expand the space for it to live in."* The benefits of this self-development work are legion. We gain increased consciousness, freedom and internal peace, and all the time we are lightening our suffering ... It is in this space of awareness, which is both fine-pointed and far-reaching, that the Enneagram comes into play.

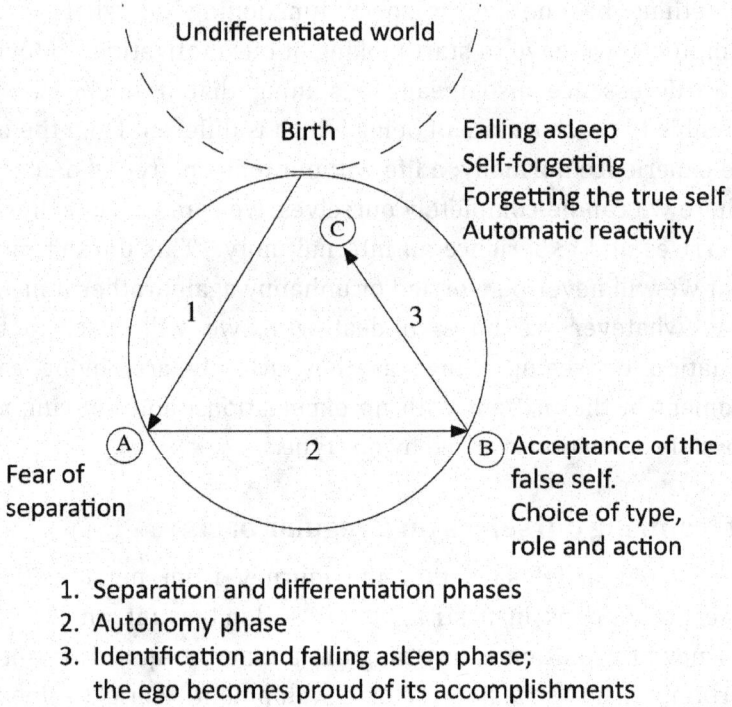

Undifferentiated world

Birth

Falling asleep
Self-forgetting
Forgetting the true self
Automatic reactivity

C

1

3

A

2

B Acceptance of the
false self.

Fear of
separation

Choice of type,
role and action

1. Separation and differentiation phases
2. Autonomy phase
3. Identification and falling asleep phase;
   the ego becomes proud of its accomplishments

Figure 20 – The construction of the false self

In Part 1 of this book we described the process during childhood that leads to the construction of the false self (Phases A, B and C). In Figure 21, phases D, E, F and G show how we can start to work with that, once we've had our wake-up call.

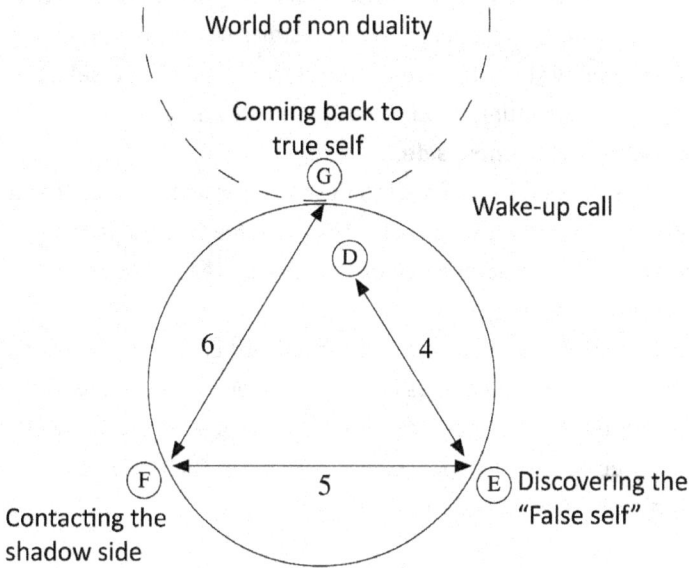

Figure 21 – Coming Back to True Self

D. The wake-up call
Something triggers an existential crisis, an awakening.

4. The "gap" phase
The sudden realisation of the gap between the "true me" and the "false me", even if we can't quite describe these ideas clearly. This leads us to undertake therapy, ask ourselves questions, be hungry to be ourselves.

E. Discovering the "false self"
This stage helps us to understand how our identity is constructed, and through the descriptions of the nine types, helps us to get to know ourselves. It throws light on to the past, the way we handle relationships and gives us routes to transformation. By finding out our dominant type we become more aware - and the signposts of the Enneagram help to make this stage of the journey clearer and easier.

5. The "warm-up" phase

This phase is about accepting and taking charge of ourselves, about taking the time to make peace with ourselves, given what we've found out about our principal failing. Our ego starts to soften and relax, and a sort of humility starts to sprout. We start to observe ourselves and become more accepting of our emotions just as they are.

F. Contacting the Shadow side

In this phase we start to be able to describe our unconscious fear and underlying tension; we start to notice where fear blocks us, when tension arises and exactly when our automatic reaction kicks in.

6. The transformation phase

We no longer run away from our most difficult emotions; we dare to stay present when pain comes up and when our whole being pushes us to flee into the conditioned behaviour of our type. And through that, we gain precious internal peace, which is one of the features of ...

G. Coming back to True Self

Using the Enneagram on this journey

The incomparable advantage of the Enneagram is that it gives a precise description of the ego and how it works. The ego and our preferred behaviour gave us the means to survive and to minimise our suffering in this world and helped develop our self-esteem. If they didn't exist, we would have no pride, no dignity. As we shall see, the ego itself is the very stuff that will help us come back to essence. In addition, I think that the map provided by the Enneagram is particularly relevant during our mid-life period; the terms that describe the ego (fixation and passion), the exact description of the role we play, the form of the original wound, the basic fear, the beliefs, all these parameters become clear in mid-life and start to make sense.

The Enneagram also sheds light on the pain that pushed us into playing a role. It leads us therefore to a better understanding and acceptance of ourselves. Our shadow sides become forgivable once they have been brought into the light, understood and accepted. By showing us the path we travelled to construct the "me", the Enneagram sheds light on the way back from the false self towards essence. I'm sure that even simply noticing the gap between essence and personality starts to set in motion an internal letting go. It certainly won't resolve all our tensions and fears, but in general it will make us want to transform ourselves, to set out on the road to reunion with the Self. Our awareness expands, we are no longer at the mercy of the fact that we are playing a role. We can start to notice when we "go on automatic" and when we don't.

But the anchors go deep. Some reflexes are deeply embedded in our genes, others in our cells. Since the age of about five, we have been refining our defences, reinforcing our armour. The conditioning has become automatic and now we have to let all that go, mentally, emotionally and instinctively! It doesn't sound like much fun, and certainly not a great way to spend your time. So why should we bother setting out on this road? Probably because the experience of completeness is like nothing else, because somewhere in ourselves we are fed up with all this wasted time, or because we want to align ourselves with the deepest part of our being. But above all, because once it has been awakened the internal force that impels us to be more ourselves gives us no choice – even if this choice upsets everyone around us!

MOVING BEYOND THE REACTIVITY OF THE SUBTYPE – THE PATTERN OF TRANSFORMATION

Converting the energy of the passion

The idea of relaxing as a response to moments when the tension is strong has always existed in all the great spiritual traditions. For most people involved in personal development, the phrase "letting go" is a classic idea, but in most cases it remains rather abstract. The usefulness of the Enneagram is that it clarifies precisely where, when and what to relax.

- Mentally, it describes exactly the direction in which the mental function focuses (see Figure 9, the *fixations*). Here is an example for Type One "*Pay particular attention when your thought starts to compare what you see with what ought to be,* and when a sort of resentment arises." With that understanding, a Type One knows exactly what to watch out for. They can link the idea of "letting go" to a specific sort of attention.

- Emotionally, through the descriptions of the *passions* the Enneagram shows which wound will be triggered, and why. Again, here an example for Type One: *"Your ideal of perfection makes you very sensitive to mistakes; anger rises, you block it and stifle it, and this heightens your internal tension."* The same advice applies; once they have identified their type, Ones will be able to focus their letting go in a particular direction.

- Behaviourally, by studying the subtypes, each person gains three landmarks to help them notice that their specific type reactivity has taken hold, and in what form.

As well as this, the Enneagram describes in detail the state of being which can exist for each of us when we have succeeded in holding our reactivity in check. When the type releases, the relaxation works on the three centres:

- *Mental* – the placement of attention expands, moves beyond its usual focus; consciousness becomes more spacious and less directed.

- *Emotional* – reactivity goes into the background, tension releases and fear goes away.

- *Behavioural* – instincts (self-preservation, one-to-one and social) can bring their true gifts in the moment rather than being driven by the type.

Figures 22 and 23 show the difference that converting the energy of the passion can make.

236

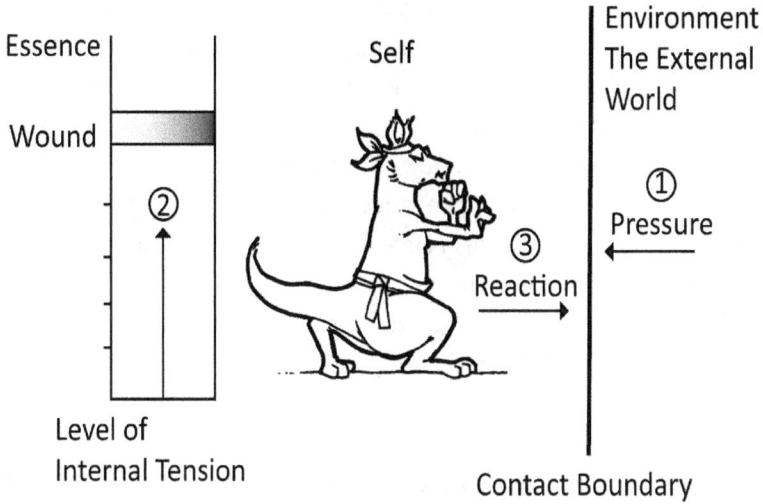

Figure 22 – Pattern of automatic reactivity

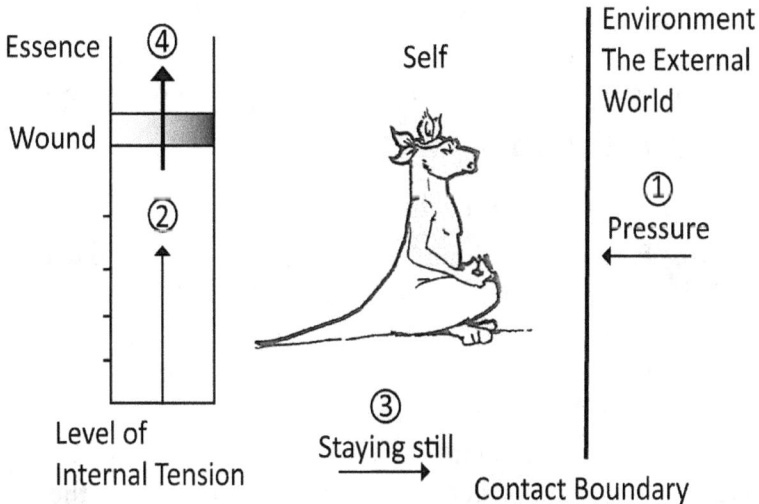

Figure 23 – Pattern of transformation

When the type releases, one consequence is that we rediscover a more creative orientation to our surroundings. We are no longer caught up in repeating learned behaviours. We are in essence; that is, we open-heartedly welcome what is happening right here and now. So we are in the right place to respond appropriately to external stimuli. In other words, essence is a state of being, a living attitude; it's a flowing, completely receptive presence, without fear, prejudice or expectation. We have released ourselves from the trap of automatic behaviour in which we shut ourselves. We have rediscovered the childhood world of non-duality, where you and I are part of the same whole. The special contribution of the Enneagram is that it describes the particular shape of essence through the nine archetypes. Each of the nine passions, when it is transcended, has its own flavour and feel. The experience of non-duality is common to all types, but the flavour of the letting go is different.

The other consequence is that we are full of energy. In effect, because we haven't reacted automatically to the external stimulus, having had the courage to come through our fear, we have retained the energy that would normally be used up by the behaviour of the subtype.

ACTIVATING THE VIRTUE AND THE HOLY IDEA – PRACTICES AND ACTION

Developing the Inner Observer

No form of spiritual development can be undertaken without effort and the will to notice our conditioning, in other words, when and where we go on automatic. The inner observer is a separate awareness that is always there, running parallel to the automatic behaviour of our type. It enables us to distance ourselves from our compulsive reactivity, so that we can stand back and evaluate whether our reaction is indeed the most appropriate response to the present situation.

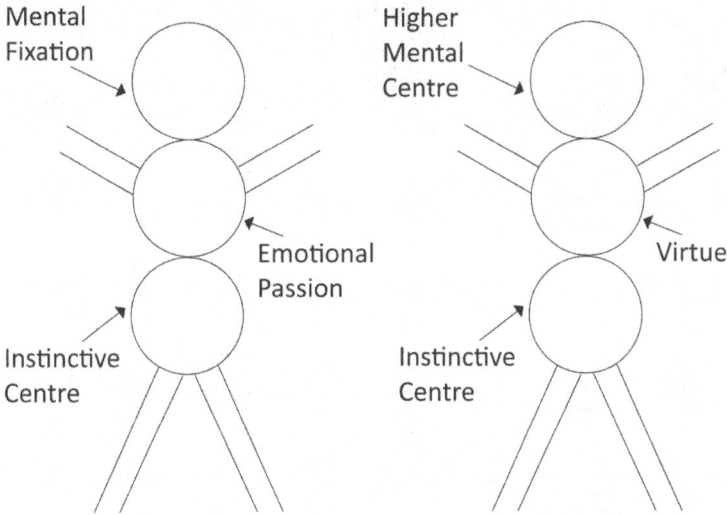

The false self on automatic pilot   The true self or essence

Figure 24 – Transforming the energy of the passion

The inner observer is separate from our thoughts, emotions and ordinary feelings. It can notice where our attention goes; it tells us what is going on. A practical example: we might suddenly notice ... "*You are thinking about something else; you are no longer present to what you are doing. Perhaps you ought to take a break*". The moment before, our attention was wandering. The inner observer, detached from our train of thought, was able, from its neutral stance, to notice that we were no longer present to ourselves. By bringing us back to ourselves, it gives us the freedom to choose either to bring our consciousness back into the present moment or to let it focus on its habitual type preoccupations.

SUBTYPES: THE KEY TO THE ENNEAGRAM

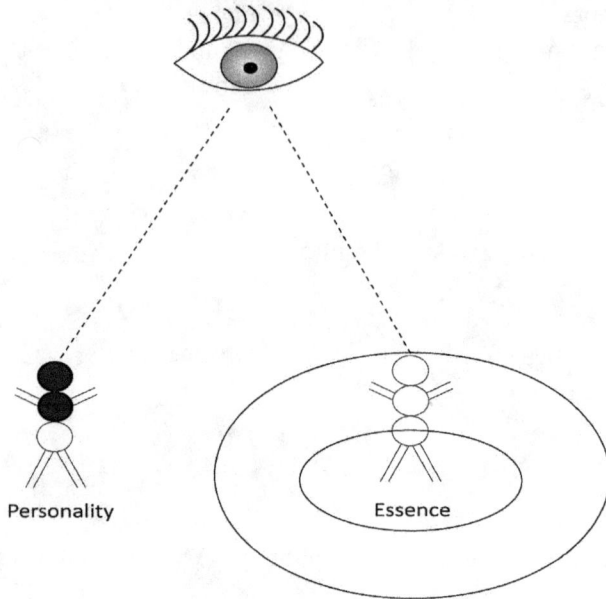

Figure 25 – The inner observer

The ego doesn't like the inner observer because it takes away the ego's automatic control of our personality. As long as the inner observer remains asleep, the ego is master of the situation; our behaviour is conditioned, our way of reacting is automatic, the alliance between the mental fixation and the emotional passion is in charge. But from the moment that we notice and cultivate the inner observer, we can call on it at will. By stopping the flow of our thoughts we can ask it whether, in this moment, we are operating according to the conditioned pattern of our personality or whether we are in the state of receptivity that belongs to essence.

It is worth mentioning that although we can train the inner observer by calling on it on a regular basis, it will never become automatic. Although the inner observer is on our side, a friend who wishes us well, calling on it will always require effort, a sort of conscious attention. Ideally it will become a travelling companion: lucid, faithful and benevolent. The inner observer has two key features: it can describe the direction of our attention and it can also evaluate the degree of awareness that we are putting into what we are doing. So once we have identified our Enneagram type, the inner observer can look at our way of reacting, at the part of ourselves which is not free, notice where our attention is going and work out whether our attention is going there freely and by choice, or automatically and compulsively.

The inner observer is never conditioned; it observes, it is a neutral witness without prejudice, opinion or inhibition. For example, when it considers what we are thinking about, it only notices *"Your attention is on thinking"*. With a bit of training, it can also notice *"Your attention finds it difficult to stay grounded when you are in thinking mode"*. Developing the inner observer is essential if we are to develop a spiritual life, assuming that part of a spiritual life is about our freedom to decide whether or not to free ourselves from our automatic behaviours.

In her book 'The Enneagram' Helen Palmer says: *"The part of consciousness that we call the inner observer enables us to relax our identification with our type habits. Seen from within the type viewpoint, relaxing our normal focus of attention makes us vulnerable; the mere fact of bringing attention to the breath for example is dangerous for the ego, because it is no longer in control. On the other hand, from the point of view of essence, a neutral consciousness contains and calms the energy normally used up by the thoughts, emotions and feelings of normal consciousness. Neutral consciousness, or consciousness with no expectations, produces significant benefits in terms of inner peace and quality of presence."*

By forcing ourselves to come out of our habitual pattern of reactivity, we can create brief moments of "emptiness" like the time-outs of relaxation practices. As we get better at it, a sense of "completeness" will start to come into these moments of emptiness.

Welcoming our balancing energy

With time and practice, the inner observer can become a force in its own right. Symbolically, the Enneagram talks about three sorts of energy: active, receptive and neutral or balancing energy. We can also find this idea in physics in the positive, negative and neutral poles of electricity.

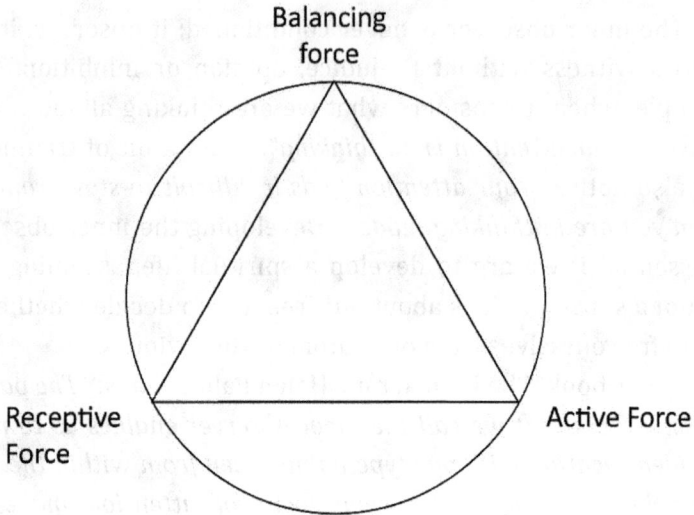

Figure 26 – Active, receptive and balancing forces

- *The active force* is action, moving towards, creating, expressing

- *The receptive force* is welcoming, evaluating, reflecting, predicting, understanding, questioning

- *The balancing force* is neither action nor reflection. It is a neutral consciousness which is both emotionally detached and immensely present to the here and now. You could say that it is meditative, if by that you mean a sort of presence which is in the moment.

Claudio Naranjo and the transformation process

In his book *Ennea-type Structures*[8] Claudio Naranjo explains the transformation process as follows: *"Enneagram types show us different variations on the loss of Being. The key moment is the instant when we realise that changing our behaviour is possible. As soon as we realise that we have had enough of this feeling of emptiness, of being lost, then we can start to observe the structure of our behaviour and free ourselves a little from the suffering which afflicts us."* The Enneagram is important because it enables us to understand how and why we went to sleep on ourselves, how the Self has been buried under the continuously humming hamster-wheel of the personality.

Elsewhere in his book Claudio Naranjo describes three states in the ego's transformation process:

* Beginning the work of self-observation and noticing the pervasiveness of reactivity
* Undertaking a sort of "holy war" against the ego, during which you force yourself to deactivate the automatic habits of the personality and cultivate the virtue which corresponds to your passion
* Setting up a contemplative practice that will help you to experience living your holy idea: the moments where the fixation relaxes and enables a much vaster consciousness.

Helen Palmer and spiritual experience

In her work at the first French-speaking Enneagram forum in Paris in June 2003[9], Helen Palmer said *"The basic question in the spiritual world is "What interferes between me and essence, between me and my internal life?" Answer: it's me, it's my type, it's my shell, it's my automatic responses. And that is experienced by everyone, whatever their religion or belief; even atheists want to be in contact with a truer reality, which we can call a spiritual experience. All my life I identified with my type, I believed that I was my type. In spiritual terms, "I was under the veil of illusion". Whereas in fact my inner observer had always been there, it had always been part of reality – but it was me that wasn't aware of it.*

I didn't realise it existed, so I had never called on it. Now that I have discovered its existence, the question becomes: why should I suffer from my emotions if I can detach myself from them and calm them? The discovery here is the existence of a receptive consciousness that can constantly observe my type, recognise fixations and passions and notice whether they are active or inactive.

The spiritual experience is probably that moment when the shell relaxes and softens and the preoccupations let go. Then we experience the presence of this receptive consciousness, which has been there all the time, which never went away, but which I had simply forgotten. In the west at the present time there are few opportunities to develop the inner observer, but in most of the spiritual traditions, the inner observer is considered an essential key to development. How can I know a greater reality if I am myself the obstacle between myself and it? ***The discovery of the shell and of the inner observer is the basis of spiritual transformation.*** *It is the key to finding what I need to do in order to let myself be guided by a consciousness which is greater than my ordinary one – how to relax the shell so that I can set it aside and become aware that the shell is not the only thing there is. If I really want to be receptive to reality, the 'I' needs to stand back, the type elements need to blur into the background."*

Daring to do nothing

Therapy and personal development are not in themselves enough to rediscover inner unity. They can pacify the past, plug the gaps, reopen some blockages, but they will never bring completeness. A much more certain way to acquire this is by backing up these "active" thought processes we are using with a daily contemplative practice – accepting that there is no guarantee of an effective result. We have to recognise that probably, unless we stop a couple of times a day to reconnect with ourselves in silence, the ego will continue to get stronger. The ego is much cleverer than we give it credit for; if we close off one mode of operation it will probably find another one, perhaps less obvious but still just as effective, to ensure that it stays in charge. It's the same sort of thing as when people feel proud of having given up smoking and then make up for it by eating chocolate, and don't want to admit that it's the same compulsion in a different form.

This necessity of doing nothing in order to relax automatic behaviour is known in many cultures as the Via Negativa. In fact, we're talking about the balancing energy that we referred to earlier – being present to the here and now, letting yourself sink into the movement of time, noticing the passage of thoughts, feelings and emotions and letting them go – in other words, meditating.

Taking precautions on the journey

Some people will continue to use the Enneagram only at its basic level, in order to understand themselves and others better – and this is a great start. Others will want to launch themselves into the great adventure of coming back to Being, using the Enneagram to clear the way. For those people, some recommendations might be helpful:

- Don't try and get through this alone. You're kidding yourself if you think you can outsmart the traps of the ego on your own. An external perspective from someone who is not going to collude with you is essential – and it's not a role for your partner …

- Don't go looking too far away to find the path. The higher dimension of our being is not hidden at the other end of the world. It is in us every moment, but it's we that are not there, because we are not present to ourselves.

- Be careful in your choice of therapies. Too often, we tend to focus on the ones that are most comfortable for our type. So Type 9s might be very proud of being good at yoga; Type 7s might enjoy clowning workshops; Type 4s might give free rein to their emotions by acting in theatre productions.

That's fine, but let's not kid ourselves! Are we taking on these activities simply to enjoy ourselves, or are we really prepared to destabilise our automatic behaviours and evolve?

- From a sensory point of view, an internal point of reference will be necessary. It will be a good idea to develop/notice a feeling in a certain part of your body when your type is relaxed, in order to be able to come back to it when the type tempest is raging[10].

- Physically, it will also be necessary to learn to recognise when tension comes up and takes root.

- Emotionally, many specialists such as Herbert Benson[11] and Daniel Goleman[12] reckon that the best cure for emotional suffering isn't fight or flight, suppressing it or distracting yourself; the best formula according to them is to relax into the pain so that it brings a relaxation of the feeling. This doesn't mean that the pain goes away; it means that you don't add extra pain to your pain because of your imagination. And if you manage to keep your attention on for example the rise and fall of the breath, eventually you will be able to send the pain into the background. The pain remains, but it "disappears behind the breath".

JOURNEYING WITH THE SUBTYPES

Many participants on our workshops have found that subtypes are a wonderful key to help them expand their consciousness and transform their being. Here are some of their stories; we have arranged them by subtype so that you can see the common themes that each subtype needs to work with, even if there isn't an example for your type. The participants are speaking their own words, but we have not put them in italics because this section is several pages long and we don't want to tire your eyes!

Self-Preservation

Self-Preservation Six – Patrick, 46, therapist and coach

When I learned about the subtypes, as you would expect from a Six, my first reaction was to see how I could use this to make myself safe! I first used the subtypes to work out others' likely reactions and prevent the risk of conflict. For self-preservation types this meant respecting the distance they need or avoiding intrusion, for one-to-one subtypes it was about accepting their intensity and withdrawal without feeling engulfed or abandoned, for social subtypes it meant being able to end a relationship with them without being annoyed with them, and without saying to myself that they had bad feelings towards me or were not interested in me. As you can see, I started to be able to thwart my slightly paranoid projections when they produced false alarms! In my professional life I also started to use my colleagues' subtype to help me decide which examples to use when talking to them, which made our conversation more relevant, and also reassured me.

Then I started to help others take advantage of this. The key word for the self-preservation Six is "warmth", which I understand to mean "being kind". I've always been good at teaching and in my professional life I've often used the subtypes to help my clients unpick and understand relationship difficulties. When I explain it and give them exercises to do, they've often been surprised at the relevance of the three subtypes.

And finally, I applied the knowledge to myself – this took a bit of time. I didn't identify my self-preservation subtype immediately because my counter-phobic side leads me to seek out different and quite often tension-producing relationships – I thought I was a one-to-one. But my security door and alarm, my need for sleep and a whole load of other clues should have made me question that one! Getting to know my subtype brought my type alive; I saw it at work in the practical details of my life and I've learned to dialogue with it when it takes over. In the past I was afraid to travel far afield or to unknown countries; I needed two computers just in case, I used to buy three packets of soap powder instead of one, I wore too many clothes just in case the temperature turned cold, I ran to the doctor for the smallest symptom. Now, I'm going to Latin America in the autumn; I've balanced the risks and I'm OK about it – I think I'm moving on!

Self-preservation Six – Elizabeth, 50, nurse

Oh crikey – being safe used always to be my highest priority! Becoming conscious of my type and subtype's preoccupations helped me to realise the amount of time that I was spending – and wasting – checking that I was safe. To give you practical examples: before leaving my flat I always used to go round checking that the windows were locked, the gas was off, any cigarette butts were completely cold – I used to do this almost automatically, unconsciously – and after locking the door I would often open it again to check a second or even third time. These days I still check that there are no risks but I've realised that once is enough. Financial security is also one of my main concerns; I've worked out my monthly expenditure and I've got a computer programme that helps me manage my accounts. I've been working as a nurse for 25 years and I get a regular salary, but in spite of that I used to need to balance my books every week. Nowadays I do it once a month – that's progress! Getting to know the other subtypes made me more tolerant and understanding of others. My partner is a one-to-one Nine, so fusion is a high priority. This might have been hard for me as I need to be alone sometimes, but once we understood the subtypes we were able to discuss what we each needed from the relationship and we managed to find a compromise – if I hadn't understood these differences we might have split up.

What I'm working on now is balancing my three subtypes. I've always had a social life outside work but it wasn't a high priority – it always came after doing the accounts, the housework and the shopping. An empty fridge really worried me, even if the cupboards were full! Thanks to understanding the subtypes I've managed (partly!) to free myself from these preoccupations, and now I find I've got more time for my social life: my sports club, my meditation class, going to workshops and discussions ... These days I find my life is much more rich and balanced.

Self-preservation Seven – Hubert, 59, osteopath

When I first found out my subtype it didn't change much in my life – ok, it gave a good description of some of my behaviours, but so what? I even discounted the Enneagram as a model; I thought that Threes and Sevens were pretty much alike and it was easier to rationalise any discomfort I felt with both of them rather than commit myself to a particular type. The panels helped me to move to a first stage of accepting myself, but I felt something was missing if I was going to commit to using the Enneagram for my personal development – it just felt very intellectual.

Recognising my subtype resolved this discomfort. Straight away I recognised my self-preservation subtype and all of a sudden the different bits of my life made sense. I was able to stand back and recognise the links between certain behaviours: the importance of belonging to a group, my focus on being organised and on managing the practical things of life, my fear of being without the things I need, my search for well-being and security, both for myself and for my loved ones, my central focus on my home, my concern for my health, my focus on my body (that's why I'm an osteopath). Accepting that I'm a Seven was a long way from really noticing how my type plays out in my everyday life. My subtype helped me to see how and where my type becomes extreme, how it stops me from sitting with my fears and how it leads me off into a vicious circle of more and more activity in this world where it's all about survival and where it's right to be anxious. It's as though I'm fleeing forwards, seeking more and more movement, at the expense of welcoming the present moment – just as it is.

Self-preservation Eight – Isabelle, 39, HR Development Manager

I came to the Enneagram only knowing my type – I was sure about this in the same way that an Eight is sure about their personal ability – I had no doubt and I could cope with anything. That was a mistake – I hadn't realised what my subtype was! I'd vaguely heard about the subtypes but I'd never really gone into it. Working out my subtype didn't happen as easily and surely as my type. I worked it out by elimination and in the end I had to give in to the evidence and accept that I'm a self-preservation; I pay attention to my body; when I'm hungry I eat, when I'm sleepy I go to bed, when I'm tired I rest and I do this whatever time it is. I don't care if it's 6 o'clock in the evening and it's not the "normal" time to have dinner or if it's 8.30 and it's "too early to go to bed" – I listen to myself.

I also find it hard to throw things away, whether it's a pair of shoes I don't wear any more, a pair of trousers that don't suit me, books I've grown tired of or a useless piece of furniture. I like having food in the house so that I'm not short of anything (I'm talking like my grandmother who lived through the last war!) My family is important to me too; I'd rather celebrate or share a meal with family than with my friends. I don't see much of my sisters or my mother; they all live a long way away but I know that they're there and that I can see them whenever I want. I don't feel the need to spend all my time phoning them because I know deep inside that they will always be there, like a lighthouse that you can see from a long way off. The self-preservation literature talks about "clan" and that speaks to me; it reassures me. But the most important part of the self-preservation subtype for me, the thing that sets me off, turned out to be "security". My safety is more important than my pleasure – I would love to do a skydive, go paragliding or bungee jumping but there are so many safety unknowns (will the parachute open, will the paraglider canopy tear, will the bungee elastic hold?) that I can't let myself give in to these desires. My physical safety is more important than my financial security and that is more important than my emotional safety. I know that I can live alone but not without a safe roof over my head. I feel good because I've got a secure job (I'm a civil servant) which means that I can house and feed myself, in short take care of my primary needs – I know that if I didn't have that security I couldn't imagine embarking on a relationship with another person. When I came to Paris it took me nine months to find a job. To give me something to do, I treated myself to an unlimited cinema pass. In all those nine months I must have gone to the cinema five or six times. I was too worried about my financial security to let myself relax into the pleasure of a good film. Ten years later I've got another cinema pass and I go at least twice a week!

It took me a year of studying the Enneagram and passing my certification to realise that my self-preservation subtype moderates my Eight. The fact that I'm obsessed by my personal safety stops me from rushing in all guns blazing. These days I can see the link between some of my behaviours and my subtype, and to be honest, I think I often act more out of my subtype than my type. Knowing that these behaviours come from my subtype makes it easier to accept them calmly.

Self-preservation Nine – Elisabeth, 51, outplacement consultant

I was very happy to find that I'm a self-preservation subtype; my enjoyment of nature and solitude, my ability to really experience the good things in life gives me a positive balance to my Nine failing, which is self-forgetting. Recognising my Type and Subtype were both a relief; it was as though I had come home. Realising this also made me notice the negative sides of being too focused on self-preservation. So now I try to give less priority to the material things that I used to use to numb myself out and procrastinate.

Understanding subtypes also helped me to understand why some people exasperated me, like my brother-in-law Jean-Pierre, who is incapable of paying attention to two people at the same time. When I'm with him and my sister, it's as though he looks straight through me. I don't see my sister very often and yet when I'm there he monopolises her. Realising that his behaviour came from his one-to-one subtype helped me to understand him and not feel rejected. My resentment towards him gives way to amusement when I catch him red-handed being too one-to-one. Once I realised that, I started seeing my sister on her own and I really value the time I spend with her alone; I've stopped worrying about it. Interestingly, one time when I happened to be alone with him we had a great time. Before I did the work on the subtypes I think that if something like that had happened it would have made me very uncomfortable, because I used to be convinced that he had no interest in me as a person because he was always focused on my sister rather than me.

One-to-One

One-to-one Subtype (Type not stated) – Cosima, 42, psychotherapist

Finding my subtype was a wake-up moment in my personal development. It was as though I came down from the stage, out of my unconscious role, and could observe the relationship games I'd been playing up to that point. The over-importance I'd given to pleasing others and being loved at all costs was the clinching proof; I realised that my subtype had been calling the shots and that I was unable to choose the appropriate level of closeness to anyone I was with – I was just like a moth fascinated by a flame. Since then I've realised that I can choose the distance I keep from others, I can actually observe them, listen to their needs and understand them better by putting myself in their shoes.

Realising the over-importance of my subtype in my life also helped me to notice my shadow side – i.e. how I neglect the other subtypes. Suddenly my arguments with my self-preservation partner made sense; yet again I came out of role and was able to observe our day-to-day tensions and misunderstandings. Now I'm more able to respect our differences and enjoy how we complement each other. If I go over the top a warning light comes on, I notice it and bring it back into balance. I'm much more able to value the interaction and richness of the three instinctual forces.

One-to-one Two – Dominique, 48, mother

Because I had known my Enneagram type for over 10 years, I came to the subtypes workshop a bit complacent – and then, boom, realising my subtype was like a tidal wave. At first, I couldn't accept my one-to-one subtype and spent a difficult time going backwards into the dark through my whole life noticing all the negative sides of my "aggression/seduction". I felt very guilty and bad about myself, but later I started to accept it, my life's film started to rewind in the other direction and the lights came back on. I realised how crucial aggression/seduction had been to my survival. I understood how my little child put this system in place in order to get through life and how it used it to help others, to forget itself, in order to love and get love.

Recognising my subtype has brought me inner peace and an enormous relief from my sense of guilt. It helps me to understand myself better; it enables me to look after myself without guilt and to communicate differently with other people. I've also realised that relationship difficulties often come more from a difference of subtype than a difference of type, and that's why it's so important to understand subtypes in order to better accept other people.

One-to-one Three – Lynda, 44, Trainer

Finding my subtype was a real revelation to me; it brought my type alive and shed light on my recurrent automatic patterns. Although this was a bit painful at first, it has become a source of joy because as I have got better at noticing my habits I can choose other more appropriate and therefore more peaceful ways of behaving.

By working on my subtypes I can try to rebalance the time, energy and attention that I spend on each of the three areas, so that I can live a fairer life for myself and for others. I've started to develop my self-preservation side; it's about being kinder to myself, listening more to my body and my emotions and living with a more appropriate rhythm (which usually means slower than my usual full-speed Three tempo!) In order to achieve that I do Tai Chi; the here and now is getting more present and is teaching me not only to slow down but also to work towards more authenticity in my movements, my stance and my feelings. This regular practice also helps me to distance myself from my need to take action. I'm also learning to modify my drive. I know that I'm always running ahead of events; I'm learning (with astonishment!) that things will happen when the right moment comes, and sometimes without any intervention from me – which is quite a relaxing thing to notice!

I'm gradually managing to give up my need to launch into everything at 100 miles an hour; I'm learning to trust my intuition more and let myself be guided by what seems right when I'm deciding whether to take action or not. In order to moderate the excesses of my one-to-one subtype, I try to ask the question: *"What role are you playing?"* It's about noticing when my automatic pilot is determining my role, and how it leads me to expend a lot of unjustified energy looking for love and acknowledgement. When I sense my subtype kicking in compulsively, I press the pause button and breathe. Then I notice that expending all this energy doesn't make sense right now. And then I can choose to sit with the discomfort, wait for the instinctive need to pass and focus on moving towards a more authentic, balanced way of being present, which is more in line with what I deeply desire and less about my image.

I neglected my social side for a long time and thought it was pointless, until I realised that there too I used to run away from uncomfortable situations where I couldn't put on a good show, for example if I was in a specialism where I couldn't shine because I wasn't competent. These days I'm developing my social side by putting people in contact with each other or by getting involved with charities. This work forces me to ground myself, be present and not to play a role with everyone I meet.

One-to-one Four – Valerie, 43, in mid-career change

Realising my subtype felt to me like a slow-motion version of discovering my type; it was as though I was overtaken by a two stage tidal wave that made me re-examine everything. Once I got over the emotion of it, I needed both to move forward into the deep water and to take a more detached view of what was happening. I quickly realised that my subtype is where I live most of the time, although mainly subconsciously. It's what I look for in every aspect of my life; it's both my obsession and my trap, my burden and my treasure, my blind spot and the gift that I've been given. I realised that it was in the space between my type and subtype that my hope of transformation could find its way forward.

At that point in my life, because of my role as mother of a family I'd just spent sixteen years in self-preservation mode – which isn't my subtype. Finding out that my real need was to be in one-to-one relationships allowed my dominant subtype to come out of the shadows. It was liberating to realise that I love being in one-to-one relationships, in communion with another person, and that I'm good at it. When I get that connection I feel good and I do good. I also found out that this talent for connection can sometimes be a tyrant, both for me and for the other person. It can take up space, in fact all the available space. Realising this changed everything; it's all about being

255

aware of it. Once you're aware, everything is easy. In my one-to-one relationships, I can now dare to be who I am, while at the same time trying to give the other person the distance they need. My self-preservation side helps me to stay anchored and present in the moment, without getting too caught up in it. In my social sphere I'm gradually learning how to move into the unknown territory of group relationships, which makes me uncomfortable and frustrates me, but which enables me to open up another side of myself. I'm not quite there yet, but I know that the beauty of this is in the journey, and the peace I seek can come just from desiring it. These days I aim to work towards balancing the three subtypes, and this aim makes me happy; I'm on the way towards a good position and place.

One-to-one Six – Suzanne, 55, HR Director

Realising my type and learning about my subtype helped me both to know myself more and understand others better. For my subtype, relationships with other people are very important, both in personal and in work life. But it's not just about people; I can also be one-to-one with my work or a book, under my little cloche, completely cut off from the outside world.

At work, I recognise my "strength and beauty" focus. When that kicks in, all my attention is on the person I'm with; I'm totally absorbed in and listening to them, super-concentrated and oblivious to my surroundings. I believe that enables the person I'm with to feel trusted, more secure and at ease – that's very important to me in my role as an HR Director. When I'm with someone, I notice the intensity that comes from my great concentration; this is reassuring when I'm trying to create trust, and it's also stimulating and almost addictive. It makes me seek out relationships with people from the same subtype, because I know that I'll find that energy, that enriching depth that I don't find in my relationships with people from other subtypes. My one-to-one preference enables me to initiate relationships, even with people I don't know. I also use my knowledge of the subtypes for my own development. As I've brought my self-preservation side to the fore, I've paid more attention to putting meals together; I focus on the taste of food and this helps me to be present in the moment and less in my head. I've also learned to value social subtype people more, and now I even enjoy meeting them. Being in a group gives me a feeling of more space and helps me to be less in my head and more in harmony with myself.

One-to-one Six – Claude, 47, therapist

I recognise how my type used to play out in my life: it was about learning karate even though I didn't want to fight anyone, always, almost obsessively, wearing pastel colours, forever smiling when I really wanted to bite or scream, wearing myself out physically or intellectually to acquire knowledge, facts and experiences, always seeking more so that I could prove that my competence was exceptional – that's what my life was like before I knew about my subtype!

Discovering my subtype made me understand the reasons behind these behaviours; I wanted to win people over through my strength, my gentleness or my warmth. These days I'm more able to express appropriate anger or my disapproval of something, and to give myself time to take care of myself. I would say that the "strength and beauty" that used to play out in extreme form in my outward life is now located inside me, and that I don't need to prove anything any more. Nowadays I'm joyfully and peacefully discovering the wonderful benefits of being authentically myself, alone, with one other person or with a crowd. I'm learning to rejoice in the moment, take advantage of the enlightenment in what's here now, look on life with benevolence and gratitude, listen to the music of every day. In a word – to love.

One-to-one Six – Mahalia, 32, trainer and therapist

I knew I was a one-to-one straight away – and that enabled me to know immediately where I needed to focus in order to move forward in my development. When I look at myself today, I know that I'm a one-to-one Six, but I also know that I'm more than that. Knowing this makes me free to play with these qualities and not get caught up in them on the occasions when life needs me to react differently.

For example, I can now get inspiration from self-preservation subtypes; they connect me back to another way of being which I know is in me, but it's been asleep. The more I realise what drives me and recognise my angst, emotions and intensity for what they are, the easier it is to let go of them much more readily. On the one hand, I love and value them dearly, but on the other hand, as I become more aware of the little voice of the other subtypes inside me, I can recognise that they are only emotions. When I notice my automatic reaction kicking in, I've learned to breathe strongly into my belly and to connect myself to my whole body, to my physical needs, and to open up my consciousness to a broader way of looking at things. As I notice how the subtypes play out in my everyday life, every day my aim is to become a bit more complete and close to the true me.

One-to-one Eight – Alix, 50, coach

I feel that the one-to-one subtype reinforces the full-on side of type Eight. Once I realised this tendency to excess, I was able to bring a bit more level-headedness into my life. It's very different from the Social Eight who can cut corners and needs to learn to be a bit less here and now and do what's needed in order to keep their friends, be accepted and even appreciated by the group. It's also very different from the self-preservation Eight who often holds themselves back in order to be self-sufficient, knows instinctively what's right for them and sticks to it. I feel that one-to-one Eights tend to make the Eight's tendency to excess even worse. I would sum up my one-to-one Eight compulsion as *"I want everything"* and this exacerbates the Eight compulsion to have what it wants *"right now"*. Putting these two together is simple and clear but it's also unyielding, excessive and even brutal – *"I want it all, right now!"*

The best illustration of this behaviour is the way in which I approach other people. When I instinctively know that there is a **strong** link between us (it's just as well that this doesn't happen with every new person I meet, otherwise I'd be exhausted!) I go straight into a particular behaviour that comes directly from my one-to-one subtype. I go off at top speed towards fusion and intensity, often wanting exclusive access to that person, sometimes to the point of manipulating them, and yet at the same time I've a sort of ambivalence towards them because I can't stand the idea that I might be refused – it's full-on! These days, now that I know how my subtype works, when I catch myself doing this I can see that my behaviour has an aspect of seduction – in the broadest sense of the word. That's why the other word that describes one-to-one, "sexual" makes absolute sense to me. And I also totally understand the phrase "possession/surrender" – I'm looking for and I experience such a strong link with you that I will give you everything – *it's all or nothing, life or death* – or I'll drop you completely, even if it means being in pain because I haven't managed to make this relationship what I wanted it to be and wasn't able to give myself up totally to your will.

In this relationship, if in addition the other person is also a one-to-one, well, phew! You'll be having endless incredibly intense conversations, and doing it again and again! For example, you could be talking until 2am, sitting in a car whose battery is running flat to the point that it breaks down; you might spend entire nights talking until dawn; you'll have lunches with girlfriends that are never long enough; you'll spend a good chunk of the night surfing the web even if your sleep and health suffer; you'll have Skype conversations that never last less than an hour; you'll be unable to end the discussion – you can't put up with the idea that someone might hang up on you, whether on purpose or not; you'll spend endless energy to achieve a professional or personal task.

My Enneagram subtype training enabled me to find out, learn and spot what the one-to-one subtype is about, to better understand how the mechanism gets set in motion, and how to thwart my automatic responses. Since then I find that I'm better able to step back and get some quiet perspective on what happens. Even if I still give in to my excesses sometimes, I have the feeling that I'm less at the mercy of them. I've got better at managing my compulsions and through my personal development I'm learning to come on less strong and to moderate my former belief that *"When I love I don't count for anything"*. The way I spend time, money and energy, which was often excessive, is calmer these days and I can watch myself with an inner smile and temper my desire to do all that stuff. I'm also starting to understand the value of the self-preservation subtype in my life; I'm taking better care of myself, watching what I eat and making sure I sleep well, living less dangerously, doing sports which are less dangerous, curbing my hyperactivity and learning when to stop and decide *"the sun will still be there tomorrow"*. These new behaviours are improving my quality of life, even more so because I'm now doing them consciously.

In my coaching work, my subtype gives me the competence to be a reassuring presence for clients and for them to feel that I won't let them down. I see my development path as learning to keep a cool head so that I don't lose my awareness of the compulsion that my Eight and my one-to-one draw me into.

Social

Social Subtype (Type not stated) – Dominique, 44, psychotherapist

Discovering my subtype was as crucial as discovering my type. It's quite something to become conscious of this lever that instinctively controls your centres of interest and the way you choose to run away every time discomfort comes up! Personally, when I'm not in a good place, I can't confront my sadness on my own – and I don't tend to seek out a one-to-one subtype to talk about my pain, because I might run the risk of losing it. Rather I tend to get very passionate about social issues, and this distracts me from myself and distances me from my real needs.

Since I noticed my subtype, my life has changed; instead of taking flight into social activity, I make myself stay in self-preservation mode. This helps me face up to my emotions, name my physical and psychological needs and learn to meet them in a balanced way. And not running away from one-to-one encounters when I'm not feeling good has also helped me to realise that the other person will still accept and love me even when the only thing I can offer them is my vulnerability. In fact, I've found that experiencing self-preservation and one-to-one have been the things that have enabled me to grow. Realising my subtype has also helped me to admire self-preservation types because they have resources that I lack, rather than simply finding them pedestrian and materialistic. With my one-to-one friends I find I can now stay in the intensity of their relationship with me, without being tempted to run away because I'm afraid of being abandoned or rejected. Of course, your dominant subtype doesn't change, and I'll always be a social subtype, but it has become less reactive and more flexible. I'm a lot less caught up in social causes and I'm not so worried about the success of the ones I do engage with. These days I take great pleasure in other aspects of life: making my home comfortable, filling the fridge and setting up a comfortable space where I enjoy spending time reading, listening to music or meditating – on my own.

Social One – Sandrine, 45, HR consultant

I didn't find it hard to recognise that I'm a One; the demands I place on myself and on others, my insistence that the job should be well done and my anger have always been part of me. All the same, when I was on panels with other Ones I often seemed to be different from them. Their emphasis on tidiness, meticulousness and extreme detailed care taken about how the task was completed didn't ring true for me. I started to wonder if I could be a Three – I'm always active, efficient, doing the best I can in a limited time: *"You want a meal for 15, sure, but don't let's take more than an hour over it."* Learning about the subtypes solved this dilemma for me. As I realised how different the subtypes' preoccupations are, I understood that my sort of One could look quite different from the meticulous concern for order associated with the ant.

My attention and energy go less to concrete things; my type comes to the fore in social settings. I need to belong to different groups, and what interests me about them is the action they take, their role in society, or their intellectual focus (it could be a youth group, a community association or a study group). I want to get involved, play a role that suits me, and this is more often defined by the needs I see rather than by my own desires. Sorting out the accounts, running a meeting or organising the purchase of a group member's birthday present are added to my daily list, to the point where I feel like a mule that's overloaded. But it doesn't matter, if I say I'll do it, I deliver; you can count on me – it's about respecting the moral contract that I've implicitly made with the group. And if I'm going to do it, I might as well be organised and efficient, which means that actually there's not a lot of room left for true physical perfectionism. So I really recognise my social One subtype. And I also realise that recognising it is not enough in itself; I need to keep working on my development path, just as all the other types do. But recognising my subtype is a relief and brings clarity, and these days I feel closer to my other subtype colleagues than I do to my Type One profile.

Social Five – Antoine, 38, engineer

If I hadn't found my subtype I would never have found my type. Most of the descriptions of Fives in the books only describe self-preservation Fives. You don't have to caricature them much to describe them as hermits living in the depths of the woods, minimalist withdrawn misanthropes who need nothing and spend their days reading. But I like people; I even feel that I'm quite sensitive and I'm really interested in what others have got to say. In my work I feel I'm very competent at everything to do with people management: inducting people, guiding their professional development, getting a small group together to think through a problem – and I'm also well in touch with key events that happen in the life of the organisation. Where's Type Five in all of that?

For me, it's about the simultaneous need to be with others and fear of being invaded by their demands or needs so that my needs get lost. I can have many human contacts in the course of a day with no problem, but I need to stay in control of who I meet and when and why I meet them. What I am looking for are meetings that only last as long as it takes to say the key things that need saying, and no longer – otherwise there always comes a point where we start small talk or my connection with the other person is broken in some way. But on the other hand, if the aim of the meeting is clearly to have a fun evening, I've no problem with that; I'm quite capable of becoming the life and soul of the party in order to make the occasion even more festive. I've got lots of friends and contacts and I go out a lot, but in certain circumstances the distant side of my Five intensifies the distant side of my subtype.

Learning about my subtype therefore enabled me to find my type, and the combination of my type and subtype shed light on the oscillation of my behaviour; I like others **and** I need time for me, on my own – realising this was such a relief. I've always found it difficult to get involved in self-preservation and one-to-one activities, but I realise that they're an important part of my development. These days I've got a different attitude to people who are from the other subtypes, and I don't condescend towards self-preservation subtypes as I did in the past. I even quite admire their ability to get totally involved in the small things of everyday life. These days I can find myself watching a gardener and envying them in a way – I'm certainly more at peace with myself and with others.

Social Seven – Isabelle, 42, civil servant

Finding my subtype was as important as finding my Seven. It removed the guilt I felt because I had so little interest in the practical aspects of life: managing bills, filling the fridge, decorating my house. Knowing this has also helped me to rebalance my life between the three subtypes

These days I'm more clear and less guilty about my behavioural preferences: my social activities and the importance of my intellectual life. Gradually I'm learning to spend more time in self-preservation activities, which I could never do a short time ago – I'm still not that keen on them, but I know that I'm working on being more balanced. Now I'm more relaxed about organising that side of my life, and I set it up so that it's not too onerous for me.

CONCLUSION:
BEING TOTALLY, SPIRITUALLY,
SACREDLY YOURSELF

One of the riches of the Enneagram is the range of its applications: daily life, personal development, spiritual practice. Until now, it had one major fault: if you only study it at a superficial level you can get the impression that it puts us in a box, which is both dangerous and superficial. I hope that this book achieves the aim both of building the Enneagram's credibility and its depth.

While I believe that the nine types are extremely useful to help us to know ourselves better, I am dubious about development recipes that rely only on the nine types. The subtypes will hopefully make up for this lack; they move the system from a base of nine to a base of twenty-seven, and the nuances that the three subtypes give to each profile open up new development opportunities.

Everyone will develop their own way of working with the information in this book: enjoying the clarification that this new dimension brings, improving their personal relationships or making use of the light that subtypes can shed on their main shortcoming. Now that we have developed the study of the subtypes, I can't see how it can any longer be said that the Enneagram is superficial.

Bringing subtypes into the light is simply about giving them their true place in the system, because they have always been part of the system. In the beginning of the rebirth of the Enneagram the subtypes were an integral part of the teaching. In his book *Enneagram Work* Peter O'Hanrahan says *"When I studied the Enneagram at Berkeley during the 1970s, we first learned the characteristics of the nine personality types, of course, but the 27 subtypes followed straight afterwards. As the course continued, over several days we really started to notice the subtype behaviours in our group. Living together, we could observe each other and notice the body language of these instinctual building blocks. We thus gathered rich information on our behaviour and that of others which shed immediate light on our principal shortcoming."*

Taking this idea further, I think that the subtypes really come into their own when we embark on personal development; they help us spot very quickly the point where we react automatically. Let's take the example of a Type One. Learning through type that *"I am someone who focuses on perfection"* is much less useful than being able to notice, several times a day, where, when and how anger comes up in my life. All spiritual traditions insist on the importance of noticing the attention we pay to the small actions of everyday life. With the subtypes, each of the 27 profiles has keys to help us notice when and in what direction our attention escapes.

After that, it is up to our personal free will, to our desire to transform ourselves. Isn't it true that we much more often find ourselves wanting to change other people rather than putting in the effort to change ourselves? That's only human; taking the risk to change ourselves is dangerous – we know what we're leaving behind, but we don't know what we're going to find. Questioning our very being is a harsh and intimate development journey; even with support, we feel alone when we are face to face with our innermost self.

So why would we bother to leave the protective shell of well-practised behaviours to dare to go naked into the world in all our vulnerability? I don't know; it's a personal choice, but I think the Enneagram's effect is to wake us up to ourselves, and once we have woken up we no longer really have a choice; the experience of being centred calls to us *"come back here"*. From my own experience, experiencing moments of being completely free from fear, acting from the centre of myself and feeling connected to a higher dimension of being is well worth the effort. In those moments, I have the impression that I am truly myself, I am being fully myself, I am being fully, spiritually, *"sacredly"* myself. This is what I wish for you: that you can apply the knowledge of the subtypes to rediscover moments of fulfilment and inner peace.

References for Part 3

1. Michel Random, author and philosopher, took part in all the international fora organised by UNESCO, and was sometimes the convenor.
2. For example *La Vision Transpersonnelle, La Mutation du Futur, La Tradition Initiatique, L'Art Visionnaire.*
3. For more detail, see C.G. Jung (1964) *Man and his Symbols*, Picador, UK
4. For more detail, see Chevalier and Gheerbrant (1997) *Dictionnaire des Symboles*, Laffont, France
5. In his book Boris Mouravieff (1990) *Gnosis,* La Baconniere, France, he analyses the Enneagram diagram in the context of Christian doctrine.
6. Some of these arguments were developed by Helen Palmer in an interview in the journal Gnosis in August 1994.
7. Another work on the mid-life crisis is Francoise Millet-Bartoli (2006) *The Mid-life Crisis*, Odile Jacob, Paris
8. Claudio Naranjo (1991) *Ennea-type Structures* Gateways Books, USA
9. This forum takes place every year – see http://www.cee-enneagramme.eu
10. See Karlfried Graf Duerckheim (1970) *Hara: the Centre of Man* George Allen & Unwin, UK
11. Doctor and professor at Harvard University. Benson (1975) *The Relaxation Response – how to resist external stress,* Harper Collins USA
12. Daniel Goleman (2003) *Destructive Emotions and how we can overcome them – a dialogue with the Dalai Lama,* Random House UK

* 9 7 8 0 9 9 3 5 9 4 7 1 7 *